The Best American
Sports Writing
2004

GUEST EDITORS OF
THE BEST AMERICAN SPORTS WRITING

1991 DAVID HALBERSTAM

1992 THOMAS MCGUANE

1993 FRANK DEFORD

1994 TOM BOSWELL

1995 DAN JENKINS

1996 JOHN FEINSTEIN

1997 GEORGE PLIMPTON

1998 BILL LITTLEFIELD

1999 RICHARD FORD

2000 DICK SCHAAP

2001 BUD COLLINS

2002 RICK REILLY

2003 BUZZ BISSINGER

2004 RICHARD BEN CRAMER

The Best AMERICAN SPORTS WRITING™ 2004

Edited and with an Introduction
by Richard Ben Cramer

Glenn Stout, *Series Editor*

HOUGHTON MIFFLIN COMPANY
BOSTON • NEW YORK 2004

ISSN 1056-8034
ISBN 0-618-25134-0
ISBN 0-618-25139-1 (pbk.)

Printed in the United States of America

MP 10 9 8 7 6 5 4 3 2 1

Contents

Foreword xi
Introduction by Richard Ben Cramer xix

JOE POSNANSKI. *Dusting Off Home* 1
from The Kansas City Star

SUSAN ORLEAN. *Lifelike* 12
from The New Yorker

STEVE FRIEDMAN. *The Race of Truth* 21
from Bicycling

LYNNE COX. *Swimming to Antarctica* 37
from The New Yorker

ROBERT DRAPER. *Beauty in the Beast* 54
from GQ

GARY SMITH. *The Secret Life of Mia Hamm* 62
from Sports Illustrated

PAUL SOLOTAROFF. *Growing Up Mantle* 86
from Men's Journal

PETER HESSLER. *Home and Away* 98
from The New Yorker

MICHAEL LEAHY. *All the King's Men: Why the Team That
Jordan Built Fell to Pieces* 119
from The Washington Post Magazine

PETER DE JONGE. *The Leap of His Life* 142
from The New York Times Magazine

LISA OLSON. *Making a Play for Players* 162
from The New York Daily News

CARLTON STOWERS. *Friday Night Lite* 167
from The Dallas Observer

CHARLES P. PIERCE. *Black Sunday* 178
from Sports Illustrated

GREG COUCH. *A Runaway Win Cubs Fans Won't Appreciate* 186
from The Chicago Sun-Times

BOB RYAN. *Misery Has More Company* 190
from The Boston Globe

IRA BERKOW. *An Unconventional Tradition of Success* 193
from The New York Times

MITCH ALBOM. *Trying to Find Yourself in the Toughest Times* 198
from The Detroit Free Press

STEPHEN RODRICK. *A Long Strange Trip* 201
from Runner's World

TOMMY CRAGGS. *Fishing the Mainstream* 214
from SF Weekly

GUY MARTIN. *Getting Slammed* 227
from Field & Stream

WILLIAM NACK. *"No, Not Again!"* 234
from ESPN.com

JOAN RYAN. *Galarraga Steals Base, Stops Time* 240
from The San Francisco Chronicle

RICK TELANDER. *Playing Against the Clock* 243
from Sports Illustrated

ANDY MEISLER. *The Fright Stuff* 260
from The Los Angeles Times Magazine

Contents

MICHAEL HALL. *Running for His Life* 272
  from Texas Monthly

BILL PLASCHKE. *At Ease, at Last* 286
  from The Los Angeles Times

Biographical Notes 293
Notable Sports Writing of 2003 297

Foreword

Sportswriters have never had a higher profile. Although most of us dwell deep within the nether reaches of the field, a great many are "famous," and a few are six- and even seven-figures rich, autograph-scrawling celebrities nearly as well known as those they write about.

But, generally speaking, not because of anything they have written.

Over the last two decades or so, as the really big money has come into sports and helped spawn things like cable channels, Internet sites, and all-sports radio, there has been a lot of spillover for those who write about sports for a living. There may not be more jobs or more markets, but there is unquestionably more opportunity to become famous and make money. Not too long ago, the only sportswriters whose names meant anything away from their home territory were those on staff at a certain few magazines, the handful whose work was widely syndicated, the strays who crossed over into network broadcasting, and the odd duck or two who managed to write a best-selling book.

All those rooms are crowded now. This is not altogether bad, for in the past few years blockbuster books by sportswriters have become something of a staple of the best-seller list, and there is a steady market even for those books that don't reach blockbuster status. Nothing wrong with that, particularly for those of us who try to eke out a living in the book world. A generation ago, that was all but impossible. Now it is only implausible.

Oddly, though, many of today's best-known sportswriters are not celebrated for the quality of their work on the page, but for the volume of their words spoken on the airwaves. Off the top of my head I can name a couple of dozen whose fame — as far as I can tell — stems neither from their written words nor even from anything specific they have ever said. Their notoriety comes almost entirely from the fact that they seem to appear on cable or radio twenty-four hours a day and apparently never shut up. I'm not sure if some of these writers were actually any good at their initial craft to begin with, or in some cases if they even write at all anymore.

But I do know this — they may have become famous and they may have become rich, but very few have become *better writers*. More successful? Perhaps. Richer? Certainly. But better? Not many.

To be fair, there are some distinctions in broadcasting media — it is not *all* the same. Sometimes the broadcast media serves the written word, as in documentaries, which are scripted so that a writer either reads what he or she has written, reports, comments about his or her own work, or is asked to comment on a topic on which, clearly, he or she has a certain specific and unique expertise. But the real glory in the industry today seems to stem from something else entirely — personality-based punditry, or the ability to yammer on endlessly about whatever happens to be coming down the pike.

I must admit that despite my personal appearance and tendency to cough at inopportune times, I have been on television and radio myself, both as a true contributor and as one of these amorphous pundits. It is difficult to say no to the broadcast media, particularly because exposure on the airwaves can help sell books or promote one's writing, and when one has a particular expertise about a given topic, such appearances are totally appropriate. But I'm no innocent. On a few occasions I have also been asked to appear on television or radio because — well, I'm not sure exactly why I was asked. As far as I could tell, (a) there was airtime to be filled and (b) I answered the phone when called by some twelve-year-old producer who didn't know better. Fortunately, talking is not very hard — ask any two-year-old.

One is understandably flattered to be asked, and when the invitation comes with the promise of a check, there is added motivation to accept because talking generally pays a great deal better than writing. The last time I was asked to talk on air it was at the exorbitant rate of about $1,200 per hour — most writing pays closer to minimum wage. There is also a certain cachet that comes along with such requests. A great many more people, particularly players and athletes, watch TV or listen to the radio than read newspapers, books, or magazines. Incorrectly, however, the writer who regularly appears on TV or radio is assumed to be both better and more important than the poor scribe who appears only in print, rearranging the same twenty-six letters over and over again.

But for some this creates an awkward dilemma. I know a few writers who are contractually required by their alphabet employers to make appearances on other media, even though they hate it, aren't very good at it, and would prefer not to. They look and sound like they detest every moment and resent the time and energy it takes from their primary job as a writer. I know others for whom such appearances are not required yet they are nevertheless pressured to accept them, no matter what effect it might have on their writing responsibilities.

At the same time, there are others — and more of them every day — for whom talking is the end goal of their writing career. They remind me of the kid who abandons the classroom for the gym in the wan dream of becoming a superstar. Rather than spending time on the craft, there are many in this industry who write only because of the dim hope that it will allow them to pole-vault into the easy money and celebrity benefits that come from making it on television and radio.

And why not, apart from the deception and desperation inherent in such a quest? After all, each of us has bills to pay, families to take care of, and retirement to think about. While those motivations are understandable, there is still something unseemly, even disingenuous, about abandoning the written word in favor of the spoken while still flaunting one's chops as a writer. It is reminiscent of the ill ease one experiences in the presence of a former athlete who demands to be recognized or shills autographs and anecdotes at a card show, cashing in on what he used to be. So, too, for many a writer-turned-pundit. It is a crude admission that writing, well, just isn't *that* important, and that attitude often shows in the print work of the professional pundit, who isn't a writer anymore so much as some inarticulate kind of "authority." From my experience, I understand that to mean a person who answers the phone when it rings and afterward is recognized at the bar.

Many seem either to forget or to be completely unaware that there is an enormous difference between writing and speaking. On the airwaves — deservedly — the words just disappear. They are rarely, if ever, recalled. To read the transcribed words of a pundit is like eating air. There isn't a collection entitled *The Best American Sports Smack*, and I don't think there ever will be. Most of it comes off as so much verbal dog-paddling — a loud splashing of one-liners on the surface of things. A day later — hallelujah — it is gone for good. But writing, particularly good writing, lasts here and elsewhere. Last time I checked, the public library wasn't collecting punditry and no one was clamoring for it to do so.

None of this would matter if not for two factors. One is that both television and radio try to get our attention by any means possible, usually by gravitating to the outrageous. Far too often the speaker blabbers on out of ignorance or lets slip some crude and pathetic comment with racist or sexist overtones that embarrasses not only the reputation of the speaker but the entire profession. The issue is not one of political correctness but of public stupidity. Yet even worse is the influence this has on writing, and writers, particularly those who are too young to know better or too ambitious to care and far too eager to listen rather than read. Instead of looking to other writing as a model, too many ape the worst qualities of "sports-talk" in print, presumably with the goal of making the transition from the page. The result is writing that aspires to have the same effect — writing informed not by language or literature but by schtick, by the not-so-comic or clever monologue that attempts to shock, provoke, or otherwise exhibit "edginess." Far more often than not such work is neither shocking nor edgy nor provocative but sophomoric, gossipy, trivial, predictable, disposable, and utterly forgettable, as entertaining as watching someone else's child in a pool trying to learn to swim and blubbering, "Look at *me!*"

From where I sit the best writing — regardless of style or approach — is essentially a search for the truth, however ephemeral that may be. I think one becomes a writer because putting words on the page is a document of learning, the consequence of hours and days and sometimes years of inquiry presented in a clear and coherent form that reveals something valuable, lasting, and previously unknown. As the poet Jack Spicer wrote, the best writing "has an infinitely small vocabulary" — every word matters and is necessary. Punditry, on the other hand, is usually whatever temporarily sticks when thrown against the wall — unedited thinking that would have been best left private. Elevating that into a kind of public discourse considered more consequential than writing is both to abandon learning and to diminish the craft.

This book tries to serve as a small antidote to all that. Writing remains the best way to communicate, and the best writing is far better at drawing and holding an audience than the most prolific or profound punditry. Readers of this book can and do sit and listen to the words of writers *for hours,* longer and far more carefully than they listen to anyone on radio or television — there are reasons apart from safety you can't read and drive a car. When the author has done his or her task well, those careful words are heard and returned to again and again, informing and illuminating our lives.

A long time ago I received perhaps the best single piece of advice I have ever received about writing. I was complaining ad infinitum to a friend about a writing project, about the ten thousand problems I had with both the project and the demands of the subject. When I finally finished my screed, my friend — a writer — waited a moment to make sure that I was done, then scrawled something on a napkin and pushed it to me across the table.

It read, "I think you need to shut up and write."

Every season I read every issue of hundreds of sports and general interest magazines in search of writing that might merit inclusion in *The Best American Sports Writing.* I also contact the sports editors of some three hundred newspapers and request their submissions. Similarly, I ask hundreds of magazine editors to provide complimentary subscriptions and/or submit individual stories.

But I also encourage writers, readers, and all other interested parties to send me stories they've written or read in the past year that they would like to see reprinted in this volume — please feel free to alert me to either your own work or that of someone else. Believe me, for reasons I'm not privy to there are more than a few publications that purposely withhold one writer's work in favor of another's. A good description of the selection process can be found in the December 2000 issue of the Associated Press Sports Editors newsletter.

The best seventy-five stories or so go to the guest editor for the final selection. Richard Ben Cramer approached his duties this year with enthusiasm, and the result is a volume of which we are both justifiably proud.

To be considered for inclusion in *The Best American Sports Writing 2005*, each nonfiction story will have to have been published in 2004 in either the United States or Canada and be column-length or longer. Reprints or book excerpts will not be eligible. All submissions must be received by February 1, 2005.

Submissions must include the name of the author, the date of publication, and the publication name and address. Photocopies, tear sheets, or clean copies are fine. Readable reductions to 8½-by-11 are best. Submissions from online publications must be made in hard copy, and those who submit stories from newspapers should submit the story in hard copy as published. Since newsprint generally suffers in transit, newspaper stories are best mounted on 8½-by-11 paper, and if the story also appeared online, with the appropriate URL. There is no limit to the number of submissions either an individual or a publication may make, but please be reasonable and use common sense. Owing to the volume of material I receive, no submission can be returned or acknowledged. I also believe it is inappropriate for me to comment on or critique any individual submission. Publications that want to be absolutely certain their contributions are considered are advised to provide a complimentary subscription to the address listed below. Those that already do so should make sure to extend the subscription.

Please note that all submissions should be sent by U.S. or Canadian mail to this exact address:

Glenn Stout
Series Editor
The Best American Sports Writing
PO Box 549
Alburg, VT 05440

Those with questions or comments may contact me at baswed @sover.net. No submissions of material will be accepted electronically.

Copies of previous editions of this book can be ordered through most bookstores or online book dealers. An index of stories that have appeared in this series can be found at glennstout.net.

Thanks again go out to those in the front office of Houghton Mifflin who allow me to continue to work on a project of a lifetime, particularly my former editor Eamon Dolan and my new editor Susan Canavan, Sarah Gabert, and Larry Cooper. Thanks also to Richard Ben Cramer for his gracious effort, the Web site sports journalists.com for posting submission guidelines, and Siobhan and Saorla for sharing me again with so many words. Most of all, however, my gratitude extends to those who still find writing and reading of unceasing value.

GLENN STOUT

Introduction

AT LAST, in my mid-fifties, I have the answer to a question I used to mull as a boy: what is the one thing I would need to abide on a desert island? I thought about this not well but often, and with a calisthenic seriousness — part of my program for misspending my youth. I don't mean this was obsessive — let's be clear about that — it was just a game.

See, you had to imagine how you would get to the island with the *one thing* — how, for instance, you would swim ashore with dry matches when your whole ship was scuttled in the watery deep . . . though magic was permitted: it could be an endless supply of dry matches. The problem was, if you went for something useful, like fire, then you had an endless supply of boredom — and a future in an asylum should you be rescued. So sometimes I'd struggle ashore with the corpus of Roman literature (magically restored in its complete variety), which guaranteed my sanity and a post-rescue future as the world's unchallenged Latin savant. Then again, I couldn't boil water . . .

So too often, alas, I'd have to cheat: the *real* question was the *two* things you'd need . . . At that point I'd have to start over of course — to reimagine how I'd swim ashore with the matches and all of Roman literature. (No! Even better! I swim with the matches, see, but the island used to be a *Roman island* — *the literature is squirreled away there*. They sent out the emperor's whole library when the Visigoths were beating at the gates!)

Okay, maybe it was a tad obsessive.

But that doesn't matter now. Now I have the answer. One great thing — and our island a paradise! . . . It is the satellite dish with the sports-pack subscription. I know, I know — there's a little problem about the electricity. If you must get *technical,* there's a shortage of desert islands these days, too. But it's the why, not the wherewithal, I mean to discuss here.

After all, what's the one thing needful at our new beach place once we've mastered, you know, the beginner's stuff: shelter, fire, desalination, and the finer points of cuisine (the coconut goulash, the coconut soufflé). What we need is a sure and ample connection to our fellow beings, to the human condition, to the drama (could I say meaning?) of life.

I don't mean to rewrite Genesis — to suggest that God worked for six days so Detroiters could root on the Red Wings. (Though it's tempting: how else to explain the peculiarly hurlable physiognomy of the octopus?) And I won't sell the snake oil that sports *is* life — or the best part of life, or life writ small, or life lived large, or life as it should be (if life had rules). Forget that hooey. It's only sports.

But I do contend that, on any given day, sports will offer us stories — the most human stories — in richer supply, and more reliably, than any other branch of endeavor. Stories are how we understand our lives. And if you break down the elements in stories from the sporting life, it reads like the to-do list from a screenwriting seminar. In sports we have *heroes* — attractive individuals with exemplary talents. By their grace, dedication, courage, and the luck of the draw, they have a chance to *achieve,* not just for themselves but for something larger — for their families or fans, their team, their town or the nation, or history. They must *contend,* against long odds and serial difficulties — their own human tendency to weakness or error *and the villainy of rivals* — to the end of the game, the tournament, or the season, where we have for our story clear *winners and losers.* Or they contend through a career, which we may see in its birth, its growth and prime, its downslope and demise — a small death for our delectation. But in this regard sports is much better than the rest of human existence; in sports we have stories from the afterlife.

In fact, in this collection we present a selection of treats from the afterlife or its near environs — from a scandal uncovered by the great turf writer William Nack about our equine athletes in hell to

Joe Posnanski's visit with Tony Peña at the ball fields of his youth, which is a glimpse of a man who went to heaven. Bill Plaschke (does this guy ever write anything bad?) makes us witness to the moment when an ex-Dodger learns he's gone to heaven. There is also Paul Solotaroff's empathetic portrait of Mickey Mantle's sons, who are trapped in the afterlife of an afterlife. And there's a sweet sharp line drive of a piece by Joan Ryan, who freeze-frames Andres Galarraga gleefully stealing time until his judgment day.

On the subject of sports bending time, there is a strong and rueful look back with Charlie Pierce to the NFL's worst day. And there's a strange, brave essay by Rick Telander, from *SI*, which is written from a place so deep in the interstice between sports and time (and life in its moments) that I have no words to characterize the story — except to call it one-of-a-kind and magnificent.

I should confess here to some prejudice in the selection of these pieces for reprint. I tend to like stories that treat a whole life, or at least the connection between sports and the rest of life. It makes good sense to me that *how a person is* — the conditions of his or her larger life — explains, or at least illuminates, how that person plays and competes. I have to call it a prejudice, because art is never plane geometry: I used to think the author of a great book had to be a great person. (It turns out that's not true.)

This book is rich in profiles that straddle sport and the rest of being. There are great examples of life shaping athletic excellence. The starkest is Steve Friedman's wondrous tale of manic-depression fueling a down-and-out Scotsman to ride a bike faster than any man ever had. There are rip-snorting portraits of a camera-loving young bass fisherman and the *dame terrible* of the WNBA. *SI*'s splendid Gary Smith contributes a better-than-splendid look at why Mia Hamm simply can't think of herself. Peter de Jonge's masterly profile of Amare Stoudemire shows basketball as a life's sense and salvation. And once you read Peter Hessler's study of Yao Ming at home and away, you'll wonder how the man plays basketball with a billion Chinese on his back. One of the strangest and most compelling contributions is this book's only piece of athlete autobiography: Lynne Cox describes her swimming career and its culmination, a swim to Antarctica. The plainest language shows us how hard and cold it was. And it shows us, too, the other side of the

life-and-sport coin — how a sporting dream can take over and become life.

It strikes me as wonderful what a wide swath of life these sports
stories cover. Or you could call this another prejudice of mine —
for the wide-angle view of what *is* sports writing. I'm pleased that
the book contains some glimpses of the underbelly of sports — in a
mordant *Sun-Times* account of how the Cubs are scalping their own
tickets, or in Lisa Olson's sharp-eyed look at the girls who bed
the big-time ballplayers. Michael Leahy's *Washington Post Magazine*
piece about the last days of the Michael Jordan Wizards is tight and
right on the basketball, but it's also a fine political story. Carlton
Stowers, from the *Dallas Observer,* uses six-man high school football
to tell the story of a whole Texas town. When Guy Martin writes
about flats fishing, it's sporting for sure (because the fish mostly
win), but it's about nothing less than how guys are. And when *The
New Yorker*'s Susan Orlean files from the far frontier of taxidermy
. . . well, I'm not sure if it's sport, but I know it's too good to leave
out of the book.

I have a couple more prejudices to explain here — happily without example. There's no gossip. There were a few submissions that
attempted to judge the Kobe Bryant rape case, based on stuff his
"friends" said. They're not in the book. And there are in this volume very few statistics. Big numbers are the punch line for writers
who can't write how it was.

When someone does write how it was, or how it is, it thrills us with
the same exultation that we feel when a fellow being excels on
the field, the court, the course, or the track. It shows us the possibility of perfection, the hope that we might, through grace and
grit, loose the human bonds of error and mediocrity. In fact, you
couldn't have one excellence without the other. Of course, sportswriters need great athletes to write about. But it is also true that
since the first marathon (from Marathon!), since the days of gladia-
tors and the (Winston?) Chariot Cup, there could be no dream of
athletic immortality without somebody to sing of it.

I don't think it's stretching things to say that the writers in this
book show, in their field, the same sort of hyper-acuity that athletic
heroes show in their games. Like the athletes, most of these writers
have been better at their game than their supposed peers for a long

time — since they were kids. And like the men and women they chronicle, they have bent all else to their art — doing this makes everything else seem small. (They should fall to their knees and thank God there's no one covering *their* personal lives.)

It's an honor to have a part in placing their stuff between book covers — for posterity and for thousands of readers who'll take from this collection both pleasure and inspiration . . . Come to think of it, I really should start over — I mean, in my game. Since the question is really what *two* things you'd need on that island, you know — and the entirety of Roman literature is waiting for me in urns there — I *could* keep two things dry on my swim. It could be the satellite rig — the sun will show me how to point it at the equator . . . and the entire collection of *Best American Sports Writing.* I think it's a winner. What do you say?

RICHARD BEN CRAMER

The Best American
Sports Writing
2004

Dusting Off Home

FROM THE KANSAS CITY STAR

ON THE ROAD to Villa Vasquez, Tony Peña cried, not for the first time that day and not for the last.

"No," he said. "Not that story. I will not tell that story."

His Mercedes raced through dust and bugs and waves of heat, past emptiness. Nobody lives on the road to Villa Vasquez. It is too hot and too dry. They say that when revolutionaries were killed — in the Dominican Republic, revolutionaries were often killed — their bodies were buried here.

They say that at night, you hear ghosts.

"Not that story," Peña said again. He shook his head. "I will tell you everything. But not that story. Some things, the heart cannot bear to hear."

He stared through the windshield ahead and did not talk for a moment. The silence was unlike him. Peña cannot bear quiet. He has always needed noise in his life — music, applause, laughter, bat cracks, glove pops, cheers, whistles, chatter, snores, the ringing of cell phones. Peña has three cell phones. When one does not ring for even a short while — a rare occurrence — he instinctively checks to make sure it works.

"No," he said again, and then "No" again to fill the silence. Tears trickled from beneath his sunglasses. His hands tightened on the steering wheel, and blood rushed to his fingertips. He pushed the car even faster. The cactuses blurred past. After a while, a small shack appeared. Another. A farmer. A goat. We had reached Villa Vasquez. The ghosts were behind us.

"Now," Peña said, his tears already dried, "I will show you where it all began."

Every year, Tony Peña takes this sentimental journey. It is something he must do. The journey begins at the baseball field in Villa Vasquez. Peña stood outside, wrapped his fingers around a chain-link fence. As always, dozens of children played baseball on the field. Some wore gloves. Others wrapped their hands in rags. Some threw baseballs, others threw stones swathed in tape.

"They are me," he said.

Peña had come to this field more than twenty-five years ago to try out for the legendary old Pittsburgh scout Howie Haak. In those days, in the smallest towns of Latin America, there was only Howie Haak. He was *la esperanza*. The hope. Haak was the kind of man who could chew tobacco for hours without spitting. He was the only man who would hold a tryout camp in Villa Vasquez.

"I was just a skinny little kid," Peña said. He pointed at one of the thinnest kids on the field, one who wore a torn Houston Astros T-shirt.

"Like him," Peña said.

Memories rushed back at him like 95-mph fastballs. He called over Royals general manager Allard Baird and pointed at different children, some who threw with a certain snap in their wrists, some who wore tattered sandals on their feet, some who reminded Peña so much of himself.

Look now. Peña is manager of the Kansas City Royals. He caught for almost two decades in the major leagues. He owns one of the biggest bottled-water plants in the Dominican Republic. His driveway is jammed with luxury cars that can push high speeds on the narrow two-lane roads that wind through his country. His swimming pool is shaped like a baseball. He is rich and utterly beloved.

He keeps coming back to the field in Villa Vasquez.

"I was so hungry," he said of that day when he tried out for Howie Haak. Peña lived in Palo Verde, some thirty miles away. He was eighteen. He slipped out of school early, ran part of the way, hitched a ride the rest. He had not eaten for a day and a half. When he got to the field, he felt weak. He could not have weighed even 140 pounds.

But he still hit home runs to left field, center field, and right field. He threw low and hard to second base. There were fifty dreamers there. Howie Haak chose only him.

"Mrs. Peña," Haak said to Tony's mother, Rosalia. "We want your son to play baseball in America."

"I have heard you," Rosalia said. "Now get out of my house."

"Look," Tony Peña said. He was driving away from Villa Vasquez on the bumpy two-lane road toward Palo Verde, where he grew up. People along the road recognized the car and waved wildly.

"Look," he said again, and he pointed out the window to the top of a distant mountain. "Can you see it? If you look very hard, you can see the crane up there. Can you see the crane? Can you see where they are building?"

He kept pointing to the spot.

"That is the highest spot in the Dominican Republic," he said. "From up there, you can see everything. You can see the valley. You can see the ocean. You can see the whole island. I used to look up there and dream."

"Now," he said, as he rolled up the window, "they are building my house up there."

In Palo Verde, the old woman nodded and shrugged. And Tony Peña walked in. Sunlight slipped through cracks in the roof. The walls warped inward. Peña pointed to a wall and a framed photograph of Pedro Martínez, perhaps the greatest player to come off this island. "Right there," Peña said, "there used to be a picture of Jesus."

This was his home. Six Peñas lived in this tiny house with its dirt floors. Octaviano Peña worked fourteen hours a day in an irrigation ditch. He made the equivalent of a few dollars a week. Rosalia taught school for less. Tony slept with his three brothers in the side room, about the size of a walk-in closet. From the front porch, they could see the banana trees that foretold their future.

"Hope?" asked Luis Silverio, Peña's longtime friend and the Royals' first-base coach. "What hope? This was so long ago. There were no baseball scouts in the Dominican then. There were no academies. To dream about playing baseball in America took a big imagination then."

Peña dreamed anyway. It was Rosalia who taught him baseball. Octaviano was too busy, too exhausted, too beaten down by life. Tony liked to say, with a strange pride, that his father did not even know on which hand to wear a baseball glove. "He worked," Peña said, "every minute of every day."

Rosalia taught them baseball. She had been a softball star, and she would place two little Peñas in the outfield, one in the on-deck circle, and one in the batter's box. She pitched. "She had some kind of arm," Tony said. "Hitting her was like trying to hit Nolan Ryan."

She didn't consider baseball a career option for Tony. Boys in the Dominican were supposed to play baseball — it added color to a dreary life of farming and burning sunshine. But that was all. Tony Peña's life was already laid out. His future wife, Amaris, lived three houses down. He was strong enough to work in the banana fields. He would have children and live his life in Palo Verde. When the baseball scout asked to take Tony away to America for baseball, he might as well have asked to take him on a spaceship to Pluto.

"Please," Tony said to his mother. And then he said something that can only be loosely translated to mean: "Baseball is all that is in my heart."

Rosalia remained unmoved.

"If I don't make it in one year," Tony said, "I will come home."

Rosalia considered the offer. Octaviano did not agree, but it was Rosalia who would decide. And she nodded. She was sitting right there, Tony Peña would say more than twenty-five years later, and he pointed to a table under a straw roof. His voice began to choke a little. He walked out into the sunshine.

"Thank you so much," Allard Baird said to the old woman who had let everyone into Peña's old house. "Thank you so much. That was so nice." The woman looked puzzled.

"That was nice of her, wasn't it?" Baird said to Peña.

"What do you mean?" Peña asked.

"Well, for her to let us into her home."

"I own this home," Peña said. "It is my home."

"You?"

"Yes," he said. "I let this woman live here. She is a friend."

Peña took one more look back at the little house.

"I have only one condition. She must leave it exactly the same. Exactly the way it was when I was a child here.

"Exactly the same," he said. "Forever."

Tony Peña handed out Royals caps outside his old house. Dozens gathered around him. People poured out of their homes to get a hat and to shake Peña's hand and to tell stories. Allard Baird watched from a distance.

"The first time I remember seeing Tony Peña," Baird said, "he was with Boston. He was catching. Roger Clemens was on the mound. Clemens was all over the place. He couldn't throw a strike. He had no command. He was awful.

"And all of a sudden, I see Tony Peña call timeout. Joe Morgan, the Red Sox manager, starts to walk out, but Peña told him to go back into the dugout. He's got it under control. Tony walked to the mound and just started screaming at Clemens. I mean, he went nuts. He's pointing and yelling and getting into Clemens's face. The umpire was afraid to go up there.

"And you know what? Clemens took it. I've never seen anything like it. I don't think there was anybody else on earth who could talk to Roger Clemens that way. He just listened, and when Peña went back behind the plate, Clemens pitched an unbelievable ball game."

As Baird finished, Peña walked over to get more Royals caps.

"I was just telling the Clemens story," Baird said.

"The one where I told him to (bleep bleep)?" Peña asked.

"That's what you told him?"

"Yes. That's nothing, though. You should tell the story about when I went to the mound and hit our closer José Mesa in the head."

"You hit José Mesa in the head?"

"Yes," Peña said as he went back to give out some more caps. "He wasn't paying attention."

The grass stopped growing on the field Tony Peña built in Palo Verde. Peña wanted to build a little paradise here, where he had played ball as a child. When he played, it had been a dirt field, hard as tile, with cracks and bumps and craters. He built outfield walls, carved a soft infield, planted the greenest grass to be found for forty miles.

The Dominican heat baked the field. The grass stopped growing.

"It used to be . . ." Peña began, but he stopped.

"Ah," he said. "Everything used to be something."

Tony Peña did not want to come back to his old life. That was what pushed him to play baseball with an almost deranged passion. There was this day, when he was playing in the rookie leagues — and not playing much — when Howie Haak called Peña over.

"Kid," Haak said, "you better start playing. 'Cause they're gonna cut you."

"How," Peña asked in halted English, "can I get them to give me a chance to play?"

"I don't know," Haak said. "But you better figure it out."

Figure it out how? Peña did not speak English well enough to talk to anybody. In a way, though, that shielded him from the hard truth: nobody in the Pirates organization thought he could play. They decided he was too weak to hit home runs, too impatient to lay off bad pitches, too erratic to catch in the major leagues.

He hit .214 his first season, all in part-time duty, and he was shuffled out to left field and third base, where he was completely lost. Soon after, they moved him to catcher, and he set league records for errors. They were ready to give up on him. It's a common Dominican story.

He did not know how to convince them he could play.

The answer, unexpectedly, came in Buffalo, Pittsburgh's Class AA team. Peña noticed there was a short fence in right field. And that short fence was his escape. Every winter, Peña returned home to the Dominican Republic, milked the cows, worked the land, listened to his father grumble that it was time for him to give up this baseball foolishness. "It is time for real life," Octaviano said.

Instead, Tony Peña ran the stairs in front of the biggest church in Santiago to build up his stamina. He taught himself to crouch with one leg sticking out, so he could give pitchers a low target and still spring up and throw out base runners. He would swing a heavy bat for hours every day to gain strength. He prayed at night for God to show him the path.

And when he saw that wonderful short fence in Buffalo, he understood. That was his path. He practiced poking long fly balls toward that short right-field fence. He had shown no power until then. But he hit thirty-four home runs in Buffalo — more than twice as many as he would ever hit again.

And he was noticed. Two years later, he was in the big leagues, where he would stay for eighteen seasons, win four Gold Gloves, play in five All-Star Games and two World Series.

"He and Johnny Bench were the two best catchers I ever saw," said José Cruz Sr., who played nineteen seasons in the major leagues himself. "Soft hands. Strong arm. A leader. That was what made Tony Peña special. He was a leader."

Tony Peña drove slowly on the bumpy dirt road, past banana trees. "Juan Marichal lived not so far away," he said softly. But his mind drifted elsewhere. He was quiet again. He could not stop looking at the trees.

"People don't know how heavy bananas are," he finally said. "You drag them and drag them until you cannot move. People don't know. Your whole body hurts. You can't even sleep at night because your whole body hurts."

Peña said he has never lived a day — not a single day as player or coach or manager — when he did not think about what might have been. He imagined himself pulling bananas, the way all his friends, all his loved ones, everyone he grew up knowing, ended up pulling bananas.

"People in the Dominican are so happy," he said. "That's what I love about my country. People are so poor. They have no money. They live in these little houses. Everybody thinks they must be very sad. But they are not. They are so happy."

He cried again. And he drove over a ditch into a little town.

In the center of town, there was a dirt field. Children played baseball.

"Look," he said. "My country."

He saved everything. Peña has a sentimental streak wider than the road to Santiago. He brought pieces of the Dominican with him to baseball. When he hurt his thumb, he holed out a lemon, poured salt inside, and kept his thumb in there. "This is how we heal in the Dominican," he told amused reporters. But he played that night.

Whenever he would get a new catcher's mitt, he would spend an hour or more bashing it with a baseball bat. "It's too new," he would say. "In my country, you never see a new glove."

And all during his career, he saved things. He saved every glove he ever used. He saved every bat that delivered an important hit.

He saved buckets of baseballs, often asking teammates to sign and date them. Now, the lettering on those baseballs has faded. He cannot tell which ball means what. It does not matter. He has a room in his home in Santiago with every ball, bat, glove, trophy, plaque, and photo he could bring back. They all mean something.

"Whenever I go in that room," he said, "I see something, and it makes me remember. I like to remember."

His favorite photo is of the last time he went up to hit. He was the manager of Aguilas, a team in Santiago that is probably more beloved than any other team in the Dominican Republic. Every winter, without fail, Peña played for Aguilas. His jersey is retired in Aguilas Stadium, along with the jersey of his brother, Ramón. There were years, Tony suspects, when he caught 170 games in the major leagues, including spring training, then caught 75 more in Santiago. He does not know how he did it.

"People have loved Tony Peña because of the way he played," Silverio said. "But he became a hero because he came home."

"Everybody in the Dominican," Royals second baseman Carlos Febles said, "wants to be Tony Peña."

In his favorite photograph, Peña is surrounded by his Aguilas players. And they all point toward the field. Peña had decided to send up a pinch hitter. And his players demanded that he go out and hit himself.

Peña looked at the photo. "I can hear the crowd chanting my name," he said. Flags waved. Feet stomped. Peña shook his head, "No, no, no," but eventually he did go out to the plate. The photo does not show what happened when Peña went up to hit.

"Base hit," Peña said. "Base hit off of José Mesa. And we won."

Tony Peña weaved his car in the twilight, through small towns, through a police checkpoint, around entire families riding on mopeds, past long lines of men walking along the side of the road. "They are looking for work," he said. "When they get tired, they will go to sleep by the side of the road. And tomorrow, they will walk to the next town."

He parked by the water in Monte Cristi, where he was born. He stepped out, and mosquitoes attacked with vengeance. Monte Cristi is one of the oldest towns in the new world — Christopher Columbus landed not so far away. Peña walked out to the water, to the largest boat on the docks that overlooked the north Atlantic Ocean. The boat is his. He climbed in and leaned against the railing and looked over the water. He talked about how the Royals would win, despite everybody picking them to lose. They would win because they would believe.

Peña said he has always known how to make people believe.

"You know," he said, "after I finished playing, there were teams that offered to make me a coach. Right away. Chicago wanted me to be a coach. Houston wanted me to be a coach. I said, 'No.' I didn't want to be a coach. I wanted to be a manager. So I told them, 'Send me back to the minor leagues.'

"And they said, 'You don't want to go back to ride buses and all that.' And I said, 'Yes, I do. Send me back.' They sent me to New Orleans for three years. It was hard. But I learned so much. You have to go back to learn. You have to go back to the beginning."

He nodded and swatted at mosquitoes. In the Dominican, as the old line goes, they treat Tony Peña as something larger than a man and something smaller than a saint. He played baseball with joy, made millions, became a manager, and then, most important, he came home.

He still comes home. Every day all winter, strangers come to his door. They need medicine or food. He offers it to them quietly. Politicians seek his approval. Mothers push their children toward him to reach for his hand so maybe something will rub off. His Royals play on television all summer.

"I'm not sure that people in Kansas City," one Dominican journalist said, "realize who Tony Peña is. You have hired our national hero."

"I have seen people forget where they came from," Peña said. "They buy expensive things — houses, cars, boats — and they forget. I cannot forget. I must not forget. I tell myself this every day. If you forget where you came from, you forget who you are."

"All right," Peña said softly as he drove through the dark, back to his home. "I will tell you the story now."

The sun had gone down. The air was cool on the road back to Santiago.

"When I signed with the Pittsburgh Pirates," he said, "my signing bonus was $4,000. That was more money than my father made in

a year. It was so much money, there was no place near my home
to cash the check. We had to go to Santiago, to the bank there, to
cash it.

"When we got there, we cashed the check, and I tried, I tried
to . . ."

Peña started to cry again. He stumbled on. He tried to give the
money to his mother. But Rosalia would not take it. The money was
his, she said, to save, to use if baseball failed, to give to his children.
Tony told her that he would make it. She did not believe him. And
she would not take the money.

"Proud," Peña said softly and angrily. "So proud."

A few days later, some men came and took away what little furniture filled the Peña home. Octaviano could not make the payments. Tony ran up to the men and offered his money, but Rosalia
shouted at him. "No," she said. "That's yours. That's yours for your
life."

Then, to the men, she said, "You may not have his money."

Tony pleaded with her. He said they could not live in an empty
home. He could not leave knowing that the house was empty. He
begged her to take the money. But she would not listen. So one day,
he quietly slipped out of the house and went to the company that
took back the furniture. He gave them $800 and bought back all
the furniture. He had it delivered to the house.

Rosalia was so angry, she would not speak to him.

"Bye, Mama," he said to her as he headed to America to play
baseball. She said nothing at all.

Years later, long after such things were forgotten or at least not
talked about, Tony Peña and his mother went driving. They often
went driving after Peña bought his first car. By then, he was one of
the best catchers in baseball, a rich man, a Dominican hero.

They drove around a beautiful community near Santiago. "Isn't
this nice?" he asked his mother.

"Yes," she said. "It is beautiful."

They then drove through a neighborhood of homes. It was a
neighborhood they had driven through before, many times. "I love
these homes," Rosalia said.

"I know," Tony said. "I know."

And they pulled up to the nicest home.

"What do you think of this one?" he asked her.

"It is the home of my dreams," she said.

He reached into his pocket, pulled out a key, gave it to her.

"It is yours," he said. They both cried for a long time.

"All the things I have done in my life," Tony Peña said, "that is the greatest. I bought my mother a home. It is the greatest thing a man can do."

Rosalia Peña still lives in that home. Tony Peña still returns to the Dominican every winter.

And, in Santiago, there is an open bank account. In it is $3,200 plus twenty-five years or so of interest. It is every remaining penny of the bonus the Pittsburgh Pirates gave Tony Peña a long time ago.

SUSAN ORLEAN

Lifelike

FROM THE NEW YORKER

As SOON AS the 2003 World Taxidermy Championships opened, the heads came rolling in the door. There were foxes and moose and freeze-dried wild turkeys; mallards and buffalo and chipmunks and wolves; weasels and buffleheads and bobcats and jackdaws; big fish and little fish and razor-backed boar. The deer came in herds, in carloads, and on pallets: dozens and dozens of whitetail and roe; half-deer and whole deer and deer with deformities, sneezing and glowering and nuzzling and yawning; does chewing apples and bucks nibbling leaves. There were millions of eyes, boxes and bowls of them; some as small as a lentil and some as big as a poached egg. There were animal mannequins, blank-faced and brooding, earless and eyeless and utterly bald: ghostly gray duikers and spectral pine martens and black-bellied tree ducks from some other world. An entire exhibit hall was filled with equipment, all the gear required to bring something dead back to life: replacement noses for grizzlies, false teeth for beavers, fish-fin cream, casting clay, upholstery nails.

The championships were held in April at the Springfield, Illinois, Crowne Plaza hotel, the sort of nicely appointed place that seems more suited to regional sales conferences and rehearsal dinners than to having wolves in the corridors and people crossing the lobby shouting, "Heads up! Buffalo coming through!" A thousand taxidermists converged on Springfield to have their best pieces judged and to attend such seminars as "Mounting Flying Waterfowl," "Whitetail Deer — From a Master!," and "Using a Fleshing Machine." In the Crowne Plaza lobby, across from the concierge desk, a grooming area had been set up. The taxidermists were bent over their animals, holding flashlights to check problem areas like tear ducts and nostrils, and wielding toothbrushes to tidy flyaway fur. People milled around, greeting fellow-taxidermists they hadn't seen since the last world championships, held in Springfield two years ago, and talking shop:

"Acetone rubbed on a squirrel tail will fluff it right back up."

"My feeling is that it's quite tough to do a good tongue."

"The toes on a real competitive piece are very important. I think Bondo works nicely, and so does Super Glue."

"I knew a fellow with cattle, and I told him, 'If you ever have one stillborn, I'd really like to have it.' I thought it would make a really nice mount."

That there is a taxidermy championship at all is something of an astonishment, not only to the people in the world who have no use for a Dan-D-Noser and Soft Touch Duck Degreaser but also to taxidermists themselves. For a long time, taxidermists kept their own counsel. Taxidermy, the three-dimensional representation of animals for permanent display, has been around since the eighteenth century, but it was first brought into popular regard by the Victorians, who thrilled to all tokens of exotic travel and especially to any domesticated representations of wilderness — the glassed-in miniature rain forest on the tea table, the mounted antelope by the front door. The original taxidermists were upholsterers who tanned the hides of hunting trophies and then plumped them up with rags and cotton, so that they reassumed their original shape and size; those early poses were stiff and simple, and the expressions fairly expressionless. The practice grew popular in this country, too: by 1882, there was a Society of American Taxidermists, which held annual meetings and published scholarly reports, especially on the matter of preparing animals for museum display. As long as taxidermy served to preserve wild animals and make them available for study, it was viewed as an honorable trade, but most people were still discomfited by it. How could you not be? It was the business of dealing with dead things, coupled with the questionable enterprise of making dead things look like live things. In spite of its scientific value, it was usually regarded as almost a black art, a wholly owned subsidiary of witchcraft and voodoo. By the early part of the twentieth century, taxidermists such as Carl E. Akeley,

William T. Horneday, and Leon Pray had refined techniques and begun emphasizing artistry. But, the more the techniques of taxidermy improved, the more it discomfited: instead of the lumpy moose head that was so artless that it looked fake, there were mounts of pouncing bobcats so immaculately and exactly preserved they made you flinch.

For the next several decades, taxidermy existed in the margins — a few practitioners here and there, often self-taught, and usually known only by word of mouth. Then, in the late 1960s, a sort of transformation began: the business started to seem cleaner and less creepy — or maybe, in that messy, morbid time, popular culture started to again appreciate the messy, morbid business of mounting animals for display. An ironic reinterpretation of cluttered, bourgeois Victoriana and its strained juxtapositions of the natural and the man-made was in full revival — what hippie outpost didn't have a stuffed owl or a moose head draped with a silk shawl? — so, once again, taxidermy found a place in the public eye. Supply houses concocted new solvents and better tanning compounds, came out with lightweight mannequins, produced modern formulations of resins and clays. Taxidermy schools opened; previously, any aspiring taxidermist could only hope to learn the trade by apprenticing or by taking one of a few correspondence courses available. In 1971, the National Taxidermy Association was formed (the old society had moldered long before). In 1974, a trade magazine called *Taxidermy Review* began sponsoring national competitions. For the first time, most taxidermists had a chance to meet one another and share advice on how to glue tongues into jaw sets or accurately measure the carcass of a squirrel.

The competitions were also the first time that taxidermists could compare their skills and see who in the business could sculpt the best moose septum or could most perfectly capture the look on a prowling coyote's face. Taxidermic skill is a function of how deft you are at skinning an animal and then stretching its hide over a mannequin and sewing it into place. Top-of-the-line taxidermists sculpt their own mannequins; otherwise they will buy a ready-made polyurethane-foam form and tailor the skin to fit. Body parts that can't be preserved (ears, eyes, noses, lips, tongues) can be either store-bought or handmade. How good the mount looks — that is, how alive it looks — is a function of how assiduously the taxidermist has studied reference material (photographs, drawings, and actual live animals) so that he or she knows the particular creature literally and figuratively inside out.

To be good at taxidermy, you have to be good at sewing, sculpting, painting, and hairdressing, and mostly you have to be a little bit of a zoology nerd. You have to love animals — love looking at them, taking photographs of them, hunting them, measuring them, casting them in plaster of Paris when they're dead so that you have a reference when you're, say, attaching ears or lips and want to get the angle and shape exactly right. Some taxidermists raise the animals they most often mount, so they can just step out in the back yard when they're trying to remember exactly how a deer looks when it's licking its nose, especially because modern taxidermy emphasizes mounts with interesting expressions, rather than the stunned-looking creations of the past. Taxidermists seem to make little distinction between loving animals that are alive and loving ones that are not. "I love deer," one of the champions in the whitetail division said to me. "They're my babies."

Taxidermy is now estimated to be a $570 million annual business, made up of small operators around the country who mount animals for museums, for decorators, and mostly for the thirteen million or so Americans who are recreational hunters and on occasion want to preserve and display something they killed and who are willing to shell out anywhere from two hundred dollars to mount a pheasant to several thousand for a kudu or a grizzly bear. There are state and regional taxidermy competitions throughout the year and the world championships, which are held every other year; two trade magazines; a score of taxidermy schools; and three thousand visits to Taxidermy.net every day, where taxidermists can trade information and goods with as little self-consciousness as you would find on a knitting website:

"I am in need of several pair of frozen goat feet!"

"Hi! I have up to 300 sets of goat feet and up to 1000 set of sheep feet per month. Drop me an email at frozencritters.com. . . . or give me a call and we can discuss your needs."

"I have a very nice small raccoon that is frozen whole. I forgot he was in the freezer. Without taking exact measurements I would guess he is about twelve inches or so — very cute little one. Will make a very nice mount."

"Can I rinse a boar hide good and freeze it?"

"Bob, if it's salted, don't worry about it!"

"Can someone please tell me the proper way to preserve turkey legs and spurs? Thanks!"

"Brian, I inject the feet with Preservz-It. . . . Enjoy!"

The word in the grooming area was that the piece to beat was Chris Krueger's happy-looking otters swimming in a perpetual circle around a leopard frog. A posting on Taxidermy.net earlier in the week declared, "EVERYTHING about this mount KICKS BUTT!!" Kicking butt, in this era of taxidermy, requires having a mount that is not just lifelike but also artistic. It used to be enough to do what taxidermists call "fish on a stick" displays; now a serious competitor worries about things like flow and negative space and originality. One of this year's contenders, for instance, Ken Walker's giant panda, had artistry and accuracy going for it, along with the element of surprise. The thing looked 100 percent pure panda, but you can't go out and shoot a panda, and you aren't likely to get hold of a panda that has met a natural end, so everyone was dying to know how he had done it. The day the show opened, Walker was in the grooming area, gluing bamboo into place behind the animal's back paws, and a crowd had gathered around him. Walker works as a staff taxidermist for the Smithsonian. He is a breezy, shaggy-haired guy whose hands are always busy. One day, I saw him holding a piece of clay while waiting for a seminar to begin, and within thirty seconds or so, without actually paying much attention to it, he had molded the clay into a little minklike creature.

"The panda was actually pretty easy," he was saying. "I just took two black bears and bleached one of them — I think I used Clairol Basic. Then I sewed the two skins together into a panda pattern." He took out a toothbrush and fluffed the fur on the panda's face. "At the world championship two years ago, a guy came in with an extinct Labrador duck. I was in awe. I thought, *What could beat that — an extinct duck?* And I came up with this idea." He said he thought that the panda would get points for creativity alone. "You can score a 98 with a squirrel, but it's still a squirrel," he said. "So that means I'm going with a panda."

"What did you do for toenails, Ken?" someone asked.

"I left the black bear's toenails in," he said. "They looked pretty good."

Another passerby stopped to admire the panda. He was carrying a grooming kit, which appeared to contain Elmer's glue, brown and black paint, a small tool set, and a bottle of Suave mousse. "I killed a blond bear once," he said to Ken. "A two-hundred-pound sow. Whew, she made a beautiful mount."

"I'll bet," Ken said. He stepped back to admire the panda. "I like doing re-creations of these endangered animals and extinct animals, since that's the only way anyone's going to have one. Two years ago, I did a saber-toothed cat. I got an old lioness from a zoo and bleached her."

The panda was entered in the Re-Creation (Mammal) division, one of the dozens of divisions and subdivisions and sub-subcategories, ranging from the super-specific (Whitetail Deer Long Hair, Open Mouth Division) to the sweepingly colossal (Best in World), that would share in $25,000 worth of prizes. (There is even a sub-sub-subspecialty known as "fish carving," which uses no natural fish parts at all; it is resin and wood sculpted into a fish form and then painted.) Nearly all the competitors are professionals, and they publicize their awards wherever possible. For instance, instead of ordering just any Boar Eye-Setting Reference Head out of a taxidermy catalog, you can order the Noonkester's #NRB-ERH head sculpted by Bones Johnson, which was, as the catalog notes, the 2000 National Taxidermy Association Champion Gamehead.

The taxidermists take the competition very seriously. During the time I was in Springfield, I heard conversations analyzing such arcane subjects as exactly how much a javelina's snout wrinkles when it snarls and which molars deer use to chew acorns as opposed to which ones they use to chew leaves. This is important because the ultimate goal of a taxidermist is to make the animal look exactly as if it had never died, as if it were still in the middle of doing ordinary animal things like plucking berries off a bush or taking a nap. When I walked around with the judges one morning, I heard discussions that were practically Talmudic, about whether the eyelids on a bison mount were overdetailed, and whether the nostrils on a springbok were too wide, and whether the placement of whiskers on an otter appeared too deliberate. "You do get compulsive," a taxidermist in the exhibit hall explained to me one afternoon. At the time, he was running a feather duster over his entry — a bobcat hanging off an icicle-covered rock — in the last moments before the judging would begin. "When you're working on a piece, you forget to eat, you forget to drink, you even forget to sleep. You get up in the middle of the night and go into the shop so you can keep working. You get completely caught up in it. You want it to be perfect. You're trying to make something come back to life."

I said that his bobcat was beautiful, and that even the icicles on the piece looked completely real. "I made them myself," he said. "I used clear acrylic toilet-plunger handles. The good Lord sent the idea to me while I was in a hardware store. I just took the handles and put them in the oven at four hundred degrees." He tapped the icicles and then added, "My wife was pretty worried, but I did it on a nonstick cookie sheet."

So who wants to be a taxidermist? "I was a meat cutter for fifteen years," a taxidermist from Kentucky said to me. "That whole time, no one ever said to me, 'Boy, that was a wonderful steak you cut me.' Now I get told all the time what a great job I've done." Steve Faechner, who is the president and chairman of the Academy of Realistic Taxidermy, in Havre, Montana, started mounting animals in 1989, after years spent working on the railroad. "I had gotten hurt, and was looking for something to do," he said. "I was with a friend who did taxidermy and I thought to myself, *I have got to get a life.* And this was it." Larry Blomquist, who is the owner of the World Taxidermy Championships and of *Breakthrough*, the trade magazine that sponsors the competition, was a schoolteacher for three years before setting up his business. There are a number of women taxidermists (one was teaching this year's seminar on Problem Areas in Mammal Taxidermy), and there are budding junior taxidermists, who had their own competition division, for kids fourteen and younger, at the show.

The night the show opened, I went to dinner with three taxidermists who had driven in from Kentucky, Michigan, and Maryland. They were all married, and all had wives who complained when they found one too many antelope carcasses in the family freezer, and all worked full-time mounting animals — mostly deer, for local hunters, but occasional safari work, for people who had shot something in Africa. When I mentioned that I had no idea that a person could make a living as a taxidermist, they burst out laughing, and the guy from Kentucky pointed out that he lived in a little town and there were two other full-time taxidermists in business right down the road.

"What's the big buzz this year?" the man from Michigan asked.

"I don't know. Probably something new with eyes," the guy from Maryland answered. "That's where you see the big advances. Remember at the last championship, those Russian eyes?" These were glass animal eyes that had a reflective paint embedded in them, so that if you shone a light they would shine back at you, sort of like the way real animals' eyes do. The men discussed those for a while, then talked about the new fish eyes being introduced this year, which have photographic transfers of actual fish eyes printed on plastic lenses. We happened to be in a restaurant with a sports theme, and there were about a hundred televisions on around the room, broadcasting dozens of different athletic events, but the men never glanced at them, and never stopped talking about their trade. We had all ordered barbecued ribs. When dinner was over, all three of them were fiddling around with the bones before the waitress came to clear our plates.

"Look at these," the man from Kentucky said, holding up a rib. "You could take these home and use them to make a skeleton."

In the seminars, the atmosphere was as sober and exacting as a tax-law colloquium. "Whiskers," one of the instructors said to the group, giving them a stern look. "I pull them out. I label them. There are left whiskers and there are right whiskers. If you want to get those top awards, you're going to have to think about whiskers." Everyone took notes. In the next room: "Folks, remember, your carcass is your key. The best thing you can do is to keep your carcass in the freezer. Freeze the head, cast it in plaster. It's going to really help if your head is perfect." During the breaks, the group made jokes about a T-shirt that had been seen at one of the regional competitions. The shirt said "PETA" in big letters, but when you got up close you saw that PETA didn't spell out People for the Ethical Treatment of Animals, the bane of all hunters and, by extension, all taxidermists; it spelled out "People Eating Tasty Animals." Chuckles all around, then back to the solemn business of Mounting Flying Waterfowl: "People, follow what the bird is telling you. Study it, do your homework. When you've got it ready, fluff the head, shake it, and then get your eyes. There are a lot of good eyes out there on the market today. Do your legwork, and you can have a beautiful mount."

It was brisk and misty outside — the antler venders in the parking lot looked chilled and miserable — and the modest charms of

Springfield, with its mall and the Oliver P. Parks Telephone Museum and Abraham Lincoln's tomb, couldn't compete with the strange and wondrous sights inside the hotel. The mere experience of waiting for the elevator — knowing that the doors would peel back to reveal maybe a man and a moose, or a bush pig, or a cougar — was much more exciting than the usual elevator wait in the usual Crowne Plaza hotel. The trade show was a sort of mad tea party of body parts and taxidermy supplies, things for pulling flesh off a carcass, for rinsing blood out of fur — a surreal carnality, but all conveyed with the usual trade-show earnestness and hucksterism, with no irony and no acknowledgment that having buckets of bear noses for sale was anything out of the ordinary. "Come take a look at our beautiful synthetic fur! We're the hair club for lions! If you happen to shoot a lion who is out of season or bald, we can provide you with a gorgeous replacement mane!" "Too many squirrels? Are they driving you nuts? Let us mount them for you!" "Divide and Conquer animal forms — an amazing advance in small-mammal mannequins, patent pending!"

The big winner at the show turned out to be a tiny thing — a mount of two tree sparrows, submitted by a strapping German named Uwe Bauch, who had grown up in the former East Germany dreaming of competing in an American taxidermy show. The piece was precise and lovely, almost haunting, since the more you looked at it the more certain you were that the birds would just stop building their nest, spread their wings, and fly away. Early one morning, before I left Springfield, I took a last walk around the competition hall. It was quiet and uncanny, with hundreds of mounts arranged on long tables throughout the room; the deer heads clustered together, each in a slightly different pose and angle, looked like a kind of animal Roman forum caught in mid-debate. A few of the mounts were a little gory — a deer with a mailbox impaled on an antler, another festooned with barbed wire, and one with an arrow stuck in its brisket — and one display, a coyote whose torso was split open to reveal a miniature scene of the destruction of the World Trade Center, complete with little firemen and rubble piles, was surpassingly weird. Otherwise, the room was biblically tranquil, the lion at last lying down with the Corsican lamb, the family of jackdaws in everlasting, unrequited pursuit of a big green beetle, and the stillborn Bengal-tiger cub magically revived, its face in an eternal snarl, alive-looking although it had never lived.

STEVE FRIEDMAN

The Race of Truth

FROM BICYCLING

CHOOSING IS AN ORDEAL. Chicken korma versus chicken rogan josh should not matter so much. To the ravaged cyclist, though, it is a matter of life and death. He needs to be vigilant. How can he afford not to be? Ten years ago, just a short bike ride from here, the racer peered through a chilly, driving rain and glimpsed the future of his sport in a blinding instant and what he saw brought him fame and riches and love. And then, for the past ten years, the mad vision tortured him.

He can't afford such prescience anymore. He can't survive the agonies it exacts. His doctors have warned him. His wife has pleaded with him. Even his former competitors and detractors, the ones he spent years challenging and vanquishing and mocking, with the hubris only a Prometheus on pedals could summon, even they wish him nothing but peace, because they have witnessed the disfiguring price of revelation.

He was an inventor and a visionary and a champion, who twice stood atop the cycling world by riding farther in one hour than anyone ever had, and, today, he needs to forget all that. He needs to concentrate on the moment. The doctors have told him that, too. Otherwise, what happened that Christmas might happen again. He couldn't bear doing that to his family. He needs to calm down, to take care of himself. He needs to order dinner.

But how can he? Korma versus rogan josh is just one of the agonizing choices facing him. His eight-year-old son wants Kashmiri naan, and though there will be plenty to share with his ten-year-old brother, the eight-year-old isn't much of a sharer. The older boy deserves his own bread, to make him feel special. Garlic bread — that might be the answer. How does the older boy feel about garlic bread? He doesn't feel so great about it, but he *really* doesn't feel great about sharing. The older boy is dyslexic, like the cyclist was when he was a child, and he is clumsy, too, just like his father. The cyclist wants to protect his firstborn. He wishes someone had protected him. He will take a chance: garlic bread.

The decision has cost the cyclist. He is blinking, squinting, grinding his jaw. It is September, chilly and damp in this coastal Scottish village, even inside the restaurant. But he is sweating. First his brow moistens, then beads appear on his broad forehead, and before long — even with him gulping at his pint of Diet Coke — sweat drips down his aquiline nose and onto the table.

His eyes are grayish blue, and he squints and blinks and clenches his jaw during times of stress, like ordering dinner, or when he hears a question that causes him pain, like one about that Christmas. He is olive-skinned, dark-haired, five-foot-eleven and 161 pounds, with broad shoulders and heavy, muscled thighs. In racing close-ups, his high cheekbones and angular jaw combine with an unusually full lower lip to exude lupine menace. At thirty-seven, he has gained about six pounds, taking the edges from his face. Combined with the nervous tics, the effect now is more prey than predator.

The bread arrives and the boys are squabbling and the first pint of Diet Coke is gone and the sweat continues to drip from the racer's nose onto his appetizers, which he has ordered with enormous, excruciating difficulty.

"Oh, for God's sake," his wife says, doing a brave imitation of a laugh. "Wipe your brow."

The racer laughs, too, a small, helpless sound.

"It's a mark of health, you know," he says. "Sweating like that."

"Not Including the Man-Hours"

Bicycling's giants strap on heart monitors and watt-measuring computers and hire coaches who calculate maximal oxygen uptake and calibrate recovery time to the millisecond. They travel with nutritionists, and they ride state-of-the-art machines produced by sophisticated engineering costing hundreds of thousands of dollars.

Graeme Obree lived in Irvine, Scotland, a grim little town in a green, hilly district hard on the Irish Sea. When he was twenty-eight years old, broke, in debt, and on welfare, he announced that he was going to break one of cycling's most prestigious and time-honored records. He said he would do it on a bicycle he had built himself, for $200 ("not including the man-hours, naturally"). He ate canned sardines and chili con carne, vegetables and marmalade sandwiches ("a pretty good diet, I'd say") and boasted that he trained by "riding when I feel like it."

What followed over the next few years — world hour records in 1993 and 1994, world pursuit championships in 1993 and 1995, domination of time-trialing in the mid-'90s — infuriated cycling's image-conscious racing aristocracy as much as it inspired the sport's fans, dreamers and wheel-happy Walter Mittys. Obree's bike was as ungainly as it was original, his riding style as awkward as it was effective. He was funny and, on his bike, funny-looking. He was also something of a loudmouth, often complaining about rampant blood doping in professional biking, years before the highly publicized French and Italian drug investigations of 1998 and beyond proved him right.

After his first and most shocking world championship, in 1993, the British Broadcasting Company (BBC) conducted a telephone poll and named Obree "Scotland's most intriguing sports personality." That's when bicycling's bureaucrats set out to destroy him. Or he began to destroy himself. He's still not sure.

"Don't Worry About That Boy"

He was a clumsy child, falling into streams, knocking into walls, cracking his head open so often that "the blood poured out every other week." His brother, Gordon, older by fourteen months, was the smart one. His little sister, Yvonne, was tougher than either. Graeme was dyslexic and sensitive, terrible at sports, terrible in the classroom. He liked building things, and would have enjoyed metal-work class if it weren't the central gathering place for his huskiest tormentors. Rather than working, he often stood with his back against a wall, a chisel in hand to ward off attackers. "It took me a year to make a trowel and half of a plant-holder bracket. I could have finished both in half a day," he says. "I hated most of my childhood. The only way I had any social interaction was by getting in fights."

His father, John, says, "As far as we're concerned, he was just a normal boy. I wouldn't go so far as to say he was dyslexic. We just thought he was lazy about reading."

He wished his parents loved him more. Sometimes, he wished he were dead.

"I have no idea how I managed to pass as normal in school," writes Kay Redfield Jamison in *An Unquiet Mind*, her memoir of manic-depression, "except that other people are generally caught up in their own lives and seldom notice despair in others if those despairing make an effort to disguise the pain."

Obree pedaled. He'd discovered that by riding as hard as he could, he could almost forget that he didn't have any friends, that his parents always seemed disappointed in him. He began racing by fifteen, on a burgundy, pre-war bike, and at seventeen he won his first race, the eighteen-mile Ayr to Girvan time trial. Total haul: £50, or about $100. He kept conquering local races, but he never won what he really wanted.

In 1985, when Obree was twenty and had found enough success on the local racing circuit that he'd parlayed his winnings into ownership of a local bike shop, his father came home early from work one afternoon and found his son sucking on the pipe of a canister of welding gas.

"He assured us it was an accident," John Obree says, "and he seemed to be perfectly all right afterwards. I tried to get him to seek medical attention, but he seemed to be all right."

This was all right for Obree: hopelessness, terror, a crushing fatigue that sent him to his bedroom, where he would wait under the covers — sometimes weeks and months — for the miraculous moment when the blackness lifted and was replaced with delight and otherworldly energy that made the horror show almost worth it. In good times, he never slept more than two or three hours a night. He hatched business schemes. He read Victorian novels, biology texts, essays, dozens of books at a time (never finishing any). He met a local girl, Anne, got married, won scores of time trials. He twice set the British record for distance in an hour. He sold the shop and joined with an investor to start a bike business.

For seven years, he alternately endured and reveled. By 1992, when he was twenty-six years old, it was mostly about enduring. His business had failed. Obree was broke, in debt, and Anne was pregnant. They often scrabbled through kitchen drawers looking for coins to buy bread. He was taking government-sponsored typing and filing lessons — welfare — so he could become a receptionist.

He watched on television that summer as an Englishman named Chris Boardman rode to first place in the 4,000-meter pursuit at the Barcelona Olympics. Obree had raced Boardman many times. He was one of the few who usually defeated Obree, but not always, and not by much. And now Boardman had a gold medal. What did Obree have? Debt. Disappointed parents. An obscure place in local biking history, reserved for provincial oddballs who crouched when they pedaled.

"Everything," he says, "was bleak. Pointless."

His salvation came on a chilly Saturday afternoon when he was sitting alone, staring at his bike, in the Irvine bike shop where he still occasionally worked. A cold, horizontal rain was blowing in from the Irish Sea, beating against the storefront window. A slow reader, a lazy student, Obree nevertheless possessed an instinctive grasp of physics. He knew there were only two ways to increase speed: boost power output or reduce resistance. He was already pedaling as hard as he could. He stared out into the rain, then back at his bike. He kept staring at the bike.

What if he adjusted the handlebar? Moved the seat closer to the front, and rode with his arms completely folded under his body so air flowed cleanly around his torso? He'd have to learn to keep his entire body rigid. . . . But that would also increase pedal power. . . . But he could train his muscles. . . . And he would need. . . . But what if. . . ?

It took him three months to build the bike he envisioned. He used pieces of scrap metal from the bike shop and bearings he pulled from a washing machine.

In one of his first races, a ten-miler in Port Glasgow, he circled the roundabout at the halfway mark, where the race marshal stood with a local cop.

The cop had never seen anything like the bike — or Obree. He thought he was watching a handicapped racer trying to keep up with the others. "Look at that poor guy," the cop said. "Somebody's gone and built a special bike for him."

"Don't worry about that boy," the marshal said. "I think he's going to win this thing."

"There Are No Words"

Obree's radical new bike was faster than anything he'd ever ridden, faster, maybe, than any other bike on earth.

To the gentlemen of the sport, Obree and his bike were a freak show — a lucky tinkerer on a monstrosity rather than an athlete. Professionals at the races called him the Praying Mantis, because of his riding position.

He'd come home from his receptionist training, wheel out his odd bike at dark, and ride as hard as he could, over the biggest hills, in the biggest gears, in the pitch black. If he pushed faster and harder, sometimes the black mood would lift, and *that* was the bike's real magic. "Everything made sense. It made more sense than it had ever made before. I was invincible. I could do anything."

Afterward, he'd lie in bed awake, fantasizing about the next evening's ride in an effort to quiet the question he could never completely ride away from: "What's the point," he says he thought, over and over. "What's the point? What's the point?"

One night he saw the point. He saw what would forever stop the pain. He would ride his strange bicycle farther in an hour than any human being ever had. Graeme Obree — clumsy, dyslexic receptionist-in-training on the dole — would triumph in an event so forbidding that most of cycling's greatest professionals avoided it, a challenge so ravenous it consumed even its champions. He would seek the Hour Record.

The race that Obree hoped would save him is merely a sixty-minute sprint around a banked track. In its utter simplicity lies its irreducible brutality. There are no coddling slipstreams, no coasting strategies, no tactical slowdowns. A man simply gets on a bike and pedals as fast as he can, as far as he can.

The Tour de France brings its champions worldwide acclaim, deep and flowing income streams, the hallowed yellow jersey. But it

is the Hour Record, not the Tour, that is known among biking co-
gnoscenti, simply and starkly, as The Race of Truth.

"The absence of wind, the regularity of terrain, and the depth of
self-knowledge necessary to maintain a near-peak effort for 60 minutes have chopped through the ranks of great cyclists like a tsu-
nami across a coconut-festooned atoll," wrote Owen Mulholland, a
prolific bike scribe, in 1991.

"How much hubris must you have to say, 'I can ride a bike faster
in an hour than any person who has ever walked the face of the
earth, and I'm going to do it in this place, on this day, at this time?'"
says Andrew Coggan, a longtime cyclist and sports physiologist at
St. Louis's Washington University. "That's why so many champions
haven't even attempted it — they've figured out the ratio of benefit
to reputation risk."

Obree called Mike Burrows, the premier designer who'd built
Boardman's gold medal–winning bike, and asked him to improve
on his vision. Burrows's luminous, pearly white version used car-
bon, was wider in front than Obree's, and more than four pounds
heavier — but was aerodynamically more effective and mechani-
cally more efficient.

Anne urged her husband to ride the bike he'd built himself. It
was a touching sentiment, inspired by love and faith. In The Race
of Truth, though, sentiment holds the same approximate value as a
thatch hut on a coconut-festooned atoll, immediately pre-tsunami.
So at 1:50 P.M. on a Friday afternoon in July, on a wooden track in
Hamar, Norway, Obree mounted the Burrows-built machine.

Friends had warned him that he could not break the Hour Record. Journalists and biking fans on the street all told the Scotsman the same thing — he was attempting the impossible, trying to
achieve the unthinkable. They were right, but they had no idea
what he was really trying to do.

"Now take a deep breath," the starter said. "This is a very big
deal, this is [Francesco] Moser's record, now get hold of yourself."

He pedaled as hard as he could, and it wasn't enough, so he pedaled harder. And when he had finished pedaling, and the hour was
used up, Obree had traveled 50.8 kilometers (31.56 miles), farther
than anyone ever had at sea level. A French television crew rushed
him as he crossed the finish line, presenting him with a huge bou-

quet of flowers. It was a great achievement. But not great enough. He had fallen short of Moser's mark, set at high altitude in Mexico City, by three-tenths of a kilometer, less than two-tenths of a mile.

When Eddy Merckx, generally acknowledged as the greatest cyclist ever, finished his Hour Record in 1972, he could barely speak. As two thousand people cheered, including fifty-three reporters and the former king of Belgium, Merckx was asked about what he had done. When he was able to summon his voice, he said the past sixty minutes were "the longest of my career. . . . I will never try it again."

Obree told the French television crew he wouldn't accept their flowers. Then he told the track officials something else: "I'm going again."

Two Races of Truth — consecutively? Out of the question, race officials said. Obree insisted. The officials relented, but only if he returned to his hotel for the night. If he still wanted to race the next morning, if he could even *walk*, they would open the track.

He was there at 9:50 A.M., without Burrows's gleaming racer. The Scotsman mounted the dull, oil-smudged machine he'd cobbled together.

"Are you sure you're ready?" the starter said. "This is Moser's record now." It was the same pep talk.

"Are *you* ready?" Obree spat out.

"Yeah," the starter said, "but . . ."

The Praying Mantis was off.

To ride for an hour at faster than thirty miles per hour puts strain on the body that few people ever experience. A human heart can beat only so rapidly before it fails; most of us can get within ten beats or so of that rate for a few minutes before we have to cease whatever we're doing. Obree would spend an hour there. He would produce an enormous amount of pure energy as he sped around the track, but fully three-quarters of it would burn off not as propulsion but as heat — the byproduct of his effort. At rest, while the core of the human body thrums along at 98.6 degrees, skin temperature stays at about 95. Even with intense exercise, it usually doesn't get above 100. During The Race of Truth, Obree's skin would burn at close to 107. In one hour, he would burn about 1,800 calories — about three-quarters of a human's average for an entire day.

"You can't go any faster, and you also can't go much longer," Coggan says. "It's like you're flying a jet, and you've hit your afterburners, and you're going through your jet fuel at a profligate rate. At some point, you have to slow down."

"I felt as if I'd reached the stage of death," Obree says. "I think I rode right through it."

He pedaled 51.596 kilometers, more than 32 miles. He broke Moser's nine-year-old record by almost half a kilometer.

A Parisian newspaper reporter wrote, "There are no words in the English or French language to do justice to this story."

The Praying Mantis had died on that track. Obree was now The Flying Scotsman. The Ayr Man. The French referred to him as "L'Homme de l'Heure" (The Man of The Hour). When he returned to Scotland, "I got fifty messages on my answering machine, many of them saying, 'We want to pay you thousands of pounds to come to a track meet.' Before, I'd make thirty to forty pounds a week if I won. Now I'd make thousands just to show up."

"I Was Art"

No one knew his secret.

He didn't want them to know. So as the reporters came calling, he created someone to greet them: a free spirit, a wild child who drank curdled yak's milk and trained only when the spirit moved him, biking's poor-kid bad-boy who made bikes with scrap scavenged from ditches and his mother's washing machine, and painted them with fingernail polish. They were half-truths, embellishments, and outright lies.

One facet of the say-anything persona wasn't artifice: the purist who pointed out, in every interview, how performance-enhancing drugs infected pro cycling, and how the governing board wasn't doing anything about it.

Biking fans adored him, never more so than when another cyclist set a new Hour Record only six days after Obree's magnificent ride, and the Scot vowed revenge. That the cyclist was Chris Boardman made the situation even more delicious.

Like Obree, Boardman was a time-trial specialist. Like Obree, he was obsessive. There, the similarities ended. Boardman was a professional, a team member, with a coach, a manager, an Olympic gold medal, and a host of sponsors. He often worked out in a lab; his roadwork involved scrupulously crafted intervals. At races, his warm-ups were scripted to the second.

"Boardman was like a robot," says England-based sports physiologist Joe Beer, who coached Obree in the late '90s. "And I don't mean that as a put-down. Graeme would roll up to a race with his kit over his shoulder, in jeans, and he'd take his fleece off, roll up and down the road chatting people up, asking how they were doing, and the next minute he'd be on the track, going for it."

"I was art," Obree says, "where he was science."

That fall, at the 1993 World Track Championships, again at the wooden track in Hamar, the men raced each other in the four-kilometer pursuit. Obree won, setting a new world record.

That's the moment when adoration changed to something more primitive and powerful. That a man who trained when he felt like it and ate what he wanted could vanquish one of the most highly trained and analyzed athletes in the world — and that he could do it with such careless panache — it wasn't just a world record. It was a victory for the human soul, a triumph for scrappy underdogs. It was a stunning display of what unalloyed joy and unbridled faith could accomplish, wondrous proof that with belief in yourself, anything was possible.

If only people had known the truth.

"It was pure fear," says Obree. "It was a feeling of 'This isn't good enough. I'm not good enough.'"

For three months after the race, unbeknownst to everyone but Anne, he spit up blood every day.

"I've never heard of that happening to a human being," says Coggan, the sports physiologist. "It's quite common in thoroughbreds, though. The pulmonary blood pressure rises so much that capillaries burst and blood gets into the lungs. That's why you see horses frothing blood-flecked foam at the end of races."

In April of 1994, Obree traveled to Bordeaux to reclaim the Hour Record. His wife and his mother were walking with him when they saw a crowd of four thousand people surging toward the stadium.

"My mother turned to me and she asked, 'What are all those people here to see?'" he remembers. "I said, 'They're here to see me, Mum.' She said, 'Ah, no. That can't be. Ah, no.'"

He set a new record that spring afternoon, of 52.719 kilometers. He had triumphed, again, in The Race of Truth.

"Where Graeme Started to Disappear"

The Union Cycliste International (UCI), the worldwide governing body that sets the rules for competitive cycling, didn't like Obree. Maybe it was because he was a working-class loudmouth in a sport of traditionalists. Perhaps UCI president Hein Verbruggen had taken Obree's drug gibes personally. Or, as his supporters claim, maybe Verbruggen was protecting the athletic purity of the sport, making sure venerable events such as the Hour Record weren't cheapened by clever cheats and tinkerers.

Obree's brother, Gordon, died in 1994, when a truck hit the car he was driving. Obree felt himself sliding into darkness. "What's the point?" he kept thinking, fixating on his familiar, grim mantra. "What's the point? What's the point?" He tried to pedal it out of his mind. Just weeks before the World Track Championships, the UCI issued new regulations. Henceforth, it said, saddle position had to be X. The top of the frame had to have angles Y and Z. There were many rules, all of them collectively outlawing Obree's bike.

He had raced till he spit blood. He'd built the fastest bike in the world out of a washing machine. Did anyone think a piece of paper would stop him?

He tinkered with the bike, adjusted angles, moved the seat, until it was in compliance. He brought it to Palermo, Sicily, to defend his world pursuit title. On the ninth lap, after two and a half kilometers, Verbruggen, wearing a blue blazer, rushed onto the track flailing his arms. He couldn't object to the bike. He was objecting to the *way* Obree was riding it.

Obree pedaled harder. "I thought, if this guy stands here, I'm gonna kill him. I'm gonna run smack into him and I'm gonna kill him. I didn't give a shit."

Verbruggen jumped out of Obree's way.

Even swerving, unnerved, Obree finished with the third fastest time. It didn't matter. He was disqualified.

"I asked for the written version of the rule," Obree says, "and they said it's unwritten. To this day, I don't know the rule I was breaking."

Shaun Wallace, silver medalist at two world championships and a former holder of the Flying Kilometer record, says, "Graeme should have been the UCI's poster child. The two main problems in cycling at the time were drugs and the escalating cost of equipment. What they did to him was arrogance, plain and simple. That an 'everyday rider,' which is how they thought of Graeme, should hold the blue riband of cycling, they just couldn't take."

Sentiments like that were common, but they wouldn't help Obree. It seemed nothing could — until, six months later, in September of 1995, when he showed up at the World Track Championships in Bogotá, Colombia, with a new bike, one with an ultra-extended handlebar that put him almost prone over the frame when he rode. He'd created another groundbreaking position. This one he called Superman.

The Ayr Man, riding Superman, took back his world pursuit title. Worse, as far as the UCI was concerned, the Superman could more easily be copied than the Praying Mantis. Before long, the design dominated velodrome races all over Europe. In 1996, Boardman used the Superman to retake the Hour Record.

The UCI banned it forever. No one could ride the Superman again.

Obree was faring little better than his invention. He'd joined a French cycling team, Le Groupement, but lasted only weeks. Team officials say they sacked him because he didn't show up to training camp on time. He claimed the team wanted him to use drugs and fired him when he refused.

He was thirty-one, poor again, with two young children now, and little in the way of marketable skills. He could design machines, but where had that gotten him? He could endure pain, but what had that produced but more pain?

He traveled to the Atlanta Olympics in 1996 to represent Great Britain. "My father said, 'Well, that's a six-day wonder; when are you getting a job?'"

Obree didn't medal, and had to be coaxed from a fifth-floor window sill by a teammate. At home over the next few years, he won a few local races, but nothing like the Hour Record or the world pursuit championship. "That," says Beer, who was trying to coach Obree at the time, "was where Graeme started to disappear."

It was injuries, newspapers said. Bad luck. A viral infection. In

1998, walking through an airport in Geneva, he entered a pharmacy, bought 112 aspirin ("that's all they would sell me"), and washed them down with water. He was hospitalized in critical condition, diagnosed with manic-depression.

Sports fans had embraced the man-child who drank yak's milk and trained by whim, the fierce and lovable idiot savant of cycling, and they even loved the idea of the champion cheated by bureaucrats in blue blazers. But could they comprehend a hero driven by shame and self-loathing, an unloved son, a frightened child? Could they understand that their hero was unskilled at anything but tinkering and racing, that he despaired of ever pleasing his parents, that the one constant in his life, his wife, forever-faithful Anne, was asking if they could please move to a small farm so she could do something *she* loved every day, which was to ride her horse, a half-Thoroughbred, half-Appaloosa named Broxy, and that even though she said it would only entail a "wee mortgage," the racing riches were gone and the notion of moving and more debt scared him, made him feel more worthless than ever, but he didn't know how to tell her, so he didn't say anything?

Biking fans had no trouble at all recalling Obree on his glorious, two-wheeled gimcrack, but could they ever envision him silent, unshaven, huddled under the covers in his bed, hour after hour, day after day?

"What Kind of Life's He Going to Have?"

In the fall of 2000, he showed up at the World Track Championships. He had been hospitalized fifteen months, on and off, since the latest suicide attempt. He was swallowing a gram of lithium a day. He told reporters he was "probably fitter than at any time in my life," and announced another impending assault on the Hour Record.

He was training again, on a conventional bike this time but in yet another new position, and at speeds he'd never obtained before. He seemed more focused. He worked with a coach. And he got faster. He added glucose polymer drinks. And he got faster. He was only half a kilometer an hour off the pace he needed for a new Hour Record, a third title that would mean no one, not even himself, could ever doubt him again. He just needed a little more speed. But no matter what he did, he couldn't find it. There was only one thing left to try.

He stopped taking the lithium. "I thought, it'll be just the way it was before."

On a Monday, December 17, 2001, eight days before Christmas, he spoke with his psychiatrist in the morning and assured him he was feeling fine. He told Anne at midday he was going out for a ride. Late in the afternoon, when he hadn't returned, she worried he'd had a flat.

He'd ridden eight miles through a steady rain to the farm where Anne boarded Broxy, then parked his bike outside the horse's stall. He'd fashioned a noose from a long piece of plastic, tied one end to a rafter, and the other to his neck.

The farmer's daughter wasn't supposed to check on the horse that day, but she did. The teenaged girl's little brother usually tagged along, but that day her father accompanied her. He'd practiced forensic law, and knew about saving lives.

At the hospital, doctors told Anne that even if Obree recovered, he might be paralyzed or brain-damaged, that if his lungs hadn't held 6.5 liters of oxygen instead of the normal human capacity of 2.5, he'd already be dead. Anne asked if she should get a priest to perform last rites. The doctor said that would be a good idea. She rubbed the bald spot on Obree's head, because she knew he liked that.

Anne says Obree's mother visited the hospital one afternoon. "She took me aside," Anne says, "and she said, 'He survived and he'll likely try again. Wouldn't it better if he just went? Wouldn't it be better to let him go? What kind of life's he going to have with mental illness?'"

Glory

It is midnight in Irvine and we are sitting in the Obree kitchen, Graeme and Anne and I. The dinner went well (he chose rogan josh and the bread scheme worked) and the boys, whom both he and Anne call the "wee fellas," are in bed. But now it's pouring and Anne announces that the roof is leaking. That gets Graeme blinking and squinting and grinding his jaw.

Anne brews tea. The horizontal rain started this week. Graeme says it will last till spring.

He's writing a book about his struggles, on the advice of his psychologist, who thinks it might help. There's also the movie based on his life, which he's helping out on, a project that's been in the works since the mid-'90s. There's a canister of gas that needs to be fetched from ten miles away so he can weld frames for the two replica bikes he's building for the movie. (The original sits in the Museum of Scotland, in Edinburgh.) And because he's going to be the body double in the film, he needs to shed the lithium flab, especially in his calves, because there will be close-ups. He needs to fix the leaking roof, of course. And he wants to compete again, but he probably won't. It's too dangerous. His therapist has warned him that salvation lies now, in this moment. But this moment is not someplace he could ever easily rest — not even when people were thrusting flowers at him. Even then, he was always pedaling toward a phantasmal future of new records and a world where he was good enough. He knows he's not supposed to dwell on what was or agonize about what might be. But how can he help it? How could he ever?

One might as well ask what led him to the barn that cold December afternoon. The UCI's persecution? Cold parents? The corrosive woe of a clumsy, dyslexic boy? Or, considering where he fashioned his plastic noose, horribly misplaced anger toward Anne for her desire to move closer to her horse?

Or maybe it was just a few synapses misfiring, a molecular exchange missed here, another one made there — the same brain chemistry responsible for his blinding cognitive leaps, remarkable endurance, and high threshold of pain, all common manifestations of the manic phase of bipolar disorder. Maybe it doesn't matter how heroic or tragic your life is, how outsized your dreams and visions, as long as you take your medicine and get enough sleep and eat right and lay off booze and talk about your feelings.

He is working his jaw harder than ever and he is squinting and blinking and even though Anne just minutes ago served tea and is smiling, it is a fixed, determined grin. The interview is over. Graeme has too much on his mind to be talking to a reporter just now.

One last question, then: He brought such delight to so many

people. Was there ever a time he felt it himself — for an instant in Norway, ten years and a lifetime ago, when he broke the unbreakable Hour Record? Did he take a moment to bask in ecstasy? I ask him what joy felt like.

"There were no celebrations," he says. "It made me feel justified. That I'd justified my existence as a person." He is still blinking and squinting.

"As a person," Anne says. She gathers up the tea cups, looks at her watch, then us, then back at her watch. She is not smiling anymore.

"I'd rather have died on the track than failed," Obree says. "I'd rather have breathed blood than failed."

"And you did," Anne says.

"This was never about sport," says the great hero, the noble champion, before he heads to his bedroom to rest. "This was never about glory."

LYNNE COX

Swimming to Antarctica

FROM THE NEW YORKER

STANDING NEAR THE STERN of the *Orlova,* a Yugoslav ship bound
for the Antarctic Peninsula, I held on tight to the metal guardrails
as five-foot waves in the Beagle Channel shattered against the bow,
rocking the ship and shooting icy spray into my face. It was eight
o'clock on a December evening, two hours before sunset, and I
watched the colorful hillside of Ushuaia, the southernmost city in
Argentina, fade into an expanding gray sea. Within minutes, sleet
and wind gusting to sixty knots drove me into my cabin, where I
changed into a warm pair of sweats and climbed up into my bunk
bed, preparing for the journey through the Drake Passage, at the
edge of the Southern Ocean. If conditions are favorable, it takes
about a day and a half to travel from Ushuaia to the Antarctic
Peninsula, but everything depends on the weather and the waves.
Storm fronts can move in rapidly and sometimes remain in a powerful holding pattern for days. The energy from these storms can
affect the entire Southern Ocean and the waters along the coasts of
New Zealand, Australia, South America, and South Africa, where
waves called cape rollers have been known to punch holes in super-
tankers.

Waves in the Drake Passage itself can reach fifty feet, and as the
Orlova sailed east toward the Atlantic I could feel them increasing
in size and frequency. In the upper bunk, where I was trying to
sleep, there was no guardrail, so I turned onto my side, stuck my
hand between the bed and the wall, and held on. Somehow I managed to sleep, until a rogue wave hit the ship and I was thrown to
the opposite edge of the bunk. It was two o'clock in the morning.

Chairs toppled, cupboards snapped open, luggage clattered to the floor. The ship's engines suddenly slowed, which meant that the waves were going to get larger still. Soon, twenty-five-foot waves were smashing against the porthole. I had spent the past two years training for a swim through some of the coldest water in the world and onto the shores of Antarctica. Now I wasn't sure if the boat would even get there.

When I was three years old, I learned how to swim in a lake called Snow Pond, in Maine, where my mother's father had taught her to swim. I swam there in the summer, and the rest of the year I took lessons in an indoor heated pool. I started entering swim meets a couple of years later, but it wasn't until my family moved to California, in 1969, and I participated in a race in the Pacific that I realized how much I loved swimming in open water. In August 1971, when I was fourteen years old, I swam twenty-seven miles, from Catalina Island, in southern California, across the Catalina Channel to the mainland. The swim took twelve hours and thirty-six minutes, and, as I touched the shore, I knew that I wanted to swim the English Channel, the Mt. Everest of distance swimming.

The water in the English Channel in summer was between 55 and 60 degrees Fahrenheit, about ten degrees colder than the Catalina Channel in August. I believed I could swim the distance — depending on the currents, it could be anything from twenty-one miles to more than thirty miles — but I had no idea whether I would be able to survive the cold. According to English Channel swimming rules, swimmers can wear only a bathing suit, a swim cap, and goggles, although they are permitted to use grease, which is thought to serve as a layer of insulation. Many Channel swimmers have suffered problems with the cold; some have gone into hypothermia, and a few have died from exposure. My father, who is a physician, believed that the more I could acclimate to cold water during the year, the less stressful my swim would be. I began swimming only in the Pacific Ocean, and I continued during the winter, when the water temperature dropped as low as 50 degrees. I wore light clothes all year long, and always slept without blankets and with the windows open. My father was right. When I was fifteen, I broke the men's and women's records for swimming the English Channel, completing a twenty-seven-mile crossing in nine hours and fifty-seven minutes. The following year, the record was broken by a man; I returned, and broke it again, finishing a thirty-three-mile swim in nine hours and thirty-six minutes.

There are swimmers who return year after year to cross the Channel, but I wanted to do something that had never been done before. I heard about a swim across the Cook Strait, between the North and South Islands of New Zealand. Three men had crossed successfully; a handful of women had tried, but none of them had finished. The islands are about ten miles apart, and I thought that I could complete the crossing in about four hours. In February 1975, after five hours of swimming, I was farther from the finish than when I had started. The waves were nine feet high, the winds gusting to forty knots, and I doubted that I could continue. The crew in the support boat next to me included a radio announcer who was broadcasting news about the swim. Listeners began calling in, and the announcer relayed their words to me. Somehow, the confidence and concern in their messages forced me on, and, after twelve hours in the water, I reached South Island. The next day, church bells rang throughout the country to celebrate the swim. I felt as though New Zealanders had shared my struggle when I was in the water, and it made me realize that a swim could be more than an athletic event. It was a way of bringing people together. A year later, in 1976, I crossed the Strait of Magellan, off the southern coast of Chile. In the following years, I swam around the Cape of Good Hope, at the southern tip of South Africa; across Lake Titicaca, from Bolivia to Peru; and through the Gulf of Aqaba, from Egypt to Israel and then from Israel to Jordan. In 1987, when I was thirty years old, I completed my most challenging swim — crossing the Bering Strait, from the United States to the Soviet Union. It had taken eleven years to secure permission from the Soviet Union, and dense fog in the strait sent me dangerously off course, but after two hours I reached the shore, where a Soviet welcoming committee was waiting.

Several times over the years, scientists have asked me if I would participate in cold studies. Most people find swimming or sitting in cold water uncomfortable, so there are few volunteers for these studies and little data on cold-water endurance. Barbara Drinkwater, an exercise physiologist at the Institute of Environmental

Stress at the University of California, Santa Barbara, wanted to find out how I was able to swim in cold water without going into hypothermia. The studies would be a way for me to understand how my body functioned, enabling me to explore my own limits. So in 1976 I became a human research subject. In one experiment at the institute, I sat for an hour in my swimsuit in water that was 50 degrees, and a rectal probe was used to measure my temperature. My response was unusual: all the other participants in the test shivered, and their core temperatures dropped; I did not shiver, and my temperature remained stable.

Heat loss in cold water happens up to twenty-five times faster than in cold air, and it can be deadly. For most people, exercise in cold water increases this heat loss. During physical activity, blood from the body's core is sent out to the working muscles in the extremities — the arms, legs, fingers, and toes. The blood close to the skin's surface is then cooled by the surrounding water and air before it's pumped back. The body attempts to combat the cold and maintain heat by vasoconstriction — closing down the blood vessels to the surface and the extremities and keeping the body's heat around vital organs like the heart and the brain. At some point, though, in a process known as vasodilation, the blood flow opens again as a way of ensuring that oxygen gets to the tissues in the extremities. Once again, colder blood is returned to the core, and people may become hypothermic, disoriented, unresponsive, severely dehydrated, develop an irregular heartbeat, and go into cardiac arrest.

That fall, I began training for a December swim across the Strait of Magellan. The biggest obstacle would be the water temperature, which was between 42 and 44 degrees Fahrenheit. No one had attempted the swim before, and little was known about how the human body would respond. Drinkwater accompanied me and gathered data on a training swim in the ocean off Santa Barbara. After four hours of swimming in 50-degree water, my body temperature actually increased, from my normal temperature of 97.6 to 102 degrees. Drinkwater believed that my body was good at closing down blood flow to its peripheral areas. This ability, coupled with the fact that, like most women, I have an even distribution of fat throughout my body, acted as an internal wetsuit. I have large muscles, and was exercising so vigorously in the water, Drinkwater said, that I was able to create more heat than I lost.

In the early 1990s, William Keatinge, one of the world's leading experts on hypothermia, asked me if I would participate in a study in his lab, at the University of London. During one part of the study, I sat in a Jacuzzi that was set at 42 degrees for an hour and a half, moving my arms back and forth. My core temperature dipped for a short time, but quickly stabilized. (The only other person whose temperature didn't plummet during this experiment was an Icelandic fisherman who had survived a shipwreck in frigid waters near the Westman Islands. All four of his shipmates had perished, but he had acclimated to extremely cold temperatures while working on the deck of a fishing boat, and he was able to swim three miles to shore.) However, my skin temperature had cooled down to the temperature of the water, and as soon as I got out my core temperature dropped. Keatinge advised me to get into a warm bath to rewarm. It was painful. My skin began to sting and itch, and it became splotchy. Being immersed in warm water caused further vasodilation, and by the time I climbed out of the warm bath the inside of my body was colder than it had been when I was sitting in the Jacuzzi.

Another part of the study examined whether blood flow could be regulated at the fingertips. Along with seventy-six premed students, I had to immerse my left hand in 32-degree water for half an hour. Fresh water freezes at 32 degrees, but in the experiment the water was constantly circulated, to prevent it from crystallizing and to maintain an even temperature. The pain was intense. Some of the students shouted and pounded on the wall, and one sang. I stayed absolutely still, and talked myself into keeping my hand in the water. Keatinge believed that, through my cold-water training, I was able to control blood flow at my fingertips, so that I didn't lose heat to the water. The results made me wonder: if I could immerse my hand in water that cold, would I be able to swim in it?

When I was seventeen and in New Zealand, preparing to attempt the Cook Strait crossing, I was met on the beach after a practice swim by a member of the local lifesaving association. He handed me a small blue penguin. It was soft, fuzzy, and warm, the size of a calico cat. The man said that it had swum all the way from Antarctica. When I asked him how a baby penguin could swim across the Pacific Ocean to New Zealand, he laughed. He was joking, he said, and explained that this breed, a fairy penguin, was indigenous to

New Zealand. I supported the penguin under its feet, and held it close to me. It wriggled, turned, and bit me hard on the neck. Afterward, every time I thought about the penguin, I thought of Antarctica.

A year later, after I'd swum across the Magellan Strait, I met two tourists in Chile who had flown across Antarctica. I longed to go there, too, but I had to get back to college in California. In 1978, when I swam around the Cape of Good Hope, I encountered twenty-foot waves generated by storms near Antarctica, more than two thousand miles away. And many years later, in 1990, when I returned to South America to swim across the Beagle Channel, which separates Argentina and Chile, an admiral in the Argentine Navy, who had provided support during the swim, offered me passage on a military supply ship heading to an Argentine base camp in the Antarctic Peninsula. It fascinated me, because it was a place without borders, but, once again, I had to get back home. I was beginning to feel like James Cook. I had completely circled Antarctica but had never been there.

Three years ago, I swam across the northern lakes of Italy. This swim was just for fun, and I even asked a friend who was an opera singer to sing to me as I swam. But afterward I felt that something was lacking. I was forty-three years old, and I needed a project that was more challenging, one that would draw on all my experience, and it suddenly occurred to me that what I wanted to do was swim to Antarctica.

The coldest water I'd swum in was in the Bering Strait, where the temperature dropped from 42 degrees to 38 degrees for the last thirty minutes of my two-hour swim. The water along the Antarctic Peninsula could be as much as four or five degrees colder. No one knew how far someone would be able to swim in those temperatures, and I wondered what the effect of the cold would be for every degree below 38 degrees. During the Second World War, pilots and submariners who were rescued from waters at these temperatures often suffered from "immersion injury," which involved swelling of the extremities and, in some cases, debilitating nerve and muscle damage. After Keatinge's hand experiment, it was three months before full sensation returned to my fingertips. I wasn't sure what would happen in Antarctic waters, but I intended to swim as fast as I possibly could.

I'm a distance swimmer, not a sprinter, and I would have to build strength and speed. Between December 2000 and December 2001, I worked out at the gym, and in the ocean, five days a week, two or three hours a day. After a year, I still wasn't strong enough, so I started working with Jonathan Moch, a trainer and former high school wrestler. In Antarctica, I planned to swim mostly with my head up, to prevent heat loss. That spring, Moch and I began with strength training, using free weights and making sure that I kept my head up throughout the workout. Then we developed stability and balance to help me in the water. And, finally, we worked on endurance. Swimming with the head up increases the drag of a swimmer's body in the water, and it can feel as though you're swimming uphill. In preparation for this, I was doing every exercise in the workout to the point of fatigue.

I also walked five or six miles a day with a friend from my hometown of Los Alamitos, Barry Binder, who had accompanied me on past swims and who was planning to come to Antarctica. In the afternoon, I swam fast for an hour in an unheated backyard pool. And every weekend I sprinted — swimming as fast as I could for three to four miles in the Pacific Ocean, off Seal Beach, in California. Between workouts, I spent hours drafting letters, making phone calls, setting up meetings, and making presentations to possible sponsors. Quark Expeditions, a Connecticut-based company that runs educational tours to Antarctica, agreed to help, allowing me to use one of its ships as the base for the swim as well as providing logistical support.

Last November, after nearly two years of training, I visited Dr. Robert "Brownie" Schoene, a pulmonary specialist at the University of Washington who had helped me prepare for previous swims. Dr. Schoene ran a series of pulmonary-function and maximum-exercise tests, which showed that I was in excellent physical shape. Still, I had some concerns about the tides, weather, ice conditions, and water temperatures in Antarctica. A friend who had spent nine seasons diving there told me that he once watched a leopard seal fling a penguin fifteen feet into the air, and then rip it out of its skin. He advised me to get out of the water quickly if I saw a leopard seal or an orca — a killer whale. There had been only one report of a killer whale attacking a person in the wild, but I decided I needed to find a swimsuit that was not black, white, or red. I didn't want to look like a penguin or signal that I was an injured animal.

I was interested, though, in the ways in which Antarctic animals adapt to the cold; perhaps I could learn something that would help me extend my time in the water. Penguins have a double layer of feathers, and the air between the layers serves as insulation. I decided to grow my hair long so that I could pile it up on my head, trapping air in my swim cap, like penguin feathers. When penguins dive into the ocean, their feathers get pressed together and no longer provide insulation, and the birds rely on their body fat to act as an internal wetsuit. Antarctic seals — Weddell, Ross, crab-eater, leopard, and elephant — stay warm by building up layers of blubber. By the time the water temperature dropped to 50 degrees in the backyard pool, I had put on twelve pounds by adding more carbohydrates and fat to my diet. John Heyning, a marine-mammal expert with the Natural History Museum of Los Angeles County, who has studied thermoregulation in whales, told me that humpback whales were able to stay warm while feeding by diverting the heat in their blood from their tongues back into their bodies. I had never considered what effect getting cold water in my mouth, or ingesting it, would have on my temperature. Another concern was the effect that intense cold would have on my teeth and ears. A friend recalled reading a book about the Antarctic explorer Apsley Cherry-Garrard which described how his teeth had shattered in minus-66-degree weather. Temperatures along the Antarctic Peninsula rarely drop much below freezing in summer, but I wondered if my teeth would conduct the cold. My dentist, Dr. William Poe, explained that because teeth have microscopic pores they are often sensitive to the cold. He gave me a series of fluoride treatments that filled these pores. He also offered to make custom earplugs out of dental impression, which would fit snugly in my ears, preventing water from seeping in and damaging my eardrums.

The period after the swim was potentially dangerous, possibly more critical than the swim itself, because I would no longer be exercising. During the Antarctic winter, male emperor penguins incubate the eggs containing their offspring, huddling together on the ice to conserve body heat. When I crossed the Bering Strait, a Russian expert on hypothermia, who had been sent from Moscow, assisted afterward. She made me get into a sleeping bag, and then placed hot-water bottles on the arteries on either side of my neck, under my arms, and in the groin area while she leaned against me to give me her body heat; it was much less painful than immediately immersing myself in a hot bath. For the Antarctic swim, one of my friends designed a scarf, top, and pants for the rewarming phase. She sewed two felt pockets into the scarf, two pockets under the arms of the top, and two in the front of the pants, where we would place hand warmers. At the end of the swim, the crew would huddle around me, to block the wind, and help me put on the warm clothes.

For knowledge about tides, weather, and currents, I relied on Susan Adie, the expedition leader for Quark Expeditions. In the past, I had started every swim from one landmass and finished on another, but for this swim there was no land I could start from. Adie and I decided that I would swim from the ship to the shore. Once the *Orlova* reached the sub-Antarctic islands and the Antarctic Peninsula, Adie and the ship's Russian ice master, Valery Eremin, would determine whether conditions were safe enough for me to attempt a swim.

Landing places would be limited. There aren't many beaches on the Antarctic continent, and icebergs sometimes flow into the ones that do exist, making them inaccessible. What's more, because the weather can change in an instant, from a calm sea with no wind to five-foot waves and fifty-knot winds, there is no way to predict the tides. Some days there are two tides in a day, Adie told me, sometimes one, and the tidal strength varies. I would be attempting the swim during a neap tide, when the moon was half full, which meant that the tide would not be as strong as it would be during a full moon. "In Antarctica, you just have to be flexible and patient," Adie said, adding that there could be platelet ice — patches of ice on top of the water — which could cut me. If there was any brash ice — broken or crumbled ice that can reach the size of a Volkswagen — I would not be able to swim. "When the icebergs break off the glaciers and hit the water, they cause mini-tsunamis," she explained. "If you're in the water with brash ice when that happens, it could kill you."

After two and a half days of sailing through violent seas in the Drake Passage, the *Orlova* encountered calmer waters, and Eremin was able to adjust his course so that we were sailing directly toward the South Shetland Islands. We began seeing large icebergs, as well as albatross and petrels gliding on the air waves created by the ship's forward movement. Some of the icebergs had sharp, jagged edges; others were smooth, their contours softened by the wind and water. We were traveling at about twelve knots, and if the weather remained stable we would reach the Antarctic Peninsula in two days. I had a crew of seven people with me, including three doctors, and most of them had been seasick for the past two days. We were relieved when we heard that there were chinstrap penguins on some of the larger ice floes. It meant we were nearing Antarctica. The *Orlova*'s other passengers had taken the expedition to see Antarctic wildlife, and we joined them on the ship's bridge to watch the penguins.

Before attempting a swim, I sat down with Adie; Dr. Anthony Bloch, the ship's doctor, who was usually based in Australia as an emergency-room physician; and two other members of my crew. We agreed that the crew would be divided among the *Orlova*'s three inflatable boats, called Zodiacs. Barry Binder would give me directions, the doctors would be collecting data and watching me for signs of hypothermia, and other crew members would be looking out for leopard seals, orcas, and icebergs. A CBS film crew would come along to document the swim. In an emergency, one crew member, wearing a dry suit — which is like a wetsuit but is sealed and filled with air to prevent water from entering — would be prepared to jump into the water, inflate his suit, and lift me to the surface.

Dr. Bloch wanted to run through an additional drill with my three doctors in case I went into cardiac arrest during the swim. When he asked me to participate in a stretcher drill to see if my crew members could carry me up the *Orlova*'s steep gangway, I declined, thinking that it would be like practicing for my own death. For two years, maybe a hundred times a day, I had been mentally rehearsing my success, not my death. Somebody volunteered to practice the drill, but the crew members couldn't lift the stretcher up the steep gangway, so we decided that in an emergency they would attach the ship's crane to a Zodiac and lift it, with me inside, on board. There was one more question: how would the crew pull me from the water if I was wearing only a swimsuit? There was very little fabric on my swimsuit for anyone to grab. I suggested to Barry that he put a six-inch-long rope through the top of my swimsuit straps and knot it. This would be an effective handhold.

I wanted to do a test swim before attempting a long swim. My goal was to swim for ten minutes, so that I could judge my endurance in the water. But the weather wasn't cooperating; winds off the South Shetlands were gusting to fifty knots, and it was sleeting. Finally, four days into our journey, when we reached King George Island, in the South Shetlands, north of the Antarctic Peninsula, conditions improved. I put on my bathing suit, and waited in the games room, looking out the window as the wind stirred the water. The two-foot waves were becoming whitecaps. I stared out the porthole at Admiralty Bay, on King George Island, and focused on the small, bright-yellow buildings that constituted Arctowski, a Polish research base. Picturing my body as a thermos, I drank four eight-ounce glasses of hot water to generate more inner heat and to prevent severe dehydration at the end of the swim. When one of the doctors took my temperature before the start of the swim, it was 99.5 degrees, well above normal, which could give me more time in the water. But, when I glanced out the window again, I saw that the waves were cresting faster. The wind had increased to thirty knots. I took a deep breath, trying to calm myself. I knew the swim could be called off at any moment. Finally, a crew member told me that everyone was ready; the boats were in position.

When I stepped outside the *Orlova*, I was hit by a blast of glacial wind. Goose pimples rose up all over my body, and my hair whorled around my head like helicopter rotors. Quickly, I retreated into the ship, trying to conserve every calorie of body heat. The water temperature in Admiralty Bay was 33 degrees Fahrenheit, and the air temperature was 34 degrees, but the wind off the surrounding glaciers made it feel as if I were standing inside a freezer. Winding my hair around my hand and pushing it into either side of my swim cap, I went back outside and stepped onto the gangway. I looked up and saw clouds rushing past the glaciers. Holding my goggles in my left hand and clutching the railing, feeling the ice-cold metal against my feet, I walked down the stairs. Pausing for a moment, I saw the crew below in the three Zodiacs, looking tense and excited. When I reached the platform at the base of the gangway, I sat down, and it felt as if I were sitting on a wet metal ice-cube tray. The platform was swaying and rolling. The waves were an icy, silvery blue, breaking inches below my feet. I leaned backward to gain momentum and then threw myself forward.

The water was searing cold. I felt as if I were naked, standing still, and being sprayed with ice water from a high-pressure hose, and it took all my focus to move. I swam with my head above water, panting. It was incredibly difficult to catch my breath; my lungs felt as if they were being squeezed in a tight corset. I couldn't get them to expand fully, but I needed oxygen. I knew that I wouldn't be able to continue for more than a couple of minutes unless I overcame my inclination to hyperventilate. I forced myself to slow down, to pull in a breath through my mouth, and then to blow it all the way out. It was extremely tiring, but concentrating on my breath prevented me from thinking about the cold. As my breathing evened out, I began to notice other sensations. The water felt different from any other water I'd swum in, as if it were more solid than fluid, as though I were swimming through a liquid Sno-Kone. I checked my hands. They were red and swollen and, like my feet, had become numb and achy. I was barely kicking, but I always swam this way: 99 percent of my propulsion through the water comes from my arms and upper body, while my legs just stabilize my stroke. One friend, who had spent years studying polar bears, told me I swam like a polar bear, which uses its feet as a rudder, probably, he said, as a means of containing heat. Because I wasn't kicking, I wasn't pumping much blood to my feet and legs. I paused in midstroke to look at my watch. I had been swimming for only a minute.

A wave shattered in my face. I choked, and started to panic. I knew I had to keep swimming; it was too cold to stop. I kept spinning my arms, trying to swallow and clear my throat. Another wave slammed into my face. I was choking harder, and feeling even more panicked. I couldn't breathe. I considered rolling over onto my back, but decided it was too cold and this would slow me down too much. Instead, I put my head into the water so that I was no longer choking on the spray. My body flattened, and I began swimming through the water instead of climbing up against it. It was easier to breathe; I could roll my head and shoulder to one side or the other. I was almost swimming normally, pulling, pushing, gliding through the water, slipping under the waves, letting them wash over me, each stroke strong and fluid. As I moved across the sub-Antarctic sea, I looked at the glaciers that encircled the harbor. My torso and head felt warm on the inside, and I relaxed just a little. Turning my head left on a breath, then right on another breath, then lifting my head up, I looked at the faces of the crew, which were filled with concern. I lifted my right foot out of the water and waved it. This was a signal that everything was okay. They grinned and waved back.

When I glanced at my watch again, I saw that I had reached my goal of ten minutes. But the more I could do now, I thought, the more confidence I would have for the final swim; indeed, if the weather turned, this could be my only opportunity to swim. When I reached the fifteen-minute mark, I glanced down and saw five or six streams of bubbles that looked like vapor trails in the sky — penguins were swimming so fast underneath me that all I could see was their bubbles. To my left were icebergs. We were moving into their float path, and the crew began shouting warnings to me, pointing at the water. I swam around the bergs, and my arms started to feel colder. I could see that we were getting closer to the beach, but the intensity of the cold was sapping my strength. Large chunks of ice were floating all around me, drifting at a rate of about a knot, parallel to the beach. The entire crew was on full alert, helping me to steer through the iceberg field. A piece the size of a soccer ball bounced off my forehead, and it brought hot tears to my eyes. Another piece, twice as big, hit me on the side of the head. I shook my head to ease the pain, and increased my speed, trying to get clear of the ice field.

The crew got out of the boats and scrambled up the embankment, waiting for me with towels and blankets. Ten feet from shore, I saw smooth gray rocks, and then the bottom rose up to meet me. I turned my head to breathe, and saw some of the passengers from the *Orlova* who had been hiking along the shore. They were running toward us, slipping a little on the ice, and waving. As I stood up, I heard cheers and muffled clapping. I had surprised everyone, including myself. I'd planned to swim for only ten minutes, but I had been in the water for twenty-two minutes and fourteen seconds. The crew surrounded me, blocking the wind and drying me off. In a few moments, I felt very cold. My legs were bright red, and bleeding from tiny scratches made by pieces of ice in the water. My feet and legs felt numb. A crew member took off his boots and helped me put them on, and we trudged across the rocks. Crossing a small brook, we entered one of the yellow buildings I'd seen from the *Orlova*, where three startled Polish researchers, who were studying water samples, greeted us. I lay down in a corner, wrapped in blankets, and shivered violently as two doctors, one on either side, helped me to rewarm. One of the doctors then measured my temperature; it had dropped only a little, to 97.7 degrees. It was much higher than expected. Still, I was shaking hard, and my teeth were chattering, but this activity was raising my metabolism and creating heat to counteract the return of cooled blood to the core. It was nearly forty-five minutes before I stopped shivering and felt warm again.

That night, I thought about what had worked and what hadn't during the swim. I knew that I could swim almost a mile in Antarctic waters, and, for the most part, I was pleased with everything my crew and I had done. Yet I also had to acknowledge that I was exhausted, and that I had lost some sensation in my fingers, toes, and skin. I didn't like feeling so cold afterward: my body had to work too hard to warm up. So I decided that next time I would swim faster, in order to generate more heat. The water would probably be a degree colder, around freezing, in part because so many glaciers were melting. Once I was in the water, I had to judge how far I could push myself, but if I made a mistake I trusted my crew.

The next day, the weather was so bad that no one was able to land on Deception Island, eighty miles southwest of King George Island, so we continued sailing south, hoping there would be a break in the storm. The following morning, the weather had improved, and Adie told me that there were three possible sites for the swim. The first was Waterboat Point, on the Antarctic Peninsula, 150 miles southwest of Deception Island; the second, a few miles to the north, was Neko Harbor; and the third, to the south, was Paradise Bay. Waterboat Point was filled with icebergs, and there was no beach to land on. We turned and headed for Neko Harbor. Two hours later, we anchored offshore, and things looked good. The sun was appearing and disappearing through the clouds as the wind blew in short gusts off the glaciers — a signal that the weather might not hold for long. I studied the shore carefully. The beach was less than four hundred feet wide, and was surrounded by glaciers so high that I had to tilt my head all the way back in order to see the tops of them; some had fracture lines, and looked as if they might break off at any moment. The beach was clear of ice, and shaped like a half-moon. It was composed of broken, shalelike rock in shades of brown, gold, taupe, and terra-cotta. This rock could hurt my feet when I landed. There were long bands of snow on the beach; some pure white, others furrowed with what are known as penguin highways — paths where the birds had walked, streaked a rusty-orange color from their droppings. The wind was down to only ten knots, but if we strayed off course — eight hundred feet to the right or left of the beach — we would be directly below a glacier face. If the glacier calved while we were under it, falling ice could kill us, or the wave created by the splash could cause the boats to capsize. In any case, we wouldn't be able to land, because the glacier made a sheer drop to the water. I wished I had some idea how fast the current was moving and in what direction. If it pushed me too far in one direction or the other, I might not make it to the beach.

Barry threaded the rope through my swimsuit, and I told him that, no matter what happened, I wanted to swim a mile. He promised me that I would. Eremin watched from the bridge. He would follow our course, plot it out, and use the ship's global positioning system to calculate the precise distance we covered. The crew climbed into the Zodiacs, and I pulled off my sweatsuit and hurried down the gangway. The air temperature was 32 degrees — two degrees colder than it had been the day before — and the wind tore heat from my body. I sat down on the platform and looked at the icy gray-blue water and then at the land. It seemed a long way off.

Taking a deep breath, I lunged forward, slipped, and hit the water face first. Although the water was a degree colder than it had been the day before, it actually felt warmer. (After the swim, I realized that nerve damage from the first swim had diminished my ability to perceive the cold.) It took longer than before to catch my breath, and my breathing was much more labored. I was tired, and I couldn't understand why. One of the crew members, who was counting my strokes, told me afterward that I was spinning my arms at ninety strokes a minute, thirty strokes a minute faster than my normal rate. The crew sensed that I was struggling, and I could see doubt on some faces. I told myself that I had to sprint faster than I'd ever sprinted in my life.

I could feel my shoulders moving in circles, but my arms were numb and burning, and something else was wrong — the boats were veering to the left. We were heading directly for a glacier. "Where are we going, Barry?" I shouted. He pointed toward the glacier. It didn't make any sense, but I trusted that he knew something I didn't. The cold was moving deeper into my arms and legs. Suddenly, the boats changed course, turning sharply to the right. I was getting agitated, but I followed them. Then I realized that, by zigzagging, Barry was adding distance, to ensure that I swam a mile. I put my face into the water and felt the shock throughout my body. "Stretch out," I told myself. The water was thicker and much colder than it had been two days ago. It was also bluer, saturated with the brightness of the Antarctic sun and the reflections off the ice and snow. It was almost vibrating, and clearer than any water I'd been in.

We passed Neko Harbor, and moved toward a small peninsula. Two-foot waves were at my back, pushing me. The current was growing stronger, moving at about one knot. My normal speed was just over two knots, so when we turned around my speed would be halved. I knew we couldn't go much farther in this direction or I would never make it back. Barry and the crew signaled to me with two fingers — I had been swimming for twenty minutes. My normal mile time was between twenty-two and twenty-three minutes, and I was swimming much faster than I usually did. We started to cross a small glacial bay that was intersected by another inlet. I felt an even stronger current, moving at nearly two knots, hitting me at a right angle. If I continued forward, I wouldn't be able to make it back to the beach at Neko Harbor. I promptly turned around and started racing for the beach. For the first time during the swim, I felt strong and pulled harder, feeling the delayed pressure of my hands against the water. I tasted the water, which was very sweet, with just a hint of salt, probably because there was so much glacial melt. Barry held up his index finger and signaled one mile. The crew cheered, and I began thinking about continuing — maybe I could swim another half-mile; my head and core felt warm. But the longer I stayed in the water, the deeper the cold would penetrate, and the harder it would be to get warm again. Two hundred yards from shore, a flock of chinstrap penguins, standing on shore, started jumping into the water. They swam to within ten feet of me, and porpoised beside me. I could see their black eyes, see their beaks enter the water first, then their backs arching, and their feet pushing the water back. They must have been swimming at more than ten miles an hour.

A few minutes later, a crew member jumped into waist-deep water to help me adjust to the change in blood pressure when I made the transition from swimming to standing. On the shore, the crew embraced me, and I thought, *We did it!* I had been in the water for twenty-five minutes. The crew immediately helped me get into a Zodiac so that we could return to the *Orlova*, where I would warm up. Back on board, Eremin told me that I had swum 1.06 nautical miles — 1.22 miles. My temperature was down to 95.5 degrees, and I was shivering violently. After the three doctors helped me dress, I stood up and the doctors and other crew members hugged me. Fifteen minutes later, my temperature was up to 96 degrees, and after thirty minutes it was 96.8. Then I went into the cabin and took a long hot shower. I couldn't endure the cold like a penguin or a seal or a whale, but, having entered their world for a brief time, I had been able to experience something extraordinarily beautiful and harsh.

ROBERT DRAPER

Beauty in the Beast

FROM GQ

THE ROUGHEST PLAYER in the WNBA? "Sheeeit. Me." Latasha
Byears hovers over a devastated platter of crab like a gold-toothed,
tattooed condor. She calls out for a third apple martini and continues. "I'm the enforcer. *Enforcer* means knockin' the bitch — I
mean, 'scuse me, I'm gettin' a little ghettrix," she mumbles, falling
back with a snicker into the booth at the self-consciously sexy
Beverly Hills establishment, where her very presence constitutes a
thundering elbow to the lipsticked mouth.

Oh, but she is barely beginning, this silo-shaped woman in the
baby blue pantsuit and matching Timberland boots, which she
donned only after her dinner companion begged her to honor the
restaurant's dress code, a plea she had initially rebuffed with a rasp-
ing "Man, I'm wearin' my tennis shoes. We gettin' in." But the
mountain, having yielded just a bit, remains a mountain. "Man, I'm
a fuckin' piece of work," she announces as her neon blue drink
arrives. "I'm like a muhfuckin' Mozart, a — whatchoo call those
paintings? I'm a van Gogh. I'm a Picasso. They got the wrong idea
about me. They don't know where I came from, and they couldn't
live a day in my shoes. You know what my attitude is? Fuck the
world. I'm a winner, man. I've been a winner from day one. It's
rough and tough. I rock brave with my Afro puffs. Rock on wit yo'
bad self. This game, it's physical out there, man. If you're a pretty
girl, do your mascara before the game, because you ain't gonna
make it long in this league, babe. I been in this league six years
now. I came in through the back door. But I'm leaving through the
front, the side, and the middle. Man, roll the red velvet out for me,

'cause I'm the boss. *Born and raised in Memphis, Tennessee, / where a lot of people don't understand the eyes that I see. / Come walk a day in my shoes for those who choose to lose. / I pop my collar two times for the bitches that sing the blues. / All of these haters, it must stop. / I shine my eyes to the motherfuckin' T-O-P top.* Ahhh. And that's a check. Naw, I'm just playin', Rob. It's all love, baby. Is that Bernie Mac over there?"

It is the offseason. From one of her surprisingly supple fingers, a fat WNBA 2001 championship ring spits gold light. A twin, for the 2002 championship, is on its way. Mere costume jewelry in this city of quotidian brilliance, you could say. Say it to Byears, garbage-woman of the Los Angeles Sparks, and she will likely stomp you a new mudhole with her baby blue Timbos. To a manfully proportioned twenty-nine-year-old black chick who forged her dreams on a court of red Memphis dirt — a homegirl who "didn't go to no all-white Catholic school, didn't live next door to no doctors and lawyers. I lived next to pimps, motherfuckers pullin' up in their big Cadillacs with a lot of wimmins. *That's* what I wanted to be. I wanted to be a pimp growing up" — these rings represent the glorious golden elbow shattering the lipsticked barrier to the American Dream.

"Trust me. I'm gonna be a millionaire someday. Man, I'm gonna buy my mama the biggest house in the world. And I'm gonna open me a restaurant or a nightclub. Whether it's a strip club or a gay club, I don't give a damn. Where I can drink my apple martinis and you can drink whatever the hell that wine is you're drinking."

"Gewürztraminer."

"Whatever." Deftly she pivots, snags the fleeing waiter. "You know what, Homes? Bring me another one. Give me some love, baby."

You have not seen this woman in the WNBA commercials. No, you have seen lithe, doe-eyed, toothy sweethearts named Lisa and Sheryl and Rebecca and Sue. Moms and models and Miss Congenialitys, quasi-babe exemplars of the game. The game, that is, of Dr. James Naismith, not of Shaq and Iverson. Old Dr. James, how he would swoon over the women's fidelity to his invention. For theirs is largely an earthbound pursuit, a triumph of the horizontal, wholly reliant on teamwork. Good behavior? In the WNBA, it's legislated: all players are required to stand in a dignified posture during the national anthem and to shake hands after the game.

These players are not spoiled miscreants, for they make on average $46,000 a year (as opposed to $4.5 million for their NBA counterparts), travel on commercial airlines, and submit to twenty-two unpaid personal appearances a year on behalf of the league's sponsors. As a result of their modest trappings, it does not cost a week's salary to see a WNBA game, and thus the league displays a commoner's touch, drawing audiences of families, of seniors, of blue-collar women kissing other blue-collar women.

Alas, these audiences are not huge. They are far from sufficient. The flat attendance figures — roughly nine thousand per game over the course of the WNBA's six-year history — suggest to some that women's basketball, like grappa in the morning or a nationwide ban on firearms, is a concept for which America will never be ready. This need not be the case. In fact, the league is rife with skill and beauty. What it lacks, to a near fatal degree, is intrigue. An otherwise healthy person succumbs to sports because something out there beneath the rafters prods his imagination. He seeks out actors in the sweaty drama — heroes, villains, buffoons, and daredevils — to divert him from the ache of his everyday life. Explain, otherwise, the popularity of wrestling, NASCAR, hockey, pro football. The action itself? Please. Characters fueled the ascent of those games. Lisa Leslie, Sheryl Swoopes, Rebecca Lobo, Sue Bird, and the other poster girls of the WNBA are fine for taking home to Mom. As characters, they belong in an Akron dinner theater.

Consider, then, Latasha "Tot-o" Byears, the Dennis Rodman of the WNBA, whom you might take home if you wished to have Mom's ass kicked. Who prays before every meal, visits underprivileged neighborhoods and donates turkeys and tennis shoes (and beers), peppers her monologues with quotations from the Bible and Tupac Shakur, and refers to one of the league's most beloved players as a "bottom bitch." Who has not worn a dress since her cousin's wedding seven years ago and who drinks Courvoisier like tap water. Who brags that she's "switched agents like Rodman switches hair colors — I'll fire 'em all." Who was suspended at DePaul for inciting a riot, busted in Sacramento for driving under the influence of marijuana (she pleaded guilty to reckless driving), and suspended last July for bouncing the basketball off the face of an opponent who had hard-fouled her. Who is a most unlovely presence on the hardwood, with a highway stripe of a headband ornamenting her drowsy visage and a chaw of Juicy Fruit dangling like a rodent's withered tongue from her lips. Who last year nearly led the WNBA in field-goal percentage, was one of the league's top offensive rebounders, and, with her brawny carriage, routinely cleared the paint for her willowy teammate Lisa Leslie — who says flatly, "Without Tot-o, we don't win, and that's both championships."

But, dainty as an avalanche, Tot-o doesn't get to be on the WNBA commercials. Un-self-censoring, she is not the go-to girl to speak at youth clinics or Nike shillfests. That the league does not share her healthy estimation of her own charisma has not been lost on Latasha Byears. "The hatred's always been there, y'understand?" she says. "I guess people are just intimidated by me." God forbid, of course, that the face of the women's league be remotely frightening. Still, the WNBA is a girlfriend in a coma; nothing short of shock treatment will resuscitate its terminally perky corpus.

So bring on Tot-o, five feet eleven, 200 and change, daughter of an auto mechanic and a housekeeper, who from infancy "wasn't interested in no dolls," according to her mother. Instead she gravitated to a schoolyard north of Memphis, where she banged with the boys, playing for cases of Budweiser while emulating the post moves of Hakeem Olajuwon and Charles Barkley. The latter would one day observe the WNBA power forward in action and gush, "Girl, you got game!" But her subtler attributes — sweet spin moves, a nose for the errant ball, "the best pair of hands in the WNBA," according to Sparks coach Michael Cooper — have always been overlooked by the faint of heart. These are the haters, in Tot-o-speak. They blanch at her network of tattoos, her gold tooth with the engraved initial *L* (a family tradition begun by her grandmother), and her wide, curveless body, which when planted beneath the basket seems like an act of senseless violence. "Latasha's not a fun person to play against," says Doug Bruno, her coach at DePaul, where Tot-o's 22.8 points and 11.7 rebounds per game as a senior in 1996 should have catapulted her into the WNBA's upper echelon a year later.

Yet no team drafted her. After days of sulking, she agreed to attend the Sacramento Monarchs' training camp. "I go up there, I got on my pink Polo shirt, my black corduroy pants, my Timbo boots, because that's all I really like, y'know what I'm sayin'? You want that dress-wearing shit, you go get yourself a supermodel or one of those prissy girls. I show up to camp, and there's all the girls I done slaughtered in college. You know the definition of coleslaw? So I call my mom: 'Ma, don't even trip. I see what they got on this team.'"

Ah, but the haters dogged Tot-o throughout her four years in Sacramento. For the first two seasons, "she was a good player on a bad team," says Sonny Allen, who took charge at the beginning of Byears's third season and later relegated her to the bench. "She was a good person but didn't really dedicate herself to being in top shape." It also rankled Allen, a sixtysomething white man, that Tot-o's posse of tatted-out, ghetto-representin' homeys would accompany her to games and that she ran a nightclub where players drank and danced with fans until two in the morning. Word spread that Byears's after-hours carousing was rubbing off on her teammates, causing the Monarchs to perform poorly on the road. Her girth expanded in inverse proportion to her playing time. When a *Sacramento Bee* reporter implied that she was slow and fat, Tot-o was prompted to scream obscenities that were broadcast from the reporter's speakerphone to the entire newsroom. By 2000, she was begging general manager Jerry Reynolds to unload her — though, she added, "Whatever you do, don't trade me to no Utah. Uh-uh! I don't need that!"

"It was the Year of the Struggle," remembers Skee 64, a Sacramento rapper and Tot-o's main running buddy. "Her stats wasn't the way she wanted 'em to be. She got bullshitted around. She needed to get out. Mike [Morango, her friend and business partner] calls. 'We goin' to Vegas.' They drive up in a big 'Lac. We hit the freeway. We drinkin' Belvedere vodka, Moët, the best liquor ever. We livin' it up. Talkin' about how big it's gonna be, how if she ever gets a ring, what we gonna do. We go to Vegas, we kick it at my cousin's house. Tot was the only one gambling. Tot don't ever give up. Lost $5,000. I remember Tot came to the men's bathroom, she had to go so bad. And we all in the stalls together. All I see is Mike's hand reachin' up under the stall. Hands everybody $500. Like, 'Let's just do it, it's not gonna stop.' We went to the mall, the new Michael Jordans was out, Mike's like, 'Get whatever size you want.' Right after that, everything seems like it's happening."

Shortly after her Vegas sojourn, Tot-o landed an offseason gig playing for a team in Turkey. Early one morning, she received an overseas phone call from Penny Toler, a former L.A. Sparks player, now the team's general manager. "P.T., don't be bullshitting me!" Byears hollered into the phone when informed that the Monarchs had traded her. Los Angeles had been a finesse team, "and that's only going to get you so far," says Toler. "I played against Tot, and she was a Sparks killer. She'd get double-doubles against us. I had agents saying when we got her, 'Oh, Penny, you're gonna be up at night. Haven't you heard about her partying?' Well, she can stay up till two or four if she brings me a double-double. Maybe I should bring her more champagne. Maybe she'll bring me a triple-double. Feed the monster, I say."

"We were a long, thin team, and we needed someone to play in the trenches," says coach Cooper, himself a legendary role-player with the Lakers of the '8os. "We knew we needed a big body, and we got her for practically nothing. She has that innate recognition, like Wes Unseld or Paul Silas, of how to get the ball and put it in. Players get a stigma put on them, and at times it's not fitting. But we *like* her negative image on the court — having the fiercest elbow-throwing, talking-shit-on-the-court type of player there is. She's like Kareem [Abdul-Jabbar] — you see that scowl and you don't realize he was one of the funniest people on the team. Byears always tells a joke to start practice. Not always the cleanest joke, but they're damn funny."

As ex-players, Cooper and Toler were experienced enough to ignore the grilled-up teeth and the locker-room snitches. Their superstar, Leslie, needed someone to watch her back, just as Isiah Thomas needed Bill Laimbeer, and Larry Bird needed Robert Parish. Gender notwithstanding, basketball is a game of spatial considerations: mass sealing off mass to facilitate the ball's unharassed journey to the hoop. Had other WNBA teams inquired about Byears, DePaul's Doug Bruno would have informed them, "One of the pleasures of coaching her was that she was an All-American who wasn't above being a garbage player." But how does such an image play on a marquee? While others have passed on her, the Sparks have won a championship ring for each year Latasha Byears has done their dirty work.

"You can't stop a diamond from shining," she crows from the comfort of a black faux-leather easy chair in her modest Inglewood apartment. "That's the documentary me and Mike are doing. It's basically my life story: where I came from, my horrible years in Sacramento, to two championship rings. It'd be great for high school kids, elementary-school kids. Man, I just want to give somethin' back."

Mike is in fact filming her now as she stretches her legs all the way across the chair to the sofa, where her shoeless size 11 feet waggle over her dinner companion's lap. Watching a videotape of the decisive second game of the 2002 WNBA Finals, Tot-o gives a running critique. The visitor interrupts with probing questions.

"Who's the toughest player on the court right now?"

"Latasha Byears."

"How come you look so much bigger on the court than right here?"

"TV makes me look bigger, baby."

"Who's got the softest hands in the league?"

"Latasha Byears."

"Who's the most promising young player?"

"Mwadi Mabika. She's an incredible talent. She reminds me of myself."

"Who's the most underrated player on the Sparks?"

"Latasha Byears."

As the artistry of the women's game rolls across the TV screen, the muffled sound of a ringing cell phone brings the session to a halt. Mike and the visitor scan the room. The phone is underneath Tot-o's ass. She's snoring, adrift on a river of apple martinis.

Weeks later, she calls from a tattoo parlor in South Central L.A. Things are turning around, she reports. Back at the Beverly Hills restaurant, she had discounted her chances of playing overseas for supplemental income this winter, saying, "I thought the hatin' for me was just in the States, but it's international, man. It's an epidemic." But yesterday she learned that she will be playing for a new team in Shanghai. Fifty grand or so for four months of hoop.

"I got my visa and my airline ticket today," she says in her seen-it-all Memphis drawl. "I just came here to get these tats. On one forearm, it's gonna be a riff on Isaiah 54:17: 'No weapon formed against me shall prosper.' On the other forearm: 'Blessed.'"

Is she looking forward to the Chinese food? "Yeah, somewhat."

At present, she knows nothing whatsoever about Shanghai. But she has proved a quick study in international relations. While playing in Istanbul, she brought her CDs into the local discos and soon became the city's most coveted DJ. Another season found her in the northern Spanish town of Oviedo, where she became close friends with a bartender named Peco and the sangria he lavishly poured her. In the Sicilian city of Messina, she made nice with the pizza-makers and was quick with a jaunty *"Tutto bene?"* which she loosely translated as "What the fuck's goin' on?"

Will Latasha Byears return for the 2003 WNBA season conversant in Mandarin slang, her thick skin riddled with kanji graffiti, rotund as Buddha? Memo to the league: take her however she comes. And let the haters hate on, baby.

GARY SMITH

The Secret Life of Mia Hamm

FROM SPORTS ILLUSTRATED

THE SHOOTER'S HEART FROZE. She'd been right in front of his camera when he'd started gunning the motor drive. Dammit, he was sure of it.

See, there she was in the first few frames, but they weren't photos worthy of the front page of *USA Today* and the living hell Robert Hanashiro had gone through to arrange this high-spirited team picture. For weeks this story had ripened, and now — forty-eight hours before 90,000 people would jam the Rose Bowl to watch women play soccer, for crying out loud — every media crew in the country was chewing on it, and he'd had to beg the U.S. women's soccer team to pose on his duct-tape markers as he clicked from atop a ladder and the TV jackals jostled him from below.

He blinked at the images on his laptop. How was it possible, firing three and a half frames every second? Somehow, on the brink of the 1999 World Cup final against China, when he'd finally gathered all the girls of summer around two inflated globes and gotten all the faces of American women's soccer smiling . . . the face of American soccer was nowhere to be seen. *Poof.* The greatest goal scorer in the history of international soccer. Vanished.

Where in the world was Mia Hamm?

Don't read this story. For Mia's sake. Don't read it or even look at the pictures. It might take too long. Then she'd feel like a burden. You might get to know her. Then she'd have to agonize over what you think.

She'll be disappearing soon anyway. For good. She's got one more year, the woman who launched millions of girls across thousands of fields. Two final engagements on the world stage. The first begins this weekend, in the World Cup, which is back on U.S. soil because of the SARS epidemic in China. The second occurs in Athens, at next summer's Olympics. In between she'll marry one of the greatest shortstops in baseball, but there's *no way* you'll see that.

Perhaps, in spite of her, we'll see her place in history — the first female team-sport superstar — and finally understand how many more complications lay in her path than in those blazed by the women icons of the solo sports, the Babes and Billie Jeans, the Wilmas and Chrissies and Peggys who preceded her.

It's tricky business, being anointed queen amid a circle of female peers, having to dismantle the throne even as you sit on it. Maybe she can pull it off here, too. Maybe she can fill a dozen magazine pages without being seen. Maybe at the end you still won't know what makes a woman ignite and extinguish herself all at once.

"How will this story start?" Mia asks. She's nervous already. "Will it begin, 'I was born a poor black child . . .'?"

No. But close. She was baptized as a middle-income black couple's godchild. With a pair of misshapen feet and sharply bowed legs soon to be wrapped in casts, then in orthotic shoes connected by a steel bar. In a small African-American Catholic church in Selma, Alabama, because her fighter-pilot father wanted to taste what life was like for blacks in a segregated southern town and had already bailed out of the white Catholic church with the shallow social conscience. Just a few feet from the church garage where Mia's ballerina mother taught black girls how to pirouette because she'd seen a black man in a civil rights march carrying a crucifix with a sign on it saying, HE DIED FOR US TOO.

Find something else to do. Mia's story is too tangled. Because just when you're coming to grips with Selma, and with a dad who goes from strafing Vietcong from an F-100 to weekend retreats with his wife among rural 'Bama blacks organized by the Taizé brothers — antiwar and antimaterialist Christians dedicated to sharing their lives with victims of violence, poverty, and racial oppression — you'll be flung from town to town, country to country, all the places our heroine moves to and vanishes from. All the places where neighbors and teammates look up one day and ask, "Where is she? Where's Mia Hamm?"

She's in Florence today. That's Italy. She's two. Banging down the Hamms' long apartment hallway, delighted with the percussion of her new Italian high-tops on the hard floor. She's the Hamms' third straight daughter. It's her third home, her family having moved from Selma to Monterey, California, for a half-year so that Air Force captain Bill Hamm could learn Italian there, and then on to Florence on a two-year grant for overseas graduate study designed to improve understanding between U.S. military officers and their foreign counterparts.

Clomp, clomp, clomp. Mia has bolted out of those leg casts and orthotic shoes as if they were jail, and she hasn't stopped bolting since, except for those astonishing two weeks when she sat on the potty, as still as Buddha, surrounded by books she'd piled up in her determination to meet Mom's challenge: Mia could go to school with her two older sisters only if she was out of diapers. She did it. Turbo potty training, the awed Hamms called it. Now the family's taking its proud housebroken runt to the park. "*Andiamo!*" Mia keeps hooting, bursting ahead of them all to the next Florence street corner. "Let's go!"

She's flying down a sliding board in her purple dress and white lace tights — every detail in the formaldehyde of family lore — when she sees her first soccer ball, en route from an Italian man's foot to his five-year-old son. It's the sport her father has begun to watch on weekends, bicycling to the stadium and falling in love with the throng and the drama and the way one man with a ball on his foot can bring a city to its feet.

In one *whoosh* Mia shoots down the sliding board, leaps a puddle, and flies across the grass, intercepting the ball and kicking it again and again until the five-year-old boy loses interest and the marveling Italian papa takes up the game with her for nearly half an hour.

Bad accent. Bad clothes. Bad haircut. Those are Mia's first words at age thirty-one when she's asked what comes to mind as she looks at a picture of herself at a desk as a little girl.

All innocence and exuberance. Nothing can touch her. Those are Mia's words when it's a picture of her as a little girl playing ball.

A funny thing happens. Mia's standing on the fringe of a pack of boys in Wichita Falls, Texas, cooking in the sun and in her own self-consciousness. *What'll people think of you?* It's the question her mother asks whenever the Hamm girls — four of them now — are out of line. It's 1977. It's Mia's fourth town in her five-year life, and in each new place she has to worry about what a whole new set of people will think of her, and she gets this feeling in her gut as if she's going to vomit, this sick feeling that she's not going to fit in.

She doesn't want to play dress-up or dolls with girls, or wear tutus and dance *The Nutcracker* like her mother. Doesn't matter how many times Stephanie Hamm explains to folks that she's nicknamed her third daughter, Mariel, after a dancer with whom she studied, Mia Slavenska. Nor how many times Mom coos that Mia has the body and athleticism and pixie face to play every gamine in every ballet ever choreographed. Mia had burst into tears and stormed out of her second dance class, recoiling from a life surrounded by mirrors, a life surrounded by Mia.

She wants to do what guys do — make friends and forget about herself by playin' ball — but she can't because she's too shy and shrimpy, and the boys might hoot her off the block. Can't because her skin's so thin that if they do, this powder keg of emotion inside her might detonate right in front of everyone. Can't, most of all, because she's . . . a girl.

Suddenly this frail, dark-haired eight-year-old boy with a trace of the Orient in his eyes and skin glides into the group and begins to speak quietly to the leader. And somehow, at the end of it all, the boys break into two teams, and the Thai-American boy waves her into his huddle. He's her ticket in. He's her brand-new brother, Garrett. One of them, at least. The other one's half African American and half Puerto Rican, a newborn named Martin. The Hamms — weary after four daughters of trying to produce a son — have done the most remarkable thing: adopted two different-colored ones.

Garrett scrawls a play in the dirt. The boys nod. He's a born leader, like Mia's dad. Mia grins. It's funny how vulnerable, how separate she felt a few minutes ago over there on the sidewalk, and how connected she feels to everyone around her now, how safe, on a team. Amazing how so many strangers just turned into pals.

She's got cover now, a big bro she can draft behind on her bike every day when they race off to play ball, one who'll choose her for his side and tout her as his "secret weapon." One she can watch and try to imitate, from his sidearm pitching motion to his shrug over everything except the important stuff — like whether *that kid just stepped out of bounds . . .* or *did not!* One who can fade right, looking, looking, and launch a spiral to that little mop of brown hair that no one notices, no one even sees, darting deep . . . touchdown, Mia!

You're still reading? Cut Mia a break. Skim this part. She's twelve. Thick hair still shorn as short as a boy's. She's moved to San Antonio for three years and just moved back to Wichita Falls. She's about to walk off a soccer field where she just drilled four goals and assisted on two others, just torched a team of boys, half the spectators never realizing that the dominant player's packing a pair of X chromosomes. She's about to leave the rectangle, to cross the white stripe, the dividing line between two worlds. On this side it's okay to spill everything boiling inside her, okay to erupt, explode, dominate, celebrate, to be better than someone else. On the other. . . .

She heads to the bathroom. She's got to be careful. She's always the new kid in the hood, always starting out in a hole, always playing so hard just to feel worthy of being one of the guys, to disappear by blending in. Playing so hard that she keeps standing out, too far out, her hunger and talent carrying her clean past her objective. Now the game's over and she must start shrinking again, fast. Now she feels the opponents' parents' eyes on her, hears them wondering why the star player's waiting in line outside the *girls'* restroom, and her cheeks are flushing red and her tongue's getting tied and someone's telling her, *Hey, the boys' room is over there!*

Dad, who has just refereed three games at the same complex, gives her a one-arm hug, hands her two bucks — fifty cents a goal — and climbs in the Pumpkin, the orange camper the Hamms brought back from Italy and put a quarter-zillion miles on. He's a rare cat. A Democrat fighter-pilot. A lieutenant colonel who, years later, will plant an AMERICANS FOR PEACE poster in his front yard amid the drumbeats of war on Iraq. A perfect ref because he's so stoic and rational, but put him in the stands at one of his kids' games, and look out! He rides refs and opponents so hard that he gets the heave-ho from an official in one of Mia's games and a middle finger from one of the players in another. Mia has seen the one thing that brings out the tendons in the stoic's neck. Mia knows how much winning matters.

They pull away from the soccer fields. Dad glimpses Mia's face in the rearview mirror. She sees where they're heading: the Maternity Cottage. She sees her Saturday going up in smoke. She's turning purple. Here it comes. . . .

Fifteen minutes ago, this eruption of feeling went into a steal and a sprint and a twenty-yard *zzzzt* that the goalie never saw — into explosions that made you hold your breath each time she touched the ball. Now there's no ball and no field. How does a dad handle a furnace with so much potential to create magic — or meltdown? Bill cringes, helpless, never quite sure. He's tried sympathy, bedroom banishment, flinging a flip-flop at her, everything except the remedy his eldest daughter, Tiffany, tried once when Mia went over the edge: lashing her to the couch with pantyhose.

The family couldn't guess what might set her off. It might be a teasing remark about the hand-me-down sweater she wears on Alternate Dress Day. It could be the skirt Mom tries to funnel her into for holidays and photos, or her failed attempt to slink out of the family picture, or that damn wing of hair flapping off the left side of her head on school picture days. Or, worst of all, losing at something cataclysmic like old maid or Uno or knee football in the hallway.

She quits when she smells defeat coming, because if she waits until it arrives, she'll tear herself to shreds. Her face will contort, her eyes gush, her nose stream, and then the worst thing of all will happen: everyone will stare at the self-conscious girl. Her one hope is to twist embarrassment into anger — to scream, punch, topple the board game, or hurl her sister Lovdy's cookie batter on the floor or threaten to smash Lovdy's collection of porcelain miniature horses into a thousand pieces. To have something else disintegrate instead of her.

The Curse, she'd call her raging emotions. All the Hamm girls have it, genetic dynamite straight from Mom, but none has it more than Mia. *I'm sorry*, she keeps saying when the dust settles. *I'm so sorry.* She'll have to spend her life guarding that furnace door. God, it seems so much simpler just to be a boy on a ball field, where you can turn humiliation into a header, fury into a breakaway. Where you get a bonus, as well, a piece of what Garrett's getting so much of: Dad's attention.

The Pumpkin rumbles up in front of the Maternity Cottage. Mia stops heaving, rubs away her tears, hangs her head, and resigns herself to whiplash, this wrenching between worlds with such different rules, values . . . and equipment.

Out come the brooms, mops, buckets, scrub brushes, paintbrushes, sandpaper, rakes, shovels, clippers. Out comes Stephanie Hamm, still stunning at forty, lush dark hair flowing over her shoulders. She's a rare cat. A prospective nun who became a ballerina. The eldest of eleven children, daughter of an Air Force pilot who grew up, like Mia, bouncing from town to town, determined to exhaust her love for dance and fulfill her mother's wish that one of her children become a nun or priest, dedicated to following her Aunt Margaret into a convent. Until, at fifteen, she met Bill Hamm and fell hard.

Somehow, the nun and the ballerina inside her survived the fall. Six children to raise, a home to pack in cardboard boxes and a new town to learn every few years: they aren't alibi enough for her conscience, aren't freedom from all those expectations. She sees her children off to school, spends the day on the phone or running around town gathering funds, food, and clothing for another church campaign or community cause, making the house shine because what if someone comes to the door — *what'll people think?* — as she's preparing dinner, then rattling off instructions to Bill when he returns from the base and racing off to the theater to choreograph a recital or to perform, off to the dance studio to take or give lessons. She can't say no. She's too kind. If it's Wednesday during Lent, they'll eat peanut soup or potato meal or unseasoned rice and lentils, the blander the better, so the Hammies can learn what it's like to spoon down the grub that African children do, so they can swallow the family's prevailing ethic: *You're no better than anyone else. We're all equals in a community, all responsible for one another.* She hurries back at 10:00 P.M., brainstorming the church rummage sale that her children will captain that weekend, her eyes sweeping the floor to make sure the dinner crumbs were swept, because if not, they'll be in a pile on a plate at the offender's place at the table in the morning when the Hamms show up for their bowls of seven-grain gruel. Stephanie is the prettiest and trimmest, the most competent, selfless, and giving mother a girl could have, but it's not enough. She doubts all of it. Every one of her *mosts* should be even more. If someone like that doesn't measure up, how can her daughters begin to think that they do?

It all crests one day when Mia's mom finds herself in a hospital bed. She's a fervent Catholic, ripping herself to pieces because she's just suffered a third-month miscarriage of a baby that, God forgive her, she secretly dreaded having, that she never should've conceived because four daughters and two recently adopted sons and a half-dozen charitable causes and a dancing career have left her feeling as if she's got nothing, God forgive her, left to give. A doctor enters the room and begins to gently chastise the woman on the next bed, scolding her about the abortion she's just undergone and the failure to be responsible about birth control, and the words pierce Stephanie's ripe conscience as if they were arrows targeted for her.

Suddenly Mia's mother is in charge of the Maternity Cottage, a Wichita Falls shelter for unmarried mothers who've been a little lax about birth control as well. Suddenly the Hamms are buying and gutting a dilapidated four-bedroom house, renovating it, maintaining the property, fundraising to keep it afloat and inviting the spillover into their own home. Suddenly there are pregnant, unhappy strangers and their toddlers occupying what's left of Mia's mom's time and attention, not to mention her family's dinner table and the television set when Mia's favorite show is on. And no matter how much Mia respects her mother's golden heart and her father's generous spirit, she's a twelve-year-old kid, for goodness' sake, who just wants to go home after a soccer game, wolf down a half-dozen chocolate-chip cookies that no Ethiopian kid'll ever lay eyes on, and play two-on-two hoops with the three guys on the next block. Instead she picks up a paint scraper and starts chipping away at the misery of the world.

Oh, boy. Here comes a grenade, rolling straight toward the Hamm house: a TV truck. Word's spread about this cute little thirteen-year-old gal on Notre Dame's junior high football team. That's worth both the six and ten o'clock news, for sure, in North Texas in 1985.

Sure, her mom said, when Mia asked if she could play on the football team. Go for it, Mia. There's so much encouragement in this house. So much *Reach for the stars, girl!* But it's all beginning to grow confusing, sometimes even inside the white stripes. Guys who used to be fine about Mia's playing ball, after they saw she had the

goods, aren't so fond of the idea now that the testosterone's kicking in and she's still beating them deep on fly patterns. Some have
started singling her out, ridiculing her, steamrollering her. She
doesn't sob inside the lines, though. You can't do that if you want
to play with boys. Nobody bites her bottom lip better than Mia
Hamm.

Play on girls' teams? She tried that once. She's just not like other
girls. Some of her teammates layered on eye liner and mascara to
play soccer. Some looked at boys *during* games. A few so resented
her dominance that they stopped passing her the ball. She'd get it
anyway, but how are you supposed to feel knocking some lipsticked
center half off the ball and banging home your fourth of the day?
She felt apologetic. She felt like the kid always raising her hand in
class with the right answer, and so she pulled back sometimes, disappearing right in the middle of games.

The TV truck's nearly here. Mia's in her bedroom sobbing. Her
mom's calling, *Hey, Mia, you better pull it together fast. What'll people
think?* But she's flattened. Lovdy, avenging some previous sisterly
atrocity, has just lowered the boom, the Hamm hammer, the clan's
heaviest guilt mallet. "You think you're better than everyone else,
don't you, Mia? Just because you're gonna be on TV, you think
you're pretty hot. Well, you're arrogant." Mia? Mia hasn't puffed
or crowed in her life, but ohmygod, if that's what people might
think. . . .

She's a Hamm. She does the right thing. She exits her room
when the doorbell rings, and tries to be polite. She gives the microphone and camera a few monosyllables, so no one can possibly
think that she thinks she's hot stuff. The family gathers around the
TV that night when her big moment comes. Where in the world is
Mia Hamm? Holed up in her room.

Let her stay there. She'll loathe this section of the story, about what
a phenomenal soccer player she turns into, and how a small girl
from a small town gets discovered. It's full of compliments, which
are almost as painful to Mia as insults.

She's fourteen. It's 1986. She tries out for the North Texas Olympic Development girls' team 150 miles away in Dallas, and when
the players split up for a scrimmage and a defender belts one sky-
ward to clear it out of her end, every coach jotting notes on a clip-

board stops and stares. Some little bitty gal bolts into the path of that clearing pass, wheels, and drills it before it ever hits the ground, a thirty-five-yard rocket volley into the upper right-hand corner of the net. Whoever she is, she's on the team . . . and six months later she's jumped to the *women's* team.

The team travels to Metairie, Louisiana, to play in a regional tournament. Her coach, John Cossaboon, alerts Anson Dorrance that there's a player he needs to look at.

Dorrance is thirty-five, but already he's the lord of U.S. women's soccer. Already he's coached North Carolina to three national titles and been named coach of the U.S. national women's team. "Don't tell me which one she is," he tells Cossaboon. It's his way of testing the supposed phenom, and himself. She should *appear* to him on her own.

Dorrance watches the first minute of the first game and heads straight to Cossaboon. He nods toward the littlest one, the youngest one, the streak of light. The one who knifes right at a defender, knocks the ball a yard past her, and then beats her to it, rubbing her out in a footrace. "That's her, right?" Dorrance says.

"No," deadpans Cossaboon. "You got it wrong."

Dorrance blinks, then shakes his head. Nice try, pal. She's *his*. Just like that. On his national team at fifteen and will be on his college team the minute she finds her way out of high school. She shows up at that first national camp with a mullet haircut and a deer-in-the-headlights stare . . . and comes home with fire on her face. She can't stop babbling at the dinner table: how marvelous Michelle and April are, how wonderful Kristine and Wendy and Joy. Women who knock *her* off the ball after she knocks *them* off the ball. Vicious competitors. A whole community. They *exist*. Females just like her.

Well, not exactly like her. Lots of them wear skirts now and then, even makeup. Women she can study, women she can draft behind when they go to a restaurant or mall, women who can introduce her to sides of herself she's never met. Good Lord, in just a few years they'll have her standing in a fitting room, trying on a bikini!

Look at her, this new person in the mirror. Not bad. Legs not half so bowed as she thought. But she could lose her so easily: one mediocre tournament could make her vanish. It's not enough, the hour and a half of dribbling and shooting drills she does alone at school on summer mornings, chasing down every shot on a netless goal in the Texas heat. Mia needs to get her first pair of running shoes and go for miles. She needs to pack up and move, for the seventh time, to some place where the competition will force her game to grow. Alone this time. That's how badly she needs to be with those girls she's just discovered.

It scares the hell out of her, walking out of tiny Notre Dame High in Wichita Falls and her class of thirty-five in February of her sophomore year, with her basketball teammates fighting to recapture the state championship that she'd led them to as a freshman. She clamps back her emotions, says goodbye to her family and friends, and she's gone.

She walks into a school, Lake Braddock, with more than five thousand students. Sick to her stomach. Silent. It's in Burke, Virginia, a soccer hotbed, where she'll live with a man she barely knows, her aunt's brother-in-law. There's no Garrett anymore to give her cover. He's back in Wichita Falls, still trying to come to terms with the diagnosis that doctors gave him two years before: aplastic anemia, a bone marrow disorder that at the time was usually fatal.

If she were a boy, she wouldn't have to agonize over joining a new team, because boys understand that sports create hierarchies and that the ball will go to the dominant player the moment he asserts himself. But girls have to assess you first; they have to decide they like you before they let you fit in. How can Mia — with no time to chat because she's cramming in extra courses in order to graduate a year early and start at North Carolina, and missing entire weeks of practice because she's off training with the best women in the world — pull this one off amid a pack of teenage girls who have played together for years?

Like this: By shrinking in team meetings and schlepping the team's gear. By taking the team's worst ball for individual drills and feeding all the girls the most wonderful passes and compliments. By making it clear to the coach, Carolyn Rice, that she's only to praise Mia fleetingly, furtively, amid kudos for the other girls. By erasing herself as she imposes herself and carries Lake Braddock to the state championship.

She returns from her first trip overseas with the national team bubbling with things to tell her family — what she's just seen and done in China, and the new world opening before her. But what awaits her are two coffins, a pair of funerals, and a family lost in grief. Her mother's dad and brother have gone down together in a Cessna.

It's almost as if fate's conspiring to hammer home her life's theme, in case she forgets it for an instant: it's not about you, Mia Hamm.

"You've got the potential, Mia. You can be the best soccer player in the world. But do you know what it takes? It's a decision you make. You can't make it halfway. You have to make it in your heart and mind, completely. You don't make the decision slowly. It's like turning on a light switch."

Mia and Anson Dorrance sit in darkness in his office. She's never met anyone like this. A man handing her a hall pass from guilt, from nineteen years of conditioning about what a female owes everyone around her. A man offering her an environment, both at Chapel Hill and on the national team, where it's okay for women to be sisters off the field and cutthroats on it. Where you step on the foot of an opponent shadowing you too closely; where the results of every day's drills are posted to show who's Top Gun in each and who's breathing down her neck; where losers of intrasquad scrimmages must bend over in front of the goal and clutch their ankles so winners can blast twenty-yard bullets at their butts. Where Mia finally feels it's safe to start growing out her hair.

Mia's parents have moved to Italy, where Bill is a U.S. Air Force attaché, but first Stephanie has sent Dorrance a long letter attempting to explain in advance in case her daughter's emotions run amok. Dorrance shrugs it off. He's never had a player like Mia, who can't eat or talk at the team's pregame buffet. Who goes off alone before a game, cutting through imaginary opponents, dancing with the ball like a ballerina. Then paces the sideline inside her own private tunnel. Then, before the big games, bolts to the toilet or nearest trash can and vomits. Bile. There's nothing in her to vomit. Then brings the crowd to its feet, chanting, "Mia! Mia!" when her foot touches the ball. Then flogs herself at halftime if she hasn't scored — *Dammit, I suck, I'm worthless, the world's ending* — as if she's about to become the outcast, the stranger over on the sidewalk the next time teams are chosen; as if she owes her girls a pair of goals to prove she belongs, must dominate to feel like an equal. Then she does what's so hard for her to do outside the rectangle: exposes her soul, lets go, explodes, slams two into the back of the net, and fist-pumps or slides or bull-rushes the stands, not in celebration of Mia but in release from the pressure she keeps heaping upon herself. You *have* to take responsibility for the community. You *have* to be perfect. But you're no better than anyone else.

Dorrance doesn't want to resolve this tension inside her. He wants it to flow like molten metal on a hundred soccer fields across the globe. He wants the furnace at full blast; he'll live with the collateral damage when Mia's anxiety over losing or not scoring sends the blaze the wrong way.

"Please tell Mia to stop yelling at me!" Tar Heels teammates ask captain Angela Kelly as they race upfield.

"It's all right, Hammer!" Angela insists.

"But we're playing lousy!" Mia shouts.

"Sure, you can tell them to step it up, but not so mean, Hammer!"

Let them work it out, Dorrance figures. Let Tony DiCicco, who replaces him in 1994 as coach of the national team, pick up the pieces and the chairs after Mia hisses, "Shut up!" at him during a game in France, then gets in a screaming match with him at halftime and starts knocking over seats in the locker room.

Dorrance will live with first-stage meltdown. It's stage two that's more worrisome. That's when Mia, sometimes because she's pulled back her game for fear of doing too much and upsetting her teammates, loses her rhythm and confidence and grows so frustrated at not living up to her own standards that her whole body sags. She can't run away when failure's coming, as she used to as a child, but her heart and soul do. She stops chasing balls. "Take her out!" captain Carla Overbeck shouts at the coach when that happens.

Dorrance has players around Mia, like Kelly and Overbeck, who can act as a firewall. He builds the sisterhood strong enough to heal the wounds. He knows Mia will feel so awful the next day that she'll mend the fences. It's worth it, all of it, because this is the player he's been searching for ever since he became a coach, one who catches fire each time the flint of her values is struck: you're doing this for nineteen teammates, Mia. For American soccer. For millions of girls you can inspire. You can give by taking, Mia.

But now he wants her to take the next step — to choose athletic immortality, to give and take more. Mia's silent. He's asking something of her that happens only on the other side of the stripe: spontaneity, a light-switch decision, a go-for-broker.

It's 1991. Title IX, mandating equal opportunities for women in collegiate sports, has just begun to bear fruit. Sometimes only a few hundred people show up to watch the U.S. team play: there's no such thing as a female spectator team sport. Mia and her teammates do their own laundry, carry their own gear, sometimes drive their team vans. There's so little interest in their games that they send faxes to inform friends in the United States of how they're doing in the inaugural '91 World Cup, in China, and return with the championship to a welcoming party of three. They function in darkness.

"It's a decision, Mia," Dorrance says quietly, "that you make like *that*." His hand strikes the switch. Light floods the room. She hasn't said a word, but she's decided, she's going for it. Never dreaming how much light she'll cast, and how much of her the light will expose.

Does the face launch the movement? Or does the movement launch the face? At some point the two entwine, and no one can say. At some point little girls begin roaming the team's hotel hallways, looking for Mia, and after she poses for a picture and begins to walk away, they say, our whole team's waiting outside for you, can you come? At some point they begin falling asleep with her face on their walls and ceilings, the last image on their retinas each day, this woman who convinces them, without uttering a word, that it's okay to sweat, seethe, leap, let go. They begin writing her letters, wearing her ponytail and number 9 jersey to her games, and shrieking, "Mia! Mia!" at the same pitch and frenzy as starving baby birds.

At some point she agrees, in spite of all her misgivings, to do the Letterman show and the Pert Plus commercial and the Barbie doll and the Gatorade and the Nike sneakers, because people she trusts persuade her that doing so will liberate even more girls who stand on the sidewalk as teams are chosen. Convince more girls that anything's possible, even a Barbie doll that plays soccer.

The movement needs the face because the face, no longer a pixie tomboy's, offers the femininity, the beauty, and the naked

passion that the sport and the camera need. The face needs the
movement because it offers the sense of mission, the justification
for all those solitary three-a-day workouts, that a Hamm needs.
Where else can the lenses go when the U.S. women's team wins the
1996 Olympic gold medal on U.S. soil in front of 76,489 fans but
to the burning hazel eyes of the team's leading scorer, the woman
who led UNC to four national titles? She becomes, according to
surveys, the most recognized and appealing female athlete in
America, and the fourth-most-admired one, behind Michael Jordan, Tiger Woods, and Lance Armstrong. One of the select few
whose first name suffices. One of *People*'s 50 Most Beautiful People.
Nike names its largest building after her, and people she's never
laid eyes on begin saying, "If you need me, I'll be in Mia at 3:30 today." The shyest one becomes the anointed one.

Sometimes it's beautiful. When she knows a public moment's
coming, when she has agreed to it and prepared herself, she might
still pace and fret, but when the moment comes to perform, the
performer turns on. She's eloquent, gracious, funny. People walk
away dazzled by Mia.

Sometimes it's painful. She's walking off the practice field. A
pack of reporters she didn't expect walks right past all her teammates and surrounds her. They're asking her the question that par-
alyzes her: what's it like to be the best woman player in the world?
They're creating more responsibility, more expectations. They're
asking her to put herself first. She can't do it.

"Ask me that question when I can dominate on both offense and
defense like [teammate] Kristine Lilly does," she replies. "Ask me
when I can head a ball like Tisha Venturini, defend as well as Joy
Fawcett, play an all-around game like Julie Foudy." It's how she
feels. It's a way of disappearing. It's both.

The reporters roll their eyes. A pack of fans gathers around the
pack of reporters. Mothers and daughters begging for autographs.
Mia! Meeee-aaaaaa! Over here! A hundred baby birds to feed, and the
mother bird must choose which ones. The team bus revs. The media want more, much more, but she has no quick answers: they all
require so much thought. Her mates are waiting. They're the ones
she wants to be with. They're why she works out eight hours a day
— to be good enough just to be part of them.

The vise tightens around the woman who makes all those girls feel so free. It's all on her face. Everything's being squeezed through layers and folds of intellect and feeling, being measured once, measured twice. What'll people think? What'll her teammates think if she keeps standing here, separate, consenting to all this attention? So she *must* say no. But what'll the reporters and fans think if she spurns them, and what about her responsibility to women's soccer? So she *can't* say no. But she's determined to have boundaries. No matter how much she loves her mother, she's not going to *be* her, she's not going to live her life by other people's expectations. So she *must* say no.

Yes or no, a strange thing happens. There's so much heat inside her, people sometimes walk away thinking that Mia's cold.

She's not built for celebrity. She can't play the game — any game — lightly, can't make breezy chitchat with strangers while all that's grinding inside her; she can't fake it. She's too busy trying to decide what's the right thing to do, too caught in her own crossfire, too wary of what lurks just below it. When a girl rises in a roomful of eight- to fourteen-year-olds in Sydney and asks Mia what her main goal in life is, she replies, "Not to embarrass myself." She's kidding. Sort of. Maybe.

She finds her way into the corner or the foyer at receptions and cocktail parties, or onto the floor to play with somebody's child. She lowers a ball-cap brim over her eyes on the street. She lowers her eyes. "I'm sure I miss some things about the world," she tells people, "but I can tell you a lot about my shoes."

That's what the world misses about her, what teammates who've known her for years cherish: her wicked sarcasm, her honesty, her vulnerability, days when her guard comes down and she's positively giddy. They get her dead-on Noo Yawk and Brit and Aussie accents, her impersonations, her rocking *Rocky Top* on karaoke nights. They get long notes so heartfelt that some keep them and read them before every game. They get her on their doorstep after a five-hour flight when their parents die. They get a teammate whose eyes well up in compassion when they're feeling down and need to talk, one who crisscrosses headbands over her nose in commiseration when they suffer a fracture and have to wear a face guard. They get her hauling the equipment bag out of the bus when they're trudging to their hotel rooms at midnight. Doing all the community work. They get appearances in her commercials, they get cash, because she takes less and insists that they be included. Newcomers keep their distance at first, wary of her moods, but by their third year on the team they love her: they've seen so much goodness unfold.

The U.S. team becomes sisters, more than any team of men ever became brothers, because their star will have it no other way. They yank her onto elevators when the autograph stalkers become too much. They pretend to be her to throw the hounds off her scent. They help her disappear.

They're there for her when darkness falls. A doctor walks into the waiting room at the National Institutes of Health in Bethesda, Maryland, in 1996 and tells Mia, her mother, and her brother Garrett that there's only one chance left for him, a Hail Mary bone-marrow transplant. She reels out of that room, punishing herself for every day she chased a ball across the world and forgot about her family. Two months after the transplant in 1997, his immune system fails, his left arm goes numb, and a fungal infection attacks his brain. She feels the full power of her parents' hearts, gratitude that they opened up to a boy born in Bangkok twenty-eight years before, as the family encircles his bed. She looks at her siblings, red eye to red eye, and realizes that all the old explosions are meaningless now, and that she will never again go months without calling them.

She takes a long, hard look at stardom, too. It has never seemed more foolish. She's never wanted more to vanish. Then she looks again. Her choice in the matter is fading, just like her brother. She'll never embrace celebrity, but now she's got to grip its hand. Because she's found her higher calling, her purpose, here on this bed: to reach even deeper on the field, and off it, too, to play like Bill Hamm's daughter so she can give like Stephanie Hamm's. To use fame to channel hundreds of thousands of dollars into the Mia Hamm Foundation, to provide athletic opportunities for girls and funds to people desperate for bone-marrow transplants. To write letters to inspire sick children, to visit them and take them to arcades.

She watches her brother's breath hitch, his eyes open for an instant. "Ohhh, Garrett," she calls. And then he's gone: the boy who first brought her in from the sideline, and now won't let her go back.

*

Now place the ball on a white dot twelve yards from the goal. Fix the eyes of 90,185 people on it, the most ever to watch a women's competition, and lock the gaze of 40 million more on it on television. Turn up the heat: 105 degrees on the field, players dizzy from dehydration. Turn it up higher: World Cup final, 0–0, U.S. and China deadlocked after ninety minutes of regulation and two fifteen-minute overtimes. And higher: birth of a women's professional league possibly riding on the five penalty kicks each team will take from the white dot on the floor of the Rose Bowl to break the tie.

Call Mia Hamm's name. Put her on the spot. She can't possibly disappear, not in front of 40,090,185 people — can she?

Holy smoke! She's *trying* to. She's telling assistant coach Lauren Gregg that she doesn't want to take one of the five penalty kicks. "Why isn't Mac taking one?" she asks, referring to teammate Shannon MacMillan. "Mac should be taking one."

"Mia, you're taking one," says Gregg.

"Why?" asks Mia.

Why? Her agent's fielding, and refusing, fifteen requests a day for interviews and appearances and photo shoots of the best female player in the world as the girls of summer become the sizzle story of 1999. She's in a Gatorade commercial going one-on-one with Michael Jordan in a variety of sports as "Anything You Can Do, I Can Do Better" jingles in the background. It's crunch time. It's when superstars demand the ball. They have no conscience. They're sharks.

In a skybox sits Bill Clinton, pulled so near the edge of his seat by this game that he has nearly fallen out of it. On the sideline stands Robert Hanashiro, discovering that his front-page *USA Today* team photo isn't the failure he feared. "Nice photo," people at the Rose Bowl tell him. "It's fitting. That's Mia." In the stands, flown here from Japan by the U.S. military at President Clinton's request, is Mia's husband, Christiaan Corry.

Wait a minute. Mia's *married?* Absolutely. Well, sort of. To a quiet, intense young man she met in a class at UNC and wedded at twenty-two. His intensity and easy wit remind her of her father's, and his career choice — he becomes a Marine helicopter pilot — does, too. What she miscalculates is how much energy and time marriage takes, how little she has left for it when her soccer de-

vours so much. She and Christiaan are so busy following their
dreams that they're rarely on the same continent, let alone the
same bed. So her marriage often seems invisible, too, and she
makes sure it is to the world, pleading with reporters who write
about her to steer clear of it.

A hush falls over the Rose Bowl in anticipation of the shootout.
Mia's teammates wrap themselves in iced towels and pour water
over their heads, but it's too late for Mia, the white dot has set all
her combustibles aflame. Doesn't matter that just a few months before, she became, at twenty-seven, the leading international scorer
in soccer history, male or female; that she left Pelé in the dust
thirty-four goals ago. Doesn't count that her defense and passing
have improved so relentlessly that she no longer needs to score to
alter a game, and that opponents double-team her, freeing her pals
to score. Mia scored two goals early in the World Cup tournament,
then ran dry, and the questions have begun again, reporters digging up those stats about her dearth of offense in major tournaments, spinning their cute little MIA puns and tying her in so many
knots over failing to meet so many people's expectations that it
becomes harder and harder for her to explode. An eight-game
drought just a few months ago brought her into Tony DiCicco's office in tears. Do you know how scary it is to be Mia Hamm and not
feel like playing?

If she misses the kick that decides this World Cup, she'll have to
live inside those flames until her final breath. Her penalty kicks in
practice have been shaky. *Oh, no.* What if the coach thinks he *has* to
choose her because she's supposedly the star? She has to let him
know he's not obligated. *Oh, no.* A hierarchy's being created here, a
threat to sisterhood and equality and all the potato meal that ever
stuck to the roof of her mouth, a thing loathsome enough when it's
being foisted on the team by outsiders — the media or a sneaker
corporation or a soccer federation presenting awards — but un-
bearable when it's the coach doing it, the family's father figure.
She has to show her teammates that she doesn't feel entitled to one
of these five kicks. *Oh, no.* What if she protests too much and they
think she doesn't *want* to contribute, that she fears the responsibility, that she's foisting it on somebody else? Trust me. You don't
want to be *in Mia* at 3:51 PDT on July 10, 1999.

Mia fails. She can't airbrush herself out of the biggest moment of her career. She is chosen to kick fourth for the Americans. They're up 3–2 — the third Chinese attempt was punched away by U.S. goalkeeper Briana Scurry — when Mia approaches the white dot. If she scores, the Chinese are against the wall. She places the ball on the dot, pushes a strand of hair from her face. She will remember nothing from then until the ball strikes the net, and the Rose Bowl explodes.

She screams, but her face never relaxes, never smiles, her eyes still burning and her jaw clenched as she races back to her teammates. She is not a woman celebrating. She's a woman howling *I beat you, goddammit,* at all her fear and doubt.

She passes out in the locker room an hour and a half after the game, awakens on a table with IV tubes in her arms and spends the rest of the night in her hotel room, vomiting bile, going hot and cold, unable to speak or even open her eyes, they burn so much. Fried as much by months of anxiety over the World Cup as by the blazing sun over the Rose Bowl.

At the jubilant team party at the hotel that night, everyone asks the same question that people asked at Mia's prom, at her school sports banquet, on her high school team picture day, and at 11:30 P.M. when her college teammates hit the Chapel Hill bars to celebrate another championship: where's Mia Hamm?

"How much do they pay you to write a story?" she asks. "Maybe I could pay you that much *not* to write it." She's joking. Sort of. Maybe.

Goodness, we're on the twelfth page of a story that she hoped to God, if it *had* to be written at all, wouldn't last more than four. So let's not linger on the depressing loss to Norway in the 2000 Olympic final or the two goals Mia is limited to in the tournament. Let's skip past the new league kicking off in 2001, the Women's United Soccer Association, thanks to Mia and her national teammates' agreeing to play for peanuts. Let's zip past the burden placed on her, as the only household name, to sell her new team, the Washington Freedom, and the WUSA itself — and the feeling that she's doing too much . . . but never enough.

Let's hurry past the shoulder problem and knee surgery that hamper her during her first two seasons with the Freedom, and all the losing that miserable first summer, when the sisterhood disperses and leaves her surrounded by strangers again: the new kid who still finds it so hard to fit in. When she's named the Freedom's captain and discovers once more, as she did in her senior year at UNC, that she's not cut out for it. When she barks at players who don't know her well enough to say, "Oh, that's just Mia," the way her USA mates do; when she's too intense for teammates cowed by a captain running sprints with her own stopwatch; when she's just not sure enough that everyone wants to hear what she has to say.

Let's even jump past the turnaround, the second year with the Freedom, when she relinquishes the captaincy and plays mostly the second halves of games as she recovers from her knee injury, and still hushes the whispers that she's past her prime by leading the league in assists, tying for the lead in points, and taking her team to the title game before finally losing. Let's triple-jump past the divorce in 2001 — *yes, please,* croaks Mia — when marriage by e-mail finally collapses. Past all the sleepless and headache-racked nights holed up in her bedroom, haunted by her failure to keep a vow made in front of her family and friends.

Let's run straight to joy — unfettered, uncluttered, unmeasured. Let's fly to Nomar.

On the white dot, of all places. That's where they meet. At a promotional event in 1998 at Harvard, where she and Nomar end up in a shootout, five kicks each, to entertain the fans. He makes three. She makes four.

"Thanks for throwing it," Mia says.

"I had to let you win," Nomar replies.

Nine months later, during the most painful patch of her career. That's when they really talk for the first time, during her eight-game slump in early '99. She's so desperate that she digs up the phone number he gave her and begs his forgiveness for bothering him. "I'm struggling right now," she says. "Do you have any ideas? What do you do when you're in a slump?"

"I pick out something small," he says. "Something I can control, something I can manage. And I just focus on that."

"Okay," she says.

"Are you winning?" he asks.

"Yeah."

"Are you playing well, outside of your scoring?"

"Well . . . yeah."

"Then you've got to just enjoy the game. You've got to stop worrying."

She tries that for a change. And not long afterward, on a give-and-go with Foudy against Japan, she scores and races to midfield, screaming to Julie, "Can you get a f——ing 500-pound gorilla off my back?" When Julie pretends to grab the beast and fling it away, she cries, "Thank you!" and swoons to the ground.

Just don't spoil it. Don't ask what Nomar's last name is. That's part of his allure, that he's one of a select few athletes whose first name suffices, a star big and bright enough to eclipse her — a cover for the cover girl. God, it's a relief when slack-jawed strangers approach and walk right past her, to him. Lord, it's a lesson to see how much easier he is with fame, comfortable enough to set boundaries and live by them without anguish, to give freely without feeling threatened when it's time to, and to say no thank you when it's not. A man she can study, a man she can draft behind when they go to a restaurant or mall, a man who can introduce her to sides of herself she has never met . . . and to her oldest self, the nine-year-old whose best buddies were ballplayin' guys.

He's a freak on fitness and perfecting technique, just as she is. They spend seven-hour days together for six weeks during the winters of 2002 and '03 at Athletes' Performance, a fitness and biomechanics center in Tempe, Arizona, where they hone every muscle and movement that they use in their games, Mia even perfecting how her feet touch the ground when she runs. She doesn't need that when she's with Nomar, of course. Her feet don't touch it.

Happy-go-lucky, playful, carefree, a real goofball . . . her friends use words like those to describe Mia these days. Why, she even wears skirts and flowing dresses at the drop of a ball cap. She's begun to paint abstract shapes, sharing a canvas and colors with Nomar on one of them. She glows when she's with him, teammates marvel. It's so wonderful that neither one wants to talk about it. And on the soccer field she's sounder of body and mind than she ever was, a better all-around player.

He flies her to the Caribbean last Thanksgiving, gets down on one knee, and asks her to marry him. For once in her life, Mia answers a question without having to think.

*

"I want to enjoy this World Cup and Olympics. That's what I want to do with my last year. I'm learning to realize this is awesome, that the positives so outweigh the negatives or the pressures. It's a waste of energy and emotion to focus on what you can't control, to brood over each play. It's not the message I want to give to the younger players.

"I'm trying to make relationships my first priority. In the end the medals never say, 'I love you.' They tarnish and collect dust. People tried to tell me that before. You can read it in books and hear it on *Oprah* and say, 'Oh, yeah.' But it has to be in your gut, and I guess it wasn't. Your perception is your reality. I'm starting to trust myself."

Yes, let's let Mia talk for a change, before she hangs it up next August along with most of the other women at the heart of the sisterhood who've been playing together since the late '80s. Mia, Julie, Joy, Kristine, and Brandi Chastain are already planning reunions at which they'll gather and laugh over all the silly things they did. Like the time that everyone misinterpreted, when a teammate yanked Mia's shorts up to her chest just as that photographer was snapping that front-page picture for *USA Today*, and she felt laughter coming on so hard that she had to duck behind a teammate.

Mia actually seems to be relishing the prospect of retirement, something no one could've imagined of her two years ago. To be looking forward to making little Nomars, to sitting in a back yard with her siblings and parents and watching all the Hamm grandchildren play touch football for as long as a Hamm can bear to sit and watch.

Of course, that's when she's not worrying about getting cut from the U.S. team any moment now, or writhing over what you think about every word in this story. Remember, she's just starting to trust herself. Just starting a long trip.

Let's let her savor the WUSA championship she helped lead her team to last month, even though the league into which she poured so much of herself folded three weeks later. Let's let her get married in private after the World Cup and then vanish with the balloons and the doves and the fireworks at the closing ceremonies next summer in Athens. She's spun enough gold, forged enough steel in that furnace. Let's remember her as the bridge, the one all the ponytailed phenoms are climbing across to leave behind the twentieth century, when so many women had to feel apologetic about going for it all, in order to reach the twenty-first, when they'll all be standing on the white dot waiting for the ball, and the photo op, and the commercial.

She's thirty-one. It's time. Sometimes you've got to disappear before you can really see yourself.

PAUL SOLOTAROFF

Growing Up Mantle

FROM MEN'S JOURNAL

So, TRY THIS ON for a childhood. You are David and Danny Mantle and, for much of your youth, your father is the most admired man in America. The beautiful, blond basher from Commerce, Oklahoma, who personally invented the tape measure homer while playing on knees so wracked it took three hours to wrap them, Mickey is the avatar of greatness and goodness, power without pride or imposture. His fame, if not fortune (this was before ballplayers were barons), entitles you to all you could reasonably want — a big house in Dallas with an in-ground pool and a yard the size of a small airstrip; six weeks in Florida every February and March for the extended recess called spring training; and eight weeks each summer in a Jersey guesthouse, plus field-level boxes behind home plate to chart Dad's moonshot blasts.

You play flag football on the outfield grass with your brothers, Mickey Jr. and Billy; plant snakes in the luggage of the phobic Phil Rizzuto and hang with his gorgeous daughters; go hunting with Billy Martin and fishing with Roger Maris and golfing with an endless parade of stars, though one of you — David — is so inept that Dad chides you to wear a cup while putting. As a bonus, you draw none of the jock-sniffing press that plagues Mickey Jr., the oldest. Let him have the gatefold spreads in *Boys' Life* and film crews at his church-league games. Who needs the hassle of Dad's first name when his last name has been so good to you?

Of course, if we're being honest, there are drawbacks, too. From day one at school, kids you've never even met, all hopped up about your presumptive wealth and angling for an instant rep, want to punch you the minute you get off the bus. (Things are bigger in Texas, including class envy; neighbor kids pump your dad's Caddy with buckshot and vandalize your home when you're up north.) Naturally, you fight, coming from a line of tough Okie zinc miners, but soon it gets old to have to sleep with a twelve-gauge and find the cops camped in your drive. In the torrent of fan mail your father receives, there's a cold stream of death threats and kidnapping warnings, and even your mom, Merlyn, keeps a loaded .38 under her pillow while Mick's away. This happens, frankly, a lot, because he's gone so much, and not just during the season. It seems that being Mickey Mantle is a year-round gig, what with beer ads to tape and tourneys to host and a heap of relatives with their hands held out, coasting on his kindness.

Such time as he does spend at home is magic: Dad hitting you over the shoulder with a pinpoint spiral in backyard football games, and lavishing you with one yarn after another, like the one about the night he and Billy Martin walked a twenty-second-floor ledge to watch a teammate have sex with a woman, only to realize there was no room to turn around, forcing them to circle the entire building to come in. But then a week passes, and he's off again, to the golf course with Whitey Ford or to hunt with Yogi Berra or to the Filling Station, a rowdy country-western bar up the road, to knock back a case with Mickey Jr., because what Dad really likes to do with whoever's around is drink until it's time to play ball. And the hard part of that is you can't join him, since even the saltiest bars in Texas won't serve you till you turn fifteen.

But still and all, come on, you're the sons of number 7 — every kid in America wants your problems. To be sure, there's that small matter of lymph node cancer, which has struck down most of the men in your family by the intolerable age of fifty, and which will befall Mickey as well as your two brothers, the latter while still in their prime. And, as long as we're being thorough, there's that other despoiler, the gene that seems to render you all helpless before booze and will make a sour mash of your twenties and thirties, leading one of you to try to shoot yourself. But let's not split hairs here — that all happens later, and in the meantime there's your God-given youth, right?

So why, years later, after the divorces and the drug runs and the hard climb back to sobriety, did you say what you said to Billy

Crystal? You were on the red carpet at the premiere of *61**, his bittersweet paean to your father and Maris, and you were thanking him for getting the film made. Jokingly, he pushed you both away, saying that as a boy he'd wished for one thing in life, to have been the son of Mickey Mantle. To which the older of you, David, bit down hard and said, Hell, we wished we had, too.

Although it's cocktail hour at Mickey Mantle's, the Manhattan restaurant named for their father, the hardest thing either of his surviving sons drink now is the ice cubes in their Cokes. But they're among old friends here, and with stories this barbed and funny, who needs booze?

"Y'all remember the gecko we slipped on Rizzuto when he was lyin' out by the pool?" says David.

"It was an iguana," says Ed Ford, who, in his gray-haired forties, is a ringer for Whitey, his father. "Your dad and mine gave us the goddamn thing, then hid in the bushes and watched. We were maybe nine at the time, and here's this three-foot dragon, but Mickey said, 'No, it'll be great.' And when we dumped it on Phil, he jumped ten feet, and the lizard dug its claws in his skin. I remember him running around with this thing on his chest, screaming, 'Help, get it off me — I'm dying!'"

"Wait, I got a better one," says Billy Martin Jr., a thirty-eight-year-old player's agent. "One time, Phil falls asleep on the plane while it's going through a hailstorm. Of course, he's terrified of planes — hell, of everything, really — so my dad puts an air mask and life jacket on and waits till the plane's really rocking. He throws some ice chips on Phil and starts screaming, 'We're going down, man, we're going down!' The poor guy almost coded."

Martin, who lives in Texas, and Ford, whose home is in New York, are in town for the annual Sportswriters' dinner. So are the Mantles, though they have next to no use for the backslapping and rubber veal. They're on hand mainly to see these two, whom they've thought of as adjunct brothers since they met in spring training as children. As their real brothers are dead — Mickey Jr. of cancer at the age of forty-seven, and Billy of chemotherapy-induced heart failure at thirty-six — and their own health fails them in ominous ways, it is less and less clear how many chances they'll have to relive those lambent times. Danny, forty-three, has had his gallbladder

removed and suffers from bouts of bile-duct blockage and agonizing liver pain. David, forty-seven, has advanced hypertension and
had a strokelike episode last summer. "You'd best hurry up and
write fast," Danny cackles to me. "You might have to do a séance to
reach us next year."

A waitress stops by, ostensibly to take their order for drinks, but
really to flirt with David. Although he's plumped up some in the
past several years, he still looks astoundingly like his father and elic-
its stares and requests for autographs when out in public. "'Course,
my favorite one of all's the hunting story," he resumes when the
waitress leaves. "Our dads had drove down to Kerrville, Texas, like
they did each year, to hunt in this guy's woods. So Mick goes inside to ask permission, and the guy says, 'Sure, I'd be honored,
but could you do me a favor? I've got this old mule out back that
needs putting down, and I'm too attached to do it.' Well, Dad decides he's gonna play a trick on Billy [Martin]. He says, 'Man, that
sumbitch said no — I'm gonna go shoot his mule!' So he does,
but when he gets back to the truck, Billy isn't in it. All of a sudden, Billy runs around the barn, laughing like a hyena. 'Start the
fuckin' truck!' he yells. "I showed that little prick — I shot two of
his cows!'"

And so on and so forth, a glory-days hymn in four-part harmony.
The sweetest stories hark back to the grapefruit years in Florida,
when the Mantles and Fords and Martins and Berras connected
every spring. Those six weeks in Fort Lauderdale (and before the
team relocated, in St. Petersburg) were the one time of year these
sons of famous men were assured of seeing their fathers, and they
look back on those springs as the best months of their lives.

"Weeks in advance, I'd feel the juices pump — I'm gonna be
with friends again," says David. "The Fords, the Berras, you didn't
have to say nothing — they just understood. There was none of
that 'Do they like me for who I am, or what I could have Dad sign'
shit, which was always my thought with kids. It was, 'Well, what do
you wanna do today?' 'Let's throw oranges off the balcony, and try
to see Cindy [Rizzuto] with her top off.' And it was seeing Mom re-
lax by the pool with her friends, after all those months of being
alone. At night, she and Dad would get dressed and go dancing
with Whitey and Billy and their wives, and we'd ditch whoever they
had left to watch us and grease all the doorknobs with lotion."

But after several hours of laughter and grace notes, Ed Ford departs with his girlfriend and son, and then Martin gets up to go chaperone some players on their first trip to New York, and the air they leave behind turns patchy. Left to their memories, the Mantles sag, as if the sadness that followed those magic springs wasn't worth the telling. It is one of many things they share with their father, a gruff mistrust of complex feelings or tales that ring of complaint. Take the pain, said Mickey, who played on knees so mangled that he could twist his lower legs a full circle. Take the pain, he told his love-starved sons, and they have and do. When they speak of their losses, it is without rancor, in the flat-edged cadence of stoics.

"We were sitting in that booth there after Dad got sober and apologized for not being a father," says Danny. "He said, 'I should've been home more, should've been more attentive, given you boys direction. It wasn't right that Mom had to raise you herself. I was selfish, and I regret it.'"

"I think it was also the first time he told us he loved us, after writing the letter to Mutt," says David. "One of the hardest things you do at the Betty Ford clinic is write a letter to your father, and when Dad did it, he cried for two days. He apologized for not being a better player, for not taking care of his body. I guess that confession kinda opened him up, 'cause he was never big on expressing himself."

By now, the story of Mickey and his pile-driving father is embedded in national lore. Mutt, a miner and former semipro shortstop, nestled a baseball into Mickey's crib hours after he was born and dragged him out for batting practice before the boy could read. It wasn't enough merely to make the Bigs, to be the first Mantle up from poverty in Tom Joad Oklahoma. No, Mickey had to be the greatest ever, to hit a ball farther than any before him, and from either side of the plate. His obeisance was such that he got married at twenty because his father said bachelorhood would hurt his stats, and before that, he'd declined a full scholarship to be the quarterback at Oklahoma. Long after the death of his father, in 1952, Mick lived in something like holy terror of letting the old man down.

But there's only so much responsibility a man can bear before he becomes a slave, and with his own brood Mantle abdicated duty every chance he got. He was no sooner home after the season ended than he began to resent Merlyn and the four small boys im-

pinging on his freedom. He could be vicious when drunk to his devoted wife, pulling a chair out from under her while dining with
teammates or throwing a napkin in her face at a banquet. (He
could also be maddeningly tender at times, sitting on the couch after her sumptuous meals and saying, "I love you, Merle; you're my
gal.") And with his kids, he seemed bent on being the anti-Mutt —
genial, but almost wholly detached.

"He wasn't one for coming out to Pee Wee games or teaching us
to throw a curve," says Danny. "He got mobbed wherever he went
in public, so of course we understood. But I always got the feeling
he was afraid to push us, on account of what his dad did. It seemed
like he wanted us to have a childhood, like that was the greatest gift
he could give us."

"And the hell of it is, we never cared for baseball as much as
other sports," says David. "I played football and had a chance to be
a walk-on at Baylor. Billy was also a football player, and even though
Junior got as far as spring training [with the Yankees in '76], his
real ambition was to be a golfer — he could drive a ball farther
than Dad even. But he had no chance, being Mickey Mantle Jr. The
pressure just ate him alive."

Although his injuries were as prolific as his power to dead center,
Mantle lasted eighteen years in the Bigs — from 1951 to 1968 —
setting a team record for games played. For much of that time, the
Yanks had a run on pennants, effectively stretching the season to
eight months. That left, in theory at least, four months at home,
though as his loved ones learned, the last out of baseball merely
launched Mickey's second season: golf. The morning of his return,
he'd be up with the roosters, polishing his woods and irons. A
member of the toniest golf club in Dallas, he often spent every
daylight hour on Preston Trail's greens and barstools. His sons,
no idiots, promptly followed him there, figuring that if the Mantle wouldn't come to Mohammed, Mohammed would go to the
Mantle.

"From about four or five, I had a club in my hands, trying Dad's
crazy grip," says Danny. "It was impossible, of course — only he had
the wrists to hit three hundred yards, hands apart. But those were
great times then, some of the best we had; it seemed like we were always laughing about something."

"Yeah, and most always, it was me," says David. "I tried real hard, but I was the world's worst golfer. One time, I teed off and topped the ball bad, and it bounced up and hit me in the nuts. Another time, I swung through and musta caught it backward, 'cause it rocketed out sideways and near took Dad's head off. He'd been over by the golf cart with Junior and Danny, and all of 'em hit the dirt hard. When he got up, laughing and dusting himself off, he said, 'Well, hell, where do we stand?'"

To be sure, there were memorable times with Mick that didn't involve a driver: when, with his young boys clumped like bananas around him, he'd pull out the projector and cackle at home movies of Junior and David as toddlers; and those epic football games out back, in which the kids tackled the kids, the adults clobbered Mickey, and play continued till the sun went down or someone broke a leg. But for Mantle, home was a nice place to visit; life — and liberty — were elsewhere. After a relaxed dinner, there'd be the call from Billy Martin, and the two would race to the honkytonks, where the girls, like the beer, were heady. Soon enough, Mickey's sons followed him there, too, and were treated like royalty, or at least a retinue.

"To the women, my dad and those guys were rock stars and I was their roadie, catching the overflow," says Danny. "I was fifteen, getting laid like a rug and pounding mixed drinks with Everclear or a topper of 151. The next morning, I'd sober up and realize, 'Hey, Dad's tagging a lot of trim.' As kids, we'd just assumed he was working when he was gone, doing endorsements and stuff. Now I saw that he wasn't the family man we'd always thought he was."

If that thought roiled him, though, he won't let on; to this day, neither he nor David will utter a word against Mickey. In that, they are every bit their father's boys, taking the weight themselves. Their drinking, for instance, began before Mickey knew about it, when they'd hang out at twelve or thirteen with their backyard boys, chugging Mad Dog and Boone's Farm wine. So, too, their forays into harder things — cocaine in the cases of Danny and David, and coke and synthetic heroin in Billy's. As with baseball, Mickey had let his sons alone to make their way and choices, and for better or worse they did. Their refusal now to fault him for it is a kind of valor, and a read on their stubborn love.

By nineteen, Danny was going full-tilt, snorting coke and getting plastered at the Filling Station. David had worked there as a cook when he wasn't out front chugging beers. Junior, having walked away from baseball in 1976, made the place his outpost after supper each night and was often met for last call by Mickey and company on their blitzkrieg of Dallas bars. Those were fast times then, getting a load on with Dad and hearing his Ruthian tales of big-league life. In his playing days, Mickey had gone to some lengths to hide his exploits from the kids, coming home more or less sober from golf and sipping a glass of wine at dinner. Now, in retirement, he either let the veil drop or was too far along to care.

His own lamented tour of booze had started his rookie year. A kid of nineteen so spooked by New York that he wouldn't leave his room to eat, he was famously coaxed from his hayseed shell by the lubricious Billy Martin. Together with Whitey Ford, himself a rookie, they went on a six-year binge that ended with Martin's exile to the Kansas City Athletics in 1957. Night after night, they steamrolled the town, running tabs at Toots Shor's or the Copa or the Latin Quarter before falling into the sack around dawn. (Often, Mickey had company there; as teammates said of him in 1956, when he was chasing the single-season home run record, "He might not make it to sixty-one, but he has way more homers off the field than Ruth.") Legend, and certainly the Yankees, held Martin responsible for leading Mantle astray, but even a cursory read of his past suggests he was primed to fall. Haunted by Mutt's death, at thirty-nine, Mickey survived him in a state of dread that shaded into terror. A presentiment lingered that he'd be dead by forty, and he swore to friends that he wouldn't be cheated before cancer got him, too. Beyond that, he loathed his failure, as he saw it, to live up to his billing. No less an authority than Casey Stengel had announced to the press that here was the rightful heir to Ruth, encumbering Mick with the mother of all loads, as well as the enmity of Joe DiMaggio. His blah first seasons, the strikeouts and tantrums and constant leg problems, disposed Mick to think that he'd spit the bit, let down a nation of fathers.

He hadn't, of course; quite the reverse, he was a national totem of honor, propping up the Yankees with indelible courage after their greatness — and his tendons — gave out. But his stout refusal to confront his drinking was emphatically unheroic and wreaked all sorts of hell back home, where the family took his cues. His boys were full-blown alcoholics by their teens or twenties, and Merlyn, in a doomed bid to keep Mick close, matched him drink for drink. Billy, the third-born, was the first to crater, developing an addiction to IV drugs after being diagnosed with Hodgkin's disease. He then turned David on to coke during the throes of a bad divorce, and soon the Mantles had another addict, though the drugs were the least of it.

"I was real reclusive when I drank or snorted; I didn't want to be with people," says David. "I had to give away my guns after the bad old days, when I was playing Russian roulette with a pistol. I'd do a bunch of blow, chug some beers, and put on *The Deer Hunter* and play along with the movie. I also cut myself with razor blades, and almost OD'd once doing so much [coke] that I basically couldn't breathe."

Amazingly, his father never caught on, though the signs were as big as billboards. "Once, on the golf course, I was in the cart with Dad when my nose started bleeding something fierce. It went on and on, and I was praying for it to stop, but Dad didn't even ask about it. Another time, we were watching some show to do with drugs, and he said to me, 'Ever do cocaine, David?' and I said, 'No, I would never,' and he said, 'Good, I'm glad you haven't.' Years later, we told him we had done drugs, and it really hurt him bad. Of course, we'd actually told him about it well before that, but he was too drunk to get it."

After high school, the two brothers floated for a while, dropping out of college for armpit jobs that paid just enough to get high. Their father did little better, scrambling to stay solvent when the phone stopped ringing for endorsements. He'd tried his hand at business, opening restaurants and men's stores, but one after another they all went bust, like his hopes for a manager's job. (The current restaurant in New York and a steakhouse in Oklahoma are owned by outside parties that lease the Mantle name.) Around baseball, the word on his drinking was out, rendering the first-ballot Hall of Famer unemployable.

And then, in the mid-1980s, a nostalgia kick sent the sports collector's market through the roof, and Mickey was once more in clover. Generous as ever, he brought on his sons to help with the scut work of signing balls, and for the next eight years they traveled in style, clocking as much as six figures per weekend, more than Mickey had made in his best-paid season. Beyond the money, it was

the boys' first chance to be around Mick each day, and they celebrated like lottery winners. Every late lunch was Mardi Gras, every
dinner St. Paddy's Day. On the golf course, their cart became a rolling bar, bearing an ice chest with beer and champagne, in the
event they passed a ship that needed christening. Their parents
split up after thirty-five years of marriage (Merlyn had finally tired
of Mick's womanizing), and both Danny and David were entangled
with women who drank as hard as they did. But the cash well kept
gushing, the road kept beckoning, and as long as their suite had a
minibar, there was no such thing as last call.

Till one crazy trip to California, when Danny went out for a late-
morning drink and blacked out for three days. "Dad and I were doing this deal for Upper Deck, having him sign two thousand baseballs," he says. "Well, a friend of mine drops by, and, boom, I'm
gone; we drank till I didn't know what day it was. I stopped eating
and sleeping, and even my buddy was looking at me and going,
'Dude, what's the matter with you?' Well, that was it — I had to go
in. So I scraped myself up and took a plane to [the Betty Ford Center in] Palm Springs."

Danny wasn't the first of the sons to seek treatment. Billy had
been through rehab on four separate occasions, returning each
time to a heedless family that greeted him with drinks in hand.
That was Danny's fear when he checked himself in, that he'd be
disowned or subverted by the people he loved, especially Mickey, to
whom he had drawn close. But he was determined to finally stop
being a Mantle and become a man. He called his fiancée and asked
her to come out; the two of them detoxed side by side, getting, and
staying, sober from that day forth.

They returned to Dallas in the fall of 1993 to a household in serial crisis. Billy's cancer was back, his third bout with Hodgkin's; he
was thirty-six, three years younger than Mutt was when he had died,
and had months, if not weeks, to live. David was holing up with a
bottle of brandy, feeling dumped and betrayed by Danny. And
Mick, at sixty-two, was in such agony from his cirrhotic liver that
he'd double over at the dinner table, looking like a man of eighty.
He was desperate to stop drinking but couldn't think how. If he
had to stand up in front of a roomful of strangers and say, "I'm
Mickey Mantle, and I'm an alcoholic," the shame of it alone would
bump him off.

He finally relented two months later, in early 1994, after a doc-

tor warned that his next drink could kill him. Those first couple
of weeks at Betty Ford, Mick couldn't talk without breaking up,
choked by shame and guilt. When he did speak, the leitmotifs
of his sorrow were his failures as a son and father. He'd never become the ballplayer Mutt envisioned (it seems not to have occurred to him that no one had), and in pain and solitude he'd
walked away from the boys who so adored him. Later, in an extraordinary prime-time interview, he said as much, tearfully, to his
friend Bob Costas, sending millions of viewers lunging for the
hand towels. In sadness, as in splendor, he was once more hailed as
the most humble of tainted kings, and his popularity, which had
never flagged, rose to untold heights. Letters by the tens of thousands poured in, many from guys his age who, inspired, went in for
treatment. At card shows, long lines of grown men trembled, as if
they were waiting for the pontiff's blessing.

From then on, Mick was rarely apart from his boys. Billy died
shortly after Mick returned; later, David, then Junior, did a stint in
rehab, never to drink again. Suddenly, men who once crawled
home at dawn now changed into pajamas after dinner, trading war
stories over cookies and milk. "Before, we'd all be in a bar talking at
once, no one listening to anyone," says David. "Now we were talking about everything — our plans for the future together, our love
for each other, and how stupid we'd been to trash those years getting drunk at 11:00 A.M."

Flush with energy and big ideas — a national campaign to raise
consciousness about drinking, especially among younger kids;
a foundation to fight cancer in Billy's memory — the Mantles
skipped their tee time for the drawing board, determined to make
a dent. But just as the multiple projects got aloft, Mickey collapsed
in pain. A battery of tests showed hepatitis and late-stage liver cancer, in addition to the cirrhosis. He'd be dead in a fortnight without a new liver; when he got one, days later, an uproar ensued over
the perception of special treatment. His sons had to sneak through
a basement door to slip the siege outside; reporters bird-dogged
their homes and cars. It had been a year and five months since
their father left rehab, and the idyll was officially over; nine weeks
later, Mickey would be dead from liver cancer.

But those seventeen months were time enough to taste what few
families do — the joys of renewed affinity. Sitting around the table

after those rib-roast dinners, the Mantle boys saw their own re-
flection beaming back at them. They didn't just look and talk like
Dad; they had his wry knack for self-effacement and blunt mistrust
of vanity. (As Mick once said to the boys of the smug Pete Rose,
"Shit, if all I wanted was to hit scratch singles, I'd have worn a dress
to play.") They also shared his feeling that fame was a lever that,
used properly, could move a mountain. After Mick's death, they
rose from grief to lead a drive for organ transplants, distributing
eight million donor forms in the shape of baseball cards. Within a
year, the number of available organs shot up 200 percent. They
traveled exhaustively, taping public-service spots and drawing media to local foundations. In early 2001, just after non-Hodgkin's
lymphoma struck down Junior, they joined with the American Cancer Society to form the Mickey Mantle Family Fund. They continue
to tour on its behalf, putting together golf tourneys and celebrity
banquets with Yogi and Whitey.

But an odd thing happened to the Mantle boys in fighting the
old man's fight. They finally stepped from his giant shadow, finding their place in the light and warmth of hard-won self-distinction.
It's been a culmination of things, starting with their entry into sobriety and their dragging Mickey, bodily, with them. Whatever they
thought they may have owed the man, that alone settled all accounts, and they have added to their credit ever since. From Mutt
on down, the story of this family has been the long arm of the father, a controlling proxy from beyond the grave. With all due respect, the sons will pen their own ending, and in some books, that
makes them the heroes.

PETER HESSLER

Home and Away

FROM THE NEW YORKER

LITTLE FATTY kept leaving it short. Twice he dropped the basket-ball on the way up, and the third time, when Yao Ming finally lifted him above the rim, he held the ball too low. His name was Sun Haoxuan; he was four years old, weighed fifty-nine pounds, and had been selected by an advertising firm that had recently scouted Beijing kindergartens for a fat boy with round cheeks and big dark eyes. There was a substantial talent pool. In Chinese cities, rising standards of living have combined with the planned-birth policy in a way that recalls the law of conservation of mass: there are fewer children, but often there is more child. It's common for adults to refer to these kids as Xiao Pangzi — Little Fatty. "Get Little Fatty ready!" the director shouted whenever he needed Sun Haoxuan. "Move Little Fatty back two steps!"

We were at the Beijing Film Studios, where Yao Ming, the start-ing center for the Houston Rockets, was shooting a television com-mercial for China Unicom, a telecommunications company. The script was simple: fat child meets seven-foot-six-inch basketball player; basketball player lifts fat child; fat child dunks. What had not been factored in was Little Fatty's behavior. He squirmed away at every opportunity; sometimes he pointed directly at Yao Ming and announced, with an air of sudden revelation, "Yao Ming!" For half an hour, the adults in the studio — cameramen, assis-tants, tech guys — had been silently aiming ill wishes his way, and maybe that was why, on the fourth take, Yao stumbled and acciden-tally rammed Little Fatty's nose against the rim. The sounds came in quick succession: a soft thud, a dropped ball — *bounce, bounce, bounce-bounce* — and then the child began to wail.

The boy's mother rushed over, and Yao Ming stood helplessly, shoulders slumped. Somebody wiped Little Fatty's face — no blood, no foul. On the next take, he finally dunked the ball, and there was a thin round of applause. Yao wandered over to the edge of the set, where I was standing, and said, in English, "Weight training."

After a sensational rookie season in the National Basketball Association, Yao, who is twenty-three, had returned to China in early May with one clear objective: to lead the national team to the title in the Asian Basketball Championship, which serves as the regional qualifier for the 2004 Olympics. Usually, China dominates Asian basketball, but this year, because of political problems, Wang Zhizhi, the country's second-best player, had not come back from America. Yao Ming had become involved in a high-profile lawsuit, which was interpreted by the Chinese press as a clash between the rights of the individual and the authority of the state. Increasingly, Yao's world was divided: there was the sanctity of the sport and, off court, a whirlwind of distractions, ranging from the burdensome to the bizarre. When I had last visited him, in July, he was staying with the Chinese team in Qinhuangdao, a seaside town that was hosting an exhibition game against a squad from the United States Basketball Academy. Yao didn't play — he had just received eight stitches in the eyebrow after a teammate elbowed him in practice. Before the game, a China Unicom representative with a digital recorder coached Yao through a series of phrases that would be sold as alarm messages to mobile-phone subscribers. "Wake up, lazy insect!" Yao said obediently, and then his bandaged brow dipped when the woman asked him to repeat it ("More emphasis!").

That evening, the Chinese nearly threw the game away — in the final quarter, they couldn't handle a full-court press from the ragtag American team. "I think the center needs to come to half-court against the press," Yao told me afterward, in his hotel room. Liu Wei, the Chinese point guard and Yao's best friend, was sprawled on one bed. Yao sat on the other bed, which had been crudely extended: the head consisted of a wooden cabinet covered with blankets. We spoke in English; he talked about the NBA offseason news that he had culled from the Internet. He had not spoken to any of his Houston teammates since returning to China. "Did you hear about Rodman?" Yao said. "He might come back. I can't believe the Lakers got Payton and Malone. I can't believe they only spent six million. If Kobe is okay, it's like a Dream Team." The names sounded foreign and far away — Mark Cuban, Shaq, Kirilenko. "AK-47," Yao said, using the sports-talk nickname for Andrei Kirilenko, a Russian forward on the Utah Jazz. Yao smiled like a kid at the sound of the phrase. "AK-47," he said again.

Yao Ming weighed ten pounds at birth. His mother, Fang Fengdi, is over six-two; his father, Yao Zhiyuan, is six-ten. Both were centers: he played for the Shanghai city team, and she was on China's national team. Chinese sports couples aren't uncommon — Yao Ming is dating Ye Li, a six-two forward on the women's national team. When Yao was growing up, the apartment directly overhead was home to the Sha family; the parents had both been point guards for Shanghai teams. "My mother and father were introduced by the basketball organization," Sha Yifeng, a childhood friend of Yao Ming, told me. "In the old days, that's how they took care of your life."

Today, Yao's parents are in their early fifties, trim and black-haired, and they carry themselves with the physical dignity of athletes. But they speak about basketball with detachment. Neither played the game as a child; sports were a low priority for China in the 1960s, particularly during the early years of the Cultural Revolution. Later, officials began to restore the national sports system, scouting for height to fill out the basketball rosters. Yao Zhiyuan began to play at the age of nineteen. Fang Fengdi was discovered at sixteen. "To be honest, I didn't much like it," she told me, when I met them both in Shanghai. "I wanted to be a dancer or an actress." By 1970, she was traveling to games around the world with the national team. "I didn't think of it as something I did or didn't want to do," she said. "I thought of it as a responsibility. It was a job."

In China, competitive sport is a foreign import. Traditional physical activities like *wushu* and *qigong* are as much aesthetic and spiritual as they are athletic. Chinese historians say that modern sport began after the 1839–42 Opium War. In the following decades, as foreign traders and missionaries established themselves in treaty ports, their schools and charitable institutions introduced Western competitive sports. American missionaries brought basketball to China at the end of the nineteenth century.

During the early 1900s, as the Chinese struggled to overcome foreign occupation, they began to see sports as a symbolic way to avenge the injustices of the past century. The goal was to beat the foreigner at his own game. After the Communists came to power, in 1949, they established a state-funded sports-training system modeled on the Soviet Union's. Promising young athletes were recruited for special "sports schools."

When Yao Ming entered the third grade, he was five-seven, and Shanghai's Xuhui District Sports School selected him for its after-school basketball program. Recently, I visited Yao's first coach, Li Zhangming, who, like a traditional Chinese educator, spoke of Yao in completely unsentimental terms ("He didn't much like basketball. He was tall, but slow and uncoordinated"). After our conversation, I wandered around the basketball courts of Shanghai's No. 54 Middle School, where the Xuhui Sports School holds some of its practices. I watched a group of young girls performing basketball drills, then introduced myself to the coach, a tall woman named Tao Yanping.

"I was a teammate of Yao's mother," Tao said. "I went to their wedding. I remember giving them towels and thermoses — things you gave newlyweds back then. See that girl there?" She pointed out a red-faced child, the tallest on the court. "Her mother was also my teammate. That girl is in the third grade. Her mother is 1.83 meters tall, and she made the national team."

I asked Tao how she recruited. "We go to the schools and look at the children's height, and then we check their parents' height," she said.

The two-hour practice consisted mostly of ball-handling drills. Tao was attentive, shouting commands at her charges ("Little Swallow, you're traveling! Who taught you to do that?"). At the end of the practice, tall parents materialized at courtside. Zhang Jianrong, a woman who was nearly six feet tall, told me that basketball was just a healthy activity for her daughter; the girl's studies were more important. Like the other parents, Zhang was a basketball mom in a country that selects its basketball moms by height.

The method of early recruitment is a product of China's inability to provide every public school with coaches and sports facilities. The system has proved effective in low-participation, routine-based sports like gymnastics and diving, but when it comes to basketball it may be China's greatest weakness. In America, where community leagues and school coaches are plentiful, athletes emerge from an enormous pyramid of participants. Some, like Allen Iverson, rise to the top with remarkable passion and creativity — but if a recruiter had shown up at the Iverson home when Allen was in the third grade, he would have found no father and a short mother who had given birth at the age of fifteen. It's significant that China has yet to produce a great male guard — the position requires skill and intensity rather than height. All three Chinese players in the NBA are centers, and two are second-generation centers. The Chinese national team is notorious for choking in key games, partly because the ball-handling is inconsistent. Players rarely appear to enjoy themselves, and their character has not been formed by true competition; even as free-market reforms have changed many Chinese industries, the sports world is a throwback to socialism, with its careful planning and career stability. Once, when I asked Yao Ming how many Chinese would be in the NBA in a decade, he said only three or four.

Throughout Yao Ming's childhood, his parents emphasized that basketball was a hobby, not a career. "When I was small, I always wanted to be famous," Yao told me. "I thought I'd be a scientist or maybe a political figure. It didn't matter, as long as I was famous." In sixth grade, he grew taller than his mother. He surpassed his father's height in ninth grade. By then, he was already under contract to the Shanghai Sharks youth team. When he was seventeen, and seven-two, Yao Ming joined the Chinese national team. Relatives told me that it wasn't until then that his parents resigned themselves to his career as a professional athlete.

Once, I asked Fang Fengdi if there had been a moment when she first sensed that basketball inspired Yao Ming. It was the only time she really smiled when discussing the sport, and I sensed that she was talking about herself as much as about her son. She said, "The Harlem Globetrotters came to Shanghai when he was in elementary school. Tickets were really hard to get — I was able to find only two. I remember thinking, Americans are good at enjoying themselves! Those players took a normal sport and turned it into something else — a performance. Afterward, I could tell that it made a deep impression on Yao Ming."

*

The first male player to make the jump from mainland China to top-level American basketball was Ma Jian, a forward who played at the University of Utah for two years in the 1990s. Ma noticed that during Utah's pregame meetings, an assistant coach sometimes wrote a "W" or a "B" on the chalkboard next to an opposing player's name. "The white players were shooters," Ma explained to me, when we met recently in Beijing. "If he put a 'B' there, we knew they were athletes." Ma never saw a "C" on the board. In 1995, Ma tried out for the Los Angeles Clippers. "The first time I stepped onto the team plane in the preseason, I saw the blacks sitting on one side and the whites on the other. I looked at myself — should I go on the brothers' side or the whites' side?"

Last year, after the Rockets selected Yao Ming with the first pick in the NBA draft, it was less than a week before somebody in the league made a remark that could be construed as racist. During a television interview, Shaquille O'Neal, the NBA's dominant center, announced, "Tell Yao Ming, 'Ching chong yang wah ah so.'" O'Neal's joke went largely unnoticed at the time, but it was resurrected in January of this year, when a columnist for *Asian Week* attacked O'Neal for it.

The column sparked a media frenzy shortly before Shaq and Yao's first on-court meeting. But Yao immediately defused the controversy. "There are a lot of difficulties in the two different cultures understanding each other," he said. "Chinese is hard to learn. I had trouble with it when I was little." The NBA released a statement pointing out that the league included players from thirty-four countries. By game time, the issue was all but dead. The Rockets won by four points, in overtime; O'Neal outplayed Yao, but Yao had a spectacular start and held his own. Afterward, O'Neal told the press, "Yao Ming is my brother. The Asian people are my brothers."

In February, I spent most of the month following Yao's games, and people repeatedly brought up the O'Neal incident. None of the black fans I talked to had anything bad to say about Yao — many believed he brought something fresh to American sports. "It's not like normal, where people say, well, he's a black athlete, so he moves like this, or he's a white athlete, so he shoots like that," Darice Hooper, a physical therapist who was attending the All-Star Game, in Atlanta, told me.

Juaquin Hawkins, one of Yao's teammates on the Rockets, agreed. "It's not just people thinking, I'm rooting for him because he's African American, or I'm rooting for him because he's white," he told me. Hawkins was familiar with the outsider's role. A native of Lynwood, California, he had failed to make the NBA in 1997, and the following year he wound up playing professionally in Chongqing, deep in the Chinese interior. I had lived in the same region, and Hawkins laughed when I mentioned the basketball slang there. If a player shoots an air ball, the fans shout "*yangwei*"; in the Sichuan dialect, it means "impotent." To encourage the home team, they chant "*xiongqi*" ("erection").

There are few foreigners in Chongqing, and even fewer blacks. I asked Hawkins how he had coped with being so different. "I always felt like I was representing my heritage," he said. "Lynwood is next to Compton. There's a lot of negative things said about that area, and that's something I take with me wherever I go. But I had a good childhood. I was raised by my mother. I try to represent that."

An uncle had introduced Hawkins to basketball as a child; he never met his father. "All I know is his first name, and the fact that he didn't want to deal with having a family," Hawkins said. He met his wife through basketball — both had played at Lynwood High School, and then at Long Beach State. In addition to Chongqing, Hawkins had played professional basketball in Taiwan, Japan, and the Philippines. He had toured with the Harlem Globetrotters ("That was actually real beneficial"). In the summer of 2002, he tried one last time to make the NBA, attending the Rockets' camp, where he established himself as a defensive specialist and beat out two other unsigned players for a roster spot. At twenty-nine, he was the oldest rookie in the league to make an opening-day lineup. When Hawkins learned that he was on the team, he telephoned his mother and wept.

Successful athletes are inevitably displaced — if you're good, you leave home — and something is always lost in transition. Much of what Hawkins carried onto the court would have been invisible to Chongqing fans, who know nothing about Compton or American single-parent families. In Chongqing, Hawkins was simply an excellent player who looked completely different from everybody else in the city. When I lived in a nearby town, it was common for crowds of twenty or more to gather and gawk at me on the street. A local nightclub once hired an African dancer, knowing that his freakishness would draw customers.

Yao Ming had an excellent rookie season, and there were clear signs that eventually he'd develop into a dominant center. But the Rockets ran only about thirty plays a game to him; initially, his American fame resulted from his height and his off-court persona. He handled attention with remarkable humor and grace. He also appealed to the national missionary instinct: if Americans had failed to convert the Chinese to God and democracy, at least we were turning them into NBA fans. The American media portrayed Yao as a nonthreatening figure — a gentle giant.

But he entered another world whenever he dealt with the Chinese press. After a difficult defeat in Los Angeles, where Yao had fouled out for the first time in his NBA career, a Chinese reporter asked what it had been like to be dunked on by Kobe Bryant. Yao said evenly, "Please don't ask me about an incident in which I have no face." At an All-Star Game press conference, Yao showed up wearing an old Chinese national team sweatshirt, and a Chinese reporter asked why. "It's comfortable, that's all," Yao said. Another reporter asked, "If you could say one sentence to all of the young Chinese players back home, what would you say?" Yao's sentence: "I don't believe that I can say very much with one sentence."

Even as they idolized him, few people in China seemed to realize how different Yao was from the typical Chinese athlete. When he played, the joy was apparent on his face. He hit free throws in the clutch, and the Rockets learned to run plays to him at the end of close games. Often, he subtly deflected the patriotic questions of the Chinese media, as if sensing that such concerns were too heavy to bear on the court.

The Chinese motivation for sport is so specific and limited — the nationalism, the sports schools — that it rarely survives a transplant overseas. Athletics has meant little to most Chinese-American communities, including the one in Houston, which has grown rapidly in the past decade. The city has an estimated fifty thousand Chinese, as well as large numbers of ethnic Chinese from Vietnam. Houston's Chinese tend to be highly educated, with an average annual household income of more than $50,000 — higher than the city's average.

The largest Asian district in Houston is along Bellaire Boulevard — a six-mile strip-mall Chinatown. In February, I spent two afternoons driving along Bellaire, where some of the signs reminded me that locals were adjusting to a new culture (All Stars Defensive Driving); others reflected success (Charles Schwab, in Chinese characters); and some were distinctly Chinese (a lot of beauty parlors — the Chinese are meticulous about their hair).

But I couldn't find anything having to do with basketball. Though everybody loved Yao Ming, people told me that the children in the community didn't play sports much; they were too busy studying. I searched for hours before finding a single sporting goods store — Sports Net International, in a mall called Dynasty Plaza — and they stocked gear only for racquet sports. "The Chinese are not so interested in basketball, because of their size," David Chang, the owner, told me. "But if you're interested in Yao Ming you should talk to the people at Anna Beauty Design. They cut his hair."

Upstairs at the hair salon, a Taiwanese woman sat behind the receptionist's desk. I asked if Yao Ming got his hair cut there.

"No," she said. "Yao Ming does not get his hair cut here."

I tried again. "Does somebody from Anna's go to Yao Ming's home to cut his hair?"

"That's something I can't answer," she said coyly. A moment later, the manager walked in. "This guy's a reporter," she told him. "He wants to know if we cut Yao Ming's hair."

The manager shot me a dirty look. "Don't tell him we do that," he said.

The receptionist added, exactly five seconds too late, "He speaks Chinese."

All told, I tracked down three defensive-driving schools, six banks, and fourteen beauty salons — but no *lanqiu*. In Houston's Chinatown, it was easier to find Yao Ming's barber than a basketball.

At the end of February, the Rockets embarked on a critical East Coast road trip. Their final game was against the Washington Wizards; both teams were fighting to make the playoffs in their respective conferences, and Yao Ming was in the running to be named Rookie of the Year. This would be the final meeting between Yao

Ming and Michael Jordan, who was retiring in order to return to his position as president of the Wizards.

The night before the Washington game, the Chinese Embassy hosted a special reception for Yao. Chinese food and Yanjing beer were served — the Beijing-based brewery had signed a Rockets sponsorship after Yao Ming was drafted. The Embassy's meeting room filled quickly: diplomats and emigrés, Sinophiles and market analysts. Scraps of conversation floated in the air.

"Yanjing paid $6 million. Their distributor is Harbrew."

"Who gives a sixty-year distribution contract? But you know, from the Chinese point of view, it's a stream of production. They don't understand the concept of branding."

"He's been in China fifteen years as a value-added player."

"Actually, I'm with the White House press office."

"You know, Anheuser-Busch owns 27 percent of Tsingtao."

"There he is! Did you get a picture?"

"Imagine being that tall!"

A round of applause followed Yao into the room. Lan Lijun, the minister of the Embassy, gave a short speech. He mentioned Ping-Pong diplomacy and "the unique role sports have played in bringing our countries together." In closing, he said, "We have full confidence that China and the United States will work together to continue to improve our bilateral relations."

Yao, in a gray suit, stooped to reach the microphone. Behind him, a display case held a ceramic horse from the Tang dynasty. Red lanterns hung from the ceiling. Yao spoke for less than a minute, and he didn't say anything about Sino-American relations. "Seeing all these lanterns reminds me of home," he said softly, in Chinese. "When I was growing up, my impression of the Chinese Embassy was like a fantasy, something you see on television and in the movies."

There was a rush for autographs, and staff members hustled Yao into a back room. In the corner, a pretty Eurasian girl in a red dress was crying. Her parents said that Yao had walked past without signing her invitation. "He's her favorite player," the mother told me, adding that the girl had been adopted from Uzbekistan. A staff member took her invitation, promising to get an autograph.

Yao was at the Embassy for nearly two hours. After he left, people stood around in groups, chatting and drinking Yanjing. We had reached the Sino-American witching hour — the Chinese guests, always prompt, were gone, but the Americans lingered, in the way that Americans do. I found myself standing next to Chen Xiaogong, the defense attaché. Chen was glassy-eyed; he kept touching his watch. "I'm surprised so many Americans know Yao Ming," he said.

The next night, Kha Vo sings Francis Scott Key and Michael Jordan comes out hot. Four baskets in the first quarter: turnaround, jump shot, jump shot, turnaround. Ten days earlier, Jordan celebrated his fortieth birthday, and since then he's been averaging nearly thirty points a game. Yao works against Brendan Haywood, the Wizards' seven-foot center. Haywood looks short tonight. Six points for Yao in the first quarter; Rockets down by nine. Sold-out arena: twenty-thousand-plus. Lots of Asians — red flags in the upper levels.

Second quarter: Rudy Tomjanovich, the Rockets' coach, plays a hunch and goes with Juaquin Hawkins, who rarely sees action. Hawkins nails a twenty-footer, then a three-pointer. He draws a charge and steals a pass. Hawkins looks hungry, as if he'd just escaped from Chongqing: he hasn't scored in nine days. Moochie Norris runs the point for the Rockets. Moochie has cornrows, a barrel chest, and four Chinese characters tattooed on his left wrist: "huan de huan shi." ("Never satisfied," he told me, when I asked him what it meant, and then I crossed to the other side of the locker room and asked Yao. "It actually doesn't have a very good meaning," he said. "Basically, you'll do whatever it takes to protect yourself.") Yao doesn't score in the second quarter. Jordan has eighteen. Rockets down by twenty. Halftime show: Chinese lion dance, followed by an announcement about Black History Month.

Houston sleepwalks through the third. At one point, they trail by twenty-four. In the final quarter, Maurice Taylor, a Rockets forward, starts to hit jumpers. With six minutes to go, Houston down by fourteen, Tomjanovich brings in Yao, and the game turns. Hawkins sinks a three, then knocks the ball loose from Tyronn Lue. The two players collide, and Lue falls, writhing in pain. Separated shoulder, cut eye: good night, Tyronn. Four straight baskets by the Rockets. In the final three minutes, Yao steps to the free-throw line four times, and nails everything. Haywood fouls out. Overtime.

Hawkins guards Jordan, and they trade baskets to start the extra period. Yao makes a baby hook to give the Rockets the lead. The Wizards feed Jordan every time down the court, and now, after playing for forty-five minutes, he suddenly finds new life. Turn-around jumper over Hawkins. Next possession: Jordan crossover dribble to his left; Hawkins freezes — dunk. Next possession: Jordan hard drive; Hawkins falls, no call — jumper. Next possession: Jordan drives; Hawkins lags, Yao goes for the block — goal-tending. Jordan scores ten in overtime and finishes with thirty-five points and eleven rebounds. Yao has sixteen and eleven; Hawkins scores ten. In the final seconds, with the Rockets down by two, Yao gets a defensive rebound and, instead of calling a time-out, throws the outlet pass. Bad shot. Rockets lose.

After the game, in the Rockets' locker room, Hawkins sat alone on a bench. "It was frustrating," he told me, shaking his head. "He's the greatest player ever."

Yao sat in front of his locker, a towel wrapped around his waist; the Chinese media pressed close. He told them that he should have called the time-out.

In the Wizards' locker room, I joined a group of reporters waiting for Jordan. After the other players had left, he appeared behind a lectern, dressed in a gray pin-striped suit. Somebody asked if the Wizards would make the playoffs. "I've never had a doubt that we would," Jordan said.

Another reporter asked about the overtime period. Jordan talked about Hawkins: "I was going against a young kid who didn't really know how to play, and he tried a couple of flops."

Somebody asked about Yao. "You can sit here and talk about how good he eventually could be," Jordan said. "But at some point he's going to have to showcase what everybody expects."

Jordan spoke with an athlete's bluntness; on the court, it didn't matter where the players had come from or where they were going. For fifty-three minutes, the competition was more important than everything that surrounded it. But, like so many games, this one receded into the essence of statistics — the meaningless points, the pointless minutes. In the end, neither the Wizards nor the Rockets made the playoffs. Michael Jordan never again collected thirty points and ten rebounds in a game, and in May, after retiring, he was forced out of the Wizards organization. Less than three weeks after the Washington game, Rudy Tomjanovich was diagnosed with bladder cancer, and he stepped down as coach. Yao Ming did not win Rookie of the Year. And this season Juaquin Hawkins, after failing to make an NBA team, rejoined the Harlem Globetrotters.

Although it is difficult for a Chinese athlete to come to America, it may be even harder for him to return home. The most troubled transition has been that of Wang Zhizhi, a seven-one center, who emerged in the late nineties, when the Communist Party was restructuring many of its sports bureaus into for-profit entities. The Chinese Basketball Association hoped to become self-sufficient, through corporate sponsorships and income from its professional league, known as the CBA. In this climate, the CBA has become a strange beast: its sponsors include private companies, state-owned enterprises, and the People's Liberation Army, which runs a team called the Bayi Rockets. Wang Zhizhi played for Bayi, and in 1999 the Dallas Mavericks selected him in the second round of the NBA draft. For nearly two years, Dallas courted Wang's bosses, trying to convince them to let the player go. Wang was officially a regimental commander in the PLA.

In the spring of 2001, Dallas and Bayi finally came to an agreement, and Wang became the first Chinese to play in the NBA. He was twenty-three years old. In the offseason, Wang returned home, as promised, representing both the national team and Bayi. But after Wang's second NBA season, in which he averaged about five points a game, he requested permission to delay his return to China so that he could play in the NBA's summer league. He promised to join the national team in time for the World Championships, in August.

The Chinese national team is notorious for its grueling practice schedule — twice a day, six days a week. Fear shapes the routine; coaches know that they will be blamed if the squad loses, so they log countless hours and resist innovation. Before games, the Chinese men's team warms up by conducting the same rudimentary ball-handling drills that I watched the third-grade girls perform in Shanghai.

In the summer of 2002, Chinese authorities refused Wang's request and ordered him to return, but he stayed in the United States anyway. Dallas did not offer him a contract, reportedly in part because they did not want to ruin the good relationship that they had developed with the Chinese. In October, Wang signed a three-year, $6 million contract with the Los Angeles Clippers. Since then, Clippers games have been banned from Chinese television (NBA broadcasts often draw as many as fourteen million viewers in China). The ban has turned Wang into a marketing liability — one NBA general manager told me that teams are wary of signing him in the future.

Wang, whose military passport has expired, reportedly received a green card last season. Over the summer, he tried to negotiate a return to China, asking for a new civilian passport and a guarantee that he could come back to the NBA after the Asian Championship. The chain of communication had grown so complicated that Wang relied heavily on a Chinese sportswriter named Su Qun to contact PLA leaders and basketball officials. "I know that as a journalist I should stay out of this," Su, who writes for Beijing's *Titan Sports Daily*, told me. "But I happen to be close to Wang. We have to save him, like saving Private Ryan."

Wang, who declined my request for an interview, did not return to China. I spoke about him with Li Yuanwei, the secretary-general of the Chinese Basketball Association. "Wang has placed too much emphasis on his personal welfare," Li said. "I assured him that there is no risk. The PLA also assured him. But he doesn't believe us, and he keeps demanding conditions that are not necessary. It's very sad."

Wang's problems formed a troubling backdrop to Yao Ming's move to the NBA last year. Yao promised to fulfill his national-team commitments during the offseason, and he reportedly will pay the CBA 5 to 8 percent of his NBA salary for his entire career. He also will pay the Shanghai Sharks, his CBA team, a buyout that is estimated to be between $8 million and $15 million, depending on his endorsements and the length of his career. Yao's four-year contract with the Rockets is worth $17.8 million, and already his endorsement income is higher than his salary.

But even Yao's sponsorship potential has been threatened by the irregularities of China's sports industry. In May, Coca-Cola issued a special can in Shanghai decorated with the images of three national-team players, including that of Yao, who already had a contract with Pepsi. The basketball association had sold Yao's image to Coca-Cola without his permission, taking advantage of an obscure sports-commission regulation that grants the state the right to all "intangible assets" of a national-team player. The regulation appeared to be in direct conflict with Chinese civil law. Yao filed suit against Coca-Cola in Shanghai, demanding a public apology and one yuan — about twelve cents. The Chinese press interpreted the lawsuit as a direct challenge to the nation's traditional control of athletes.

When I spoke with Li Yuanwei, of the basketball association, he emphasized that Coca-Cola was an important source of funding, and he hoped that the company and Yao would reach an agreement out of court. Li told me that Americans have difficulty understanding the duties of an athlete in China, where the state provides support from childhood. I asked if the same logic could be applied to a public-school student who attends Peking University, starts a business, and becomes a millionaire. "It's not the same," Li said. "Being an athlete is a kind of mission. They have an enormous impact on the ideas of the common people and children. That's their responsibility."

Before I traveled to Harbin, in northeastern China, to attend the Asian Championship, I talked with Yang Lixin, a law professor at People's University in Beijing. Yang was preparing a seminar on the Coca-Cola case. "Contact with American society probably gave Yao some new ideas," Yang told me. "It's like Deng Xiaoping said — some people will get wealthy first. Development isn't equal, and in a sense rights also aren't equal. Of course, they are equal under law, but one person might demand his rights while another does not. It's a choice. In this sense, Yao Ming is a pioneer."

Displaced people have always wandered to Harbin. During the twentieth century, they came and went: White Russians, Japanese militants, the Soviet army. Even today, much of the architecture is Russian. Harbin's symbol is the former St. Sofia Church: gold crosses, green onion domes, yellow halos around white saints. The city has one of the last Stalin Parks in China.

At the end of September, sixteen teams arrived for the Asian Championship; the winner would qualify for the Olympics. The squads came from shadowy lands. Most of the Kazakhstan players were in fact Russians whose families had stayed after the collapse of the Soviet Union. The Malaysian team had a peninsular range: ethnic Chinese, Indians, Malays. Qatar's team included athletes from Africa and Canada — opponents grumbled that they had loosened the definition of a Qatari. The Syrian coach was a black man from Missouri; the Qatar coach was a white man from Louisiana. Iran's coach was a Serb who told me that his playing career had been cut short; he pulled up his sleeve to reveal a cruel scar ("Not long after that, I started coaching").

Except for the Chinese team, everybody stayed at the Singapore Hotel. Tall people in sweatsuits lounged in the lobby. The South Korean team included Ha Seung-Jin, an eighteen-year-old who is seven-three, weighs 316 pounds, and has basketball bloodlines — his father was once a center for the Korean national team. People expect Ha to be a first-round NBA draft pick next year. The league has never included a Korean. "I want to be a Korean Yao Ming," he told me, through an interpreter (who added that the young player's nickname is Ha-quille O'Neal). Ha was eager to play Yao; everybody expected China and South Korea to meet in the final. Last year, in the Asian Games, South Korea had upset the Chinese. Ha hoped to get Yao into foul trouble. "Yao Ming likes to spin to his right," Ha said. "I'll establish position there and draw the foul."

The other seven-three player in the tournament was an Iranian named Jaber Rouzbahani Darrehsari. Darrehsari had played for only three years, since being discovered in the city of Isfahan, where his father sells fruit and vegetables in a market. Darrehsari's wingspan is more than eight feet. Once, when he was leaving the court after a game, I asked him to touch the rim of the basket. He hopped ever so lightly, and then stood still: fingers curled around the metal, the balls of both feet planted firmly on the hardwood. He was seventeen years old. He had dark, long-lashed eyes, and he hadn't yet started shaving — it was as if a child's head had been attached to an elongated body with dangling arms. In Iran's first two games, Darrehsari played only a few minutes; smaller opponents shoved him mercilessly. He looked terrified on the court. Sitting on the bench, he almost never smiled.

The Chinese team stayed at the Garden Hamlet Hotel, a walled compound reserved for central-government leaders. All summer,

Yao had been unable to appear in public without attracting a mob. In August, the Chinese media reported that a medical exam had revealed that Yao had high blood pressure. His agents said the condition was temporary, and a message from Yao appeared on his official website: "I have been exhausted because of the poor security at the National Team games . . . too many public appearances and commitments by the Chinese National Team, and incessant fan disturbances at the team hotel."

A few hours before China played Iran, one of Yao's agents told me that I could meet with his client. Yao is represented by an entity known as Team Yao, which consists of three Americans, two Chinese, and one Chinese-American. Half the team had come to Harbin — Erik Zhang, Yao's distant cousin and the team leader; John Huizinga, a deputy dean at the University of Chicago Graduate School of Business, where Zhang is a student; and Bill A. Duffy, who heads BDA Sports Management. They were accompanied by Ric Bucher, a senior writer for *ESPN The Magazine*, who had signed on to write the official Yao biography. A day earlier, Yao had agreed to a multiyear endorsement contract with Reebok. A source close to the negotiations told me that the deal, which is heavy with incentives, could be worth well over $100 million — potentially the largest shoe contract ever given to an athlete.

A guard let us into the compound; we walked through rows of willows, past well-kept lawns decorated with concrete deer. It was raining hard. In Yao's room, there was little sign that the shoe contract had changed his life. The shades were drawn; discarded clothes were everywhere. Liu Wei, the point guard, lay in a tangle of sheets. The only difference from the day I'd seen Yao at his hotel room in Qinhuangdao was that this time they had put the wooden cabinet at the foot of his bed.

The night before, after China had defeated the Taiwanese team by sixty points, Yao had sprained his left ankle while boarding the team bus. Now Duffy, a former player in his forties, was examining him. The ankle was slightly swollen. He told Yao to ice it immediately after that night's game. Yao answered that there was no ice at the arena.

Duffy looked up at him, incredulous. "They don't have ice?" The games were being held in a converted skating rink in a sports complex less than two hundred miles from the Siberian border.

"No ice," Yao said again, and then he spoke in Chinese to Zhang: "I've been getting acupuncture."

After a few minutes, Team Yao left the room. Yao and I chatted about the tournament, and then I mentioned that his first coach had told me that Yao didn't like basketball as a child. "That's true," Yao said. "I didn't really like it until I was eighteen or nineteen."

I asked Yao about his first trip to the United States, in 1998, when Nike had organized a summer of training and basketball camps for him. "Before then, I was always playing with people who were two or three years older than me," he said. "They were always more developed, and I didn't think that I was any good. But in America I finally played against people my own age, and I realized that I was actually very good. That gave me a lot of confidence."

He talked about how difficult it had been when he first moved to Houston ("Everything about the environment was strange"), and I asked him about the differences between sport in China and in America.

"In China, the goal has always been to glorify the country," Yao said. "I'm not opposed to that. But I personally don't believe that that should be the entire purpose of athletics. I also have personal reasons for playing. We shouldn't entirely get rid of the nationalism, but I do think that the meaning of sport needs to change. I want people in China to know that part of why I play basketball is simply personal. In the eyes of Americans, if I fail then I fail. It's just me. But for the Chinese if I fail then that means that thousands of other people fail along with me. They feel as if I'm representing them."

I asked about the pressure. "It's like a sword," he said. "You can hold it with the blade out or with the blade pointing toward yourself." Then I mentioned Wang Zhizhi's situation.

"There's an aspect of it that I shouldn't talk about," Yao said slowly. "It's best if I simply speak about basketball. If Wang were here, it would be good for me. I just know that if he played I wouldn't feel as if so much of the pressure was falling onto one person."

I asked about the Coca-Cola lawsuit. "I always put the nation's benefit first and my own personal benefit second," Yao said. "But I won't simply forget my own interests. In this instance, I think that the lawsuit is good for my interests, and it's also good for other ath-

letes. If this sort of situation comes up in the future for another athlete, I don't want people to say, 'Well, Yao Ming didn't sue, so why
should you?'"

No pregame national anthems at the Asian Championship. Before
tonight's game, the loudspeaker plays an instrumental version of
the theme from *Titanic*. The Iranians look nervous. Sold-out arena:
four thousand–plus. The stands are full of Thundersticks — they
are, after all, manufactured in China — but nobody seems to know
how to use them. The lack of noise feels like intense concentration.
The spectators cheer both sides — enthusiastically when the Chinese score, politely for an Iranian basket.

The coach plays a hunch and starts Darrehsari. On every possession, the Iranians avoid Yao's lane, swinging the ball along the pe-
rimeter: Eslamieh to Bahrami to Mashhady. Mashhady to Bahrami
to Eslamieh. Yao does not score for nearly six minutes. At last, he
brushes Darrehsari aside, grabs an offensive rebound, and dunks
with both hands. Tie game. Next possession: China leads. Next
possession: bigger lead. Eslamieh to Bahrami to Mashhady. Somebody throws it to Darrehsari, fifteen feet out. Yao doesn't bother
to challenge. The shot develops as a chain reaction across the entire length of Darrehsari's frame: knees bend, waist drops, elbows
buckle, long hands snap — *swish*. Running back down the floor, he
tries to fight back a smile. A few possessions later, he fouls Yao hard.
Darrehsari is all elbows and knees, but for the first time in the tournament he looks like he wants to be on the court. The coach plays
him the entire half. He scores four and leads Iran with four rebounds. After the halftime buzzer, his teammates clap him on the
back.

Yao plays half the game: fifteen points, ten rebounds. He looks
bored. China wins by twenty-four. Later, Yao tells me diplomatically
that Darrehsari has potential. "It depends on environment," Yao
says. "Coaching, teammates, training." For the rest of the tournament, Darrehsari does not play half as many minutes. The day after
the China game, he beams and tells me, "It was an honor to play
against Yao Ming."

Before the final, China Unicom unveiled its new commercial at a
press conference attended by more than a hundred Chinese jour-

nalists. Scenes flashed across a big screen: the ball, the boy, the giant, the dunk. Little Fatty looked adorable. Li Weichong, China Unicom's marketing director, gave a speech. "In America, people talk about the Ming dynasty," he said. "What does this mean? Now that Michael Jordan has retired, the NBA needs another great player. Our Yao Ming could be the one." The press conference ended with the theme from *Titanic*.

South Korea and China played for the title on National Day — the fifty-fourth anniversary of the founding of Communist China. Ha Seung-Jin, the eighteen-year-old, came out inspired: after false-starting the jump ball, he immediately collected four points, two rebounds, one block, and a huge two-handed dunk. He also committed four fouls in less than four minutes. For the rest of the game, Ha sat on the bench, dejected.

The Chinese starting point guard fouled out in the third quarter, and then the backcourt began to collapse. The Korean guards tightened the press, forcing turnovers and hitting threes: Bang, Yang, Moon. Bang three, Bang three, lay-up — and with five minutes left China's lead had dwindled to one point.

On every possession, Yao came to half-court, using his height and hands to break the press. At one point, he dove for a loose ball — all seven feet six inches. With the lead back at five and less than two minutes left, Yao grabbed an offensive rebound and dunked it. Thirty points, fifteen rebounds, six assists, five blocks. After the buzzer, when the two teams met at half-court, Yao Ming shook Ha Seung-Jin's hand, touched his shoulder, and said, "See you in the NBA."

The next morning, Yao caught the first flight out of Harbin. He sat in the front row of first class, wearing headphones. First the Indian team filed past, in dark wool blazers, and then the Filipinos, in tricolor sweatsuits. The Iranians were the last team to board, Darrehsari's head scraping the ceiling. Each player nodded and smiled as he walked past Yao. During the flight, many Chinese passengers came forward to have their tickets autographed. In three days, Yao would leave for America. Later that month, he would accept an apology from Coca-Cola and settle the lawsuit out of court.

I sat in the row behind Yao, beside a chubby man in his forties named Zhang Guojun, who had flown to Harbin to watch the game. He'd bought his ticket from a scalper for nearly $200. Zhang was proud of his money — he showed me his cell phone, which used China Unicom services and had a built-in digital camera. Zhang told me that he constructed roads in Inner Mongolia. He sketched a map on the headrest: "This is Russia. This is Outer Mongolia. This is Inner Mongolia. And this" — he pointed to nowhere — "is where I'm from."

We talked about basketball. "Yao is important in our hearts," Zhang said solemnly. "He went to America, and he returned." Halfway through the flight, the man held up his cell phone, aimed carefully, and photographed the back of Yao Ming's head.

MICHAEL LEAHY

All the King's Men: Why
the Team That Jordan Built
Fell to Pieces

FROM THE WASHINGTON POST MAGAZINE

IT WAS A KIND OF DEATHWATCH. The NBA calls it "elimination" when a team falls out of playoff contention for good, but it was more a liquidation for the Washington Wizards — the life of Michael Jordan's playing career down to four April nights, the bitterness and recriminations around the team now palpable. Back in Washington, Wizards owner Abe Pollin was quietly contemplating an elimination of his own making. But the players knew nothing of that. They knew only that they had a few hours before they would be officially eliminated.

Jordan sank deep into a folding chair in a cramped visitors locker room in Miami, his eyes occluded behind designer shades with charcoal lenses. On this, the last night that one of his teams would ever be alive for a playoff spot, Michael Jordan took refuge behind a pair of big silver headphones. Stevie Wonder leaked out of them, muted and scratchy-sounding.

The sight of Jordan with the headphones on had the intended effect: it kept people away — the media, certainly, but his coach and most of his teammates, too, who knew not to approach him in this period before a game unless a matter couldn't wait. Now and then, feeling a stare or sensing footsteps getting closer, he adjusted the headphones tighter over his ears, getting deeper into his cocoon. Mostly, he watched videotape of the opponent that evening, another failed NBA team, the Miami Heat. Now and then, he just stared clear through everyone, like a man looking out on an ocean.

Across from him, staying away, Miami reporters mingled among players they didn't necessarily know, discreetly asking for names: there was Larry Hughes, sitting in front of a locker alongside Kwame Brown, who plopped into a chair next to Tyronn Lue, who was down a row from Charles Oakley and Bryon Russell, who sat across from, in order, Jerry Stackhouse, Juan Dixon, Brendan Haywood, and Bobby Simmons. Jordan, who had the locker closest to the television, sat next to no one.

He had commandeered two lockers. In the locker next to his own, he had conspicuously hung his gray herringbone suit jacket, his signal to any teammate who might be thinking of taking the stall. He generally reserved the adjoining locker on the road for a member of his entourage or a close friend not part of the team.

"I want some popcorn," Brown was saying from his own folding chair across the locker room, talking to no one in particular, talking to air — Kwame Brown, the Kid, as Jordan sometimes called him, once affectionately, now usually pejoratively. Brown's season had started brightly, then swiftly became marked by distress. In late March, he cursed Coach Doug Collins in Phoenix after being pulled from a game, and earlier had raged at Collins in Utah, where he had been benched after missing a couple of shots that Collins and the other coaches regarded as out of his range, further evidence of bad judgment. "You wouldn't take out M.J. or Stack for taking those shots," Brown had snapped at a fuming Collins. Jordan told the team that such behavior would not be tolerated: "Don't treat our coach that way."

Brown apologized for the Phoenix and Utah outbursts. But nothing in his relationship with Collins had really changed, he said, privately telling people that the respect he had tried to give Collins had not been returned. Now Collins walked over to Brown and stood over him. Fifteen feet away, Jordan lifted his head, glanced at the pair, and looked away. Collins bent over and whispered something to Brown, who did not look up to meet the coach's gaze, just stared straight ahead, in a kind of self-induced trance. Collins bent a little more, as if determined to make eye contact. It was a contest of wills by now. Brown never looked up, staring into a little slice of nothingness that he had fixed his eyes on, nodding at Collins while not really acknowledging him.

As losses and dissension had begun convulsing the team, other players had railed at Collins, none more notable than the team's second star, twenty-eight-year-old Jerry Stackhouse, who was the Wizards' major acquisition in the offseason. A two-time NBA all-star obtained at Jordan's urging from Detroit, Stackhouse arrived in exchange for Richard Hamilton, another player to have fallen out of Collins's and Jordan's favor at different times during the previous season.

Earlier that day in Miami, Stackhouse had said he hoped the Wizards would be running more next year, following what he called "the Michael Jordan farewell tour." He said this casually, without edge: he knew better than any other Wizard how best to walk the public relations tightrope when addressing questions about Jordan. Articulate and seasoned, he had the unusual ability of at once speaking respectfully about his fellow North Carolinian Jordan — "The greatest player of all time, and he played in all eighty-two games this year, which says a lot about him" — while gently declaring that their styles were "contrasting" and "did not always fit," that the idol's on-court presence limited his own play and slowed down younger Wizards wanting to fast-break more. Smiling, he summarized the season, noting that it had been built around doing "everything we can to cater" to Jordan. He made this sound pleasant and benign, which took considerable finesse. He had a future, if he wanted it, as a charming diplomat.

Stackhouse had already begun looking past the final week of Jordan veneration. "Michael can give the fans a last glimpse of greatness," he said. "But I think our focus has to be toward next year and trying to get our young guys involved."

Toward that end, he did not want to play that evening. He told Collins that his right knee was hurting him — a flare-up of tendinitis, he thought — and that, unable to jump with any effectiveness, he wanted to heed his body's message and not risk the possibility of a ligament tear. Now he only had to break the news to Jordan, who, not having moved from his folding chair, still watching game tape, was trying to extend the team's hopes beyond that night.

At 6:55 P.M., with the game about an hour off, Stackhouse walked over to Jordan wearing a plastic blue brace that ran from his right knee clear down to his instep. Stackhouse gently tapped on it and said, "Hey, Mike." He had to repeat this, just to penetrate those silver headphones — Jordan still had Stevie Wonder streaming into his ears. "Mike."

Jordan looked up from his folding chair, squinting, and slid one flap of his headphones down, slack-jawed, his face a question mark.

"Talked to Doug," Stackhouse began. "You know, I tried. Tried running. But it's bothering me when I push off on it. Just can't push off on it any good."

There was a pause. Jordan did not speak immediately. His head lowered, he faced the game tape on the television monitor. "Yeah?"

Stackhouse nodded quickly. "Feels a little weak. I plant and can't do it. It hurts when I go up."

Jordan cocked his head to regard Stackhouse. "Yeah," he said vaguely.

Stackhouse paused, as if waiting for something more. The silence lengthened, uncomfortably. Stackhouse resumed talking about his knee. Jordan languidly nodded, glancing at the television, murmuring, "Yeah." It was in the gaps between their words that the truth revealed itself: a stiff courtesy prevailed between them. They shared an alma mater, but really nothing else. They were not antagonists, but they were not close either, merely two powerful partners in an enormous business who never had made a personal connection, in large part because they wanted the same thing and only the titan between them could have it. But now the titan was on his way out. That the younger partner would not be playing that evening only increased the possibility that the end would be swifter. It was awkward. "I wanted to be out there," Stackhouse went on. "I —"

Jordan interrupted, gently, and looked at him, still holding up one of the flaps on the headphones. "Uh, you rest it," he said in his deep bass. He looked back at the television, subdued. "See tomorrow how it feels."

"Wish I could be out there."

Now Jordan wanted to wrap up. "Rest it. It's about long-term value, not short-, for you — right?" Stackhouse didn't say anything to this. Jordan went on: "See tomorrow. Long-term value. All right then." He was already repositioning his headphones, lowering his head, back in the cocoon.

"Thanks, Mike." Stackhouse walked away, unbuckling and removing the blue brace.

Everybody scheduled to play was in uniform now except Jordan, who remained on that folding chair in his gray herringbone trousers, not having so much as undone his blue tie or a single button on his crisp white shirt — waiting, as was his way, for the media and strangers to leave, when he could at last have sanctuary.

The deathwatch was on everybody's mind. A few players listened skeptically to talk of rival contenders Orlando and Milwaukee losing all their games. "Keep hope alive," an encouraging Baltimore reporter said to Russell, whose chuckle said he knew better.

Jordan spent most of the game guarded by a lean, supple six-foot-seven rookie out of LaSalle named Rasual Butler, who, not yet in kindergarten when Jordan began his NBA career, now could routinely outleap and outrun the older man, but not outthink him. Jordan abused him. It was Bobby Fischer against the chess champion of the Fort Lauderdale YMCA: there were too many moves and gambits for the kid to process. Jordan made Butler look silly a few times, no more so than when, Meadowlark Lemon–like, he extended his arm with the ball on the end of it beyond Butler's head and pulled it back as if on a wire to the oohs of twenty thousand, just before blowing by the entranced kid for a lay-up.

That would have been a windmill dunk at one time, but since the beginning of his comeback, with his athleticism eroding, he had done things on a lower plane. It made him a different kind of marvel. He still drove the lane sometimes, only to find it a shrinking aperture. Competing in ever-diminishing space, with the air around the rim virtually off-limits to him, Jordan had morphed into a habitual jump shooter.

His most artful move now came off what players call a jab step — an aggressive one-dribble move meant to scare a young defender like Rasual Butler into backing up. Jordan's version of it included a sweep-back dribble that carried him into reverse — basketball's answer to Michael Jackson's moonwalk — and, *voilà*, into free space for another jumper. Sly improvisation, and the handicap of being consigned to distant spots on the court, made what he did satisfyingly confounding. The scoring jumpers came like a flood in the first half, eight in total, and after each he ran backwards in his familiar canter. If his name had been not Jordan but Michael Jones, his on-court productivity at middle age would have been deemed miraculous. But he was competing each night not merely against a defender but against the ghost of his younger self. He ended the half with twenty-three points, with the crowd torn between marveling over the fall-away jumpers and longing for a high-altitude dunk.

It would be his career's last great half.

He'd score just two more points that night, those coming on free throws, missing all eight of his second-half field-goal attempts. A year of long stretches of forty-plus-minute nights, a regimen meant for a twentysomething, appeared to have worn him down late in the season: he admitted to being tired sometimes. Miami was his comeback in microcosm: bursts of brilliance, punctuated by a middle-aged man's limits and fatigue.

"He would have had forty-six points in his younger days," Collins said after the game.

Still, the Wizards won narrowly. And there was excitement: the deathwatch might be on hold for at least a night; a reprieve might come. Milwaukee had won, but Orlando was locked in a close game with the formidable Indiana Pacers. The Wizards' locker room remained closed as Collins and Jordan and the rest of the team waited out the returns from Indianapolis. Then word floated out that Orlando had increased its lead to eleven points with about four minutes to play. Collins appeared to say it didn't look good. He talked with the media for a few minutes, then went back inside the locker room, where the TV showed Orlando putting the game away.

"I'm very disappointed we didn't get there, Michael," Collins softly said to Jordan, according to an onlooker. "I'm very disappointed. You know how much I wanted you to get there."

Twenty minutes later, having rushed in and out of a steamy shower, Jordan emerged in his gray suit, with sweat running in rivulets alongside his left eye and down his cheek, to face the media. It had been two years since, as the Wizards' president of basketball operations, he sat in his Washington office on a dreary winter afternoon, looking like a prisoner, and began flirting with an idea. Two years since he looked out at the inglorious vista of a parking lot and distant pharmacy and, patting his paunch, said that managerial power did not compare with playing — that there was nothing in money or a title or an office that could compare with "takin' the shot, to bein' it." Two years since his eyes scanned a seafood restaurant and some panhandlers in snow, as he talked of what the "insanity" would be like if he could take on Vince Carter and Kobe Bryant. It seemed like fifteen minutes ago. It had all passed quickly, he said.

Now that quiet office back in Washington seemed to be waiting for him again. There wasn't much else to say, but Jordan found a few things. He praised Larry Hughes for playing with a bad ankle and casually noted that Stackhouse had sat out the game. ("Yeah, Stack not playing — that hurt.") And still he looked for a goal, intent on demonstrating improvement: he wanted to end this season, he said softly, with more victories than the Wizards' thirty-seven wins of last season. That would require one win in the team's remaining three games, a reasonable expectation given that two of them were at home.

But that wouldn't happen either. And Doug Collins's anger was about to spill over. And back in Washington, Abe Pollin began compiling stories of trouble between players and Collins, who had landed in Washington, two years earlier, only because Michael Jordan had chosen him.

Power relationships between superstar athletes and uncelebrated coaches do not *need* to be one-sided from the beginning. Someone must give in to create the imbalance, someone must cave. And, under pressure, Doug Collins had yielded to Michael Jordan more than a decade earlier, during the coach's three turbulent seasons at the helm of the Chicago Bulls. This explained most of their dealings and mutual decisions since — on subjects ranging from Jordan's playing time as a Wizard to the team's deliberate-paced style of offense. Deference had become habit. It was difficult to point to a single event in Chicago that triggered Collins's subservience, but several people in the Bulls organization remembered a closed-doors intrasquad scrimmage during the 1987–88 season when Jordan began complaining that Collins, the scorekeeper, had deprived his team of points. No, the score's right, said Collins. Like hell it is, the young star yelled back.

Jordan stormed out of the practice and did not return, an *enfant terrible* moment rivaling anything Kwame Brown has ever done. That evening, aboard a plane ready to take them to Indianapolis, the Bulls sat shocked, aware that Jordan had not shown up. About a minute before the plane departed, Jordan appeared and coolly walked past Collins without even acknowledging him. "Nothing was the same after that," Brad Sellers, then a Bull, said years later. "The guys knew who had control."

The relationship between coach and star changed forever. Careful not to offend, Collins turned to others to confront Jordan about sensitive matters, one day dispatching an assistant coach, Phil Jackson, to press Jordan about Jackson's conviction that a star became great only when he thought less of individual accolades and made his teammates better.

But nothing could save Collins, whose intensity and volatility alienated several players and key Bulls officials. At the end of the 1989 season, Bulls managing owner Jerry Reinsdorf fired him, replacing him with Jackson, a practitioner of Zen, not long from professional basketball's minor leagues.

Shortly before Jackson finished guiding the Bulls to six titles, Collins lost another coaching job, this time midway into his third season in Detroit, where club officials thought his emotional style — great highs followed by ranting lows — had again cost him the support of several players.

Collins went into coach's exile, doing basketball commentary for a television network. Jordan moved into the Wizards' executive suite. In 2001, when it came time to hire a new coach in Washington, Jordan — already toying with the idea of his own comeback as a player — decided to opt for a known commodity he could manage over a wild card who might exert an unwanted authority. Not having worked in the NBA for three years, Collins now owed his basketball life to Jordan.

His gratitude made him both an ideal and dangerous choice to look after Jordan's comeback. The shadow boss told Collins when he wanted to be in a game and when he wanted to come out, an arrangement that resulted in his playing so many minutes on tendinitis-plagued knees that he broke down and needed knee surgery in his first season back.

The coach even referred to Jordan as the "boss," which irked Wizards brass, prompting an organization official to send down word to Collins that Jordan, having relinquished the club presidency, was no longer an executive in the organization, simply a player; that Collins's true boss was, and would always be, owner Abe Pollin.

Collins began the past season trying to project a new authority. At training camp, he insisted that it wouldn't matter how much Jordan lobbied for more playing time, that he would hold Jordan's minutes down in the interest of protecting the questionable knees.

Collins's vow lasted one month, the same period Jordan was content to begin games on the bench while Jerry Stackhouse led the team. After telling the media during Thanksgiving week that this would be his final season and therefore he risked nothing if his body broke down, Jordan was a starter again, soon playing about forty minutes a game, as he had during crushing stages of the previous season. Jordan would win his gamble with his knees, fulfilling his personal goal of playing in all eighty-two games, but his return to the lineup presented Collins with a thorny challenge. How would the coach satisfy the demands of his team's two stars — one an aging god, the other a twenty-eight-year-old all-star and presumably in his prime — each of whom had come to expect having an offense built around his appetites and style of play?

Stackhouse wanted to be part of an up-tempo, fast-breaking offense that enabled him to soar and "attack the rim," as he put it — banging bodies, drawing fouls, scoring on drives and dunks. Privately, according to a Wizards official, Collins complained he did not have the players, particularly a sterling point guard, to fast-break often. Besides, he reasoned, Jordan was now scoring in big numbers again — and Jordan didn't want to run much, or not nearly enough to satisfy Stackhouse. Often when the Wizards had a clear opportunity to fast-break, Collins's booming voice rang out to halt them. Four players would frequently wait for Jordan to join them.

Meanwhile, Jordan began pushing for changes, wanting the team's point guard of sorts, Larry Hughes, replaced in the starting lineup by Tyronn Lue. Hughes knew how to score, Jordan said, but hadn't shown the ability to get him the ball when and where he wanted it. In time, Hughes would lose his starting job.

All along, the pressure on Collins grew. Jordan told him privately that he expected to make the playoffs, and, by late February, shared his presumption with the media, raising the stakes: "I think we're gonna make the playoffs. . . . I've never had doubts we would make the playoffs."

By then, a season and a half in Washington had left its marks on Collins. His gray crew cut looked sparser; the deep crease under his right eye deeper still. He openly admitted to not understanding his players, suggesting some lacked emotional toughness, an observation that ran the risk of stirring a terrible backlash. Jordan, pushing the theme with impunity, emboldened Collins, who would vent: "The players have to hurt when they don't win, just like the coaches do. We have to hurt together."

Saying this, his face shook ever so slightly, like a tuning fork, which happened when he became greatly moved or angered. "This is one of those wins you really remember with your team," he said, having triumphed over division-leading New Jersey, "because we have had a lot of ups and downs. . . . I've never been more proud of them. . . . I was very emotional. I became a grandpa yesterday." It seemed, for an instant, he was close to tears. His voice trembled. His baby grandson, he said, "got his first win tonight."

It was Collins, all of him, in about twenty seconds — his pride, joy, anxieties, hurt, his demand that others hurt, his emotions naked and spilling, the very impulses that led associates to worry about him sometimes, just as people had worried at different times in Chicago and Detroit.

He was mercurial. He could be kind, as when, before a March game, he praised the job done by Denver coach Jeff Bzdelik, whose dogged team's losing record left it near the bottom of the league's standings. But he had a virtually nonexistent frustration threshold for subjects he didn't want to discuss. Unlike Phil Jackson, whose amusement with sharply edged questions about Jordan had only added to an enamored media's portrait of him as the Zen Master, Collins bristled, intent on demonstrating his loyalty to Jordan, sometimes by walking through flames of his own making.

An out-of-town reporter asked Collins if players had become afraid of the legend. Collins snickered, "How would I know that? You'd have to ask them." He added, "It doesn't scare me." He looked around and, with a broadening smile, began laughing loudly, a touch mockingly, looking back at the offending reporter and then at the rest of the press corps, as if to say, *Get a load of this guy, what a question*, studying the faces, in the way of a man trying to get a read on a room.

By then — with Brown and Stackhouse already having lashed out at Collins — Jordan told his teammates that he would not tolerate any further disrespect of their coach. But never did he send a message of unqualified admiration for Collins. Few scenes so reflected Collins's status in Jordan's eyes as a practice on the morning of a late March game against the Lakers, in Los Angeles — the last time Jordan would be competing against Phil Jackson.

Wizards players and coaches lingered around a basket, idly chatting and bouncing balls while Jordan held court with reporters. He was asked about Jackson, whom, in the late '90s, Jordan had said he "loved." It seemed, now as then, such a strong word for a man with no history of lavishing affection on people in the basketball world. Jordan pursed his lips, and took his time answering. "The thing I remember greatly about Phil," he said, "is that he challenged me. He was never intimidated by me. When most coaches could easily be intimidated by me, he came in and if I played bad, he told me I played bad. If he felt I needed to improve in areas, he told me I needed to improve in those areas. I respected him for doing that. I wanted a coach who could always tell me what my weaknesses were . . . because it would only help me be a better basketball player. This is what Coach [Dean] Smith did for me. This is what Phil Jackson did for me."

Doug Collins stood a scant thirty feet away, in Jordan's line of sight. The omission of his name said much, and in the end too much. He had given Jordan his friendship, deference, and loyalty for years. But there are limits to what deference can get you. Maybe men cannot love those who need their love too much. Jordan appreciated Collins, who had given him whatever he wanted, whenever he wanted it — given Jordan everything except a reason to revere him.

At this point, not even Jordan's aura could help the coach with several players. And Jordan's remove from most of the Wizards guaranteed that he would not play peacemaker. The Collins blowup was coming, and Abe Pollin, who was never consulted on the hiring of Collins, now had a target.

Jordan had teammates, but few intimates. He had basketball discussions with teammates — which he considered business — but little else crept in. "I have a small comfort zone with people," he said in a moment of candor last year.

That comfort zone wasn't penetrated by the team's newest arriving star. Jordan and Stackhouse had met many years ago, when, as NBA gossip had it, Stackhouse beat Jordan in a summertime one-on-one contest while still a Philadelphia 76er and then suffered the payback of a Jordan torching the next time their teams met. Both graduates of the University of North Carolina and raised in the state, the two could scarcely have been more different in their personal styles. Jordan was privately assertive; Stackhouse quieter, so quiet that some considered him aloof. While Jordan avoided hands-on involvement in most community causes, Stackhouse had been driven by personal loss to establish a foundation dedicated to fighting diabetes. Two older sisters had died of the disease, and both his parents were afflicted by it. Becoming a passionate advocate for more research funding only heightened his skills with language; he would usually answer questions thoroughly, insightfully.

But Stackhouse's mien belied a competitive fierceness and an occasional temper. Disagreements in the past with players had not always ended well: he had punched out two of them over the years, including current Wizard Christian Laettner when they were teammates in Detroit. After not getting his Pistons deep enough into the playoffs, he was traded away for a younger player in Richard Hamilton.

One school of observers believed the Wizards had gotten the worst of the deal, having essentially traded young for older. But Hamilton's relationship with Jordan had made him expendable. Hamilton had dared to look forward aloud to the post-Jordan days, when he and his young Wizards teammates — "the New Jacks," Hamilton had dubbed them — could at last reveal the depth of their talents, out of the idol's shadow. There had been sniping between Jordan and the upstart, some mutual searing of egos, and Hamilton was gone, on his way to helping the Pistons finish at the top of the Eastern Conference.

But, like Hamilton a year earlier, Stackhouse was both a teammate and a rival of Jordan's. Each had expectations that doomed any chance of that magic called synergy. "I guess we gave up some things for each other," Stackhouse the diplomat said, late in the year. "But the mix of us, with our contrasting styles, didn't work out."

In essence, he had decided to wait Jordan out. To complain about him would have been pointless anyway: Jordan was the Wizards' unmistakable leader, and by January, their most productive player, on his way to becoming the first forty-year-old to score forty points in a game, and averaging about twenty points a night, in addition, often, to shutting down a foe's top shooting guard.

In Jordan's mind, his effort and resurgence gave him license to lacerate his teammates, particularly the young ones. "It's very disappointing," he said after a March loss in New York, "when a forty-year-old man has more desire than twenty-five-, twenty-six-, twenty-three-year-old people. He's diving for loose balls, he's busting his chin — and it's not reciprocated by other players on the team." Twelve days later, fuming after a crushing twenty-six-point loss in Phoenix at the start of a critical six-game western road trip, he disclosed to the media what he had told his teammates at halftime — that, if they just gave him the word, he would go home and golf. "If you want to play hard basketball, we'll play hard basketball," he told them. "If you guys want to take it off, I could be playing golf somewhere. . . . I'm not wasting my breath. . . . I can do other things with it. I can have a nice cigar."

The eruptions contrasted with his long-standing insistence that he had principally returned to the court to give the younger Wizards the benefit of his knowledge and on-court leadership. Now, in distancing himself from them in the down times and wistfully talking of abandonment, he looked less like their mentor than a temperamental rajah. "The truth hurts," Jordan said. "Sometimes you just got to say the things that may hurt."

On another occasion, he mocked his teammates as a group, rhetorically asking how they could think of being content, given their basketball histories: "Why should they? It's not like they've done anything." Aside from himself, the only one in the group who had ever won an NBA championship, he noted, was Lue, a former Los Angeles Laker. Thinking about Lue's title, Jordan added, "And he was only a reserve." Message: Jordan was the only winner.

As always, he reserved his harshest criticisms for twenty-one-year-old Kwame Brown, at whom, a year earlier, he had screamed, "Flaming faggot," when Brown complained as a rookie about being fouled in an intrasquad game. Before the 2001 NBA draft, Jordan and other Wizards brass considered trading the rights to their top pick for star forward Shareef Abdur-Rahim, now with Atlanta. But

Jordan and other Wizards officials were swayed by Georgia high school senior Brown's abilities after he dominated another highly touted prep player, Tyson Chandler, during a private one-on-one competition. But now Jordan was tired of waiting for Brown to get better.

For his part, Brown said the right things: "Anyone can learn from Michael" if that "player listens." But, privately, Brown reeled under Jordan's and Collins's criticism off and on for two seasons now, desperate to receive a slice of the encouragement Jordan had lavished on him during Brown's golden days. On many nights, he had gone from wunderkind to waste. Despairing, Brown began to seek counsel from other teammates, notably Stackhouse, who could provide solace but little else, suffering beneath the weight of his own disappointments and, like Brown, having nowhere to turn.

Lakers assistant coach Tex Winter, who had been an assistant for the Bulls under first Collins and later Phil Jackson, had seen it before. The creator of Chicago's famed triangle offense, which he and Jackson had sold to a reluctant Jordan, Winter is the rare figure from Jordan's past who speaks openly about the idol. "I think the [Wizards] are better for having had him; he sets a great example [in his play on the court] and still has the ability to make big plays for them," Winter said toward the end of the season. "But I think he expects too much from teammates because they're not Michael Jordan. . . . No doubt, an awful lot of the players that he's played with [in Chicago], at least in their own minds, believe he alienated them. They've resented the treatment they've received" from him.

Winter wondered. He sat there, on an empty practice court in Los Angeles, mulling over why Jordan routinely berated others. He viewed the questions he was being asked as comprising the great unknown about Jordan: Did he make the humiliated better? How many? At what cost?

Winter's thirteen years with Jordan meant that he had coached him longer than anyone else — including Smith, Jackson, and Collins. But Winter never understood him, saying he was mystified why a man so beloved was an antagonist to so many people in his job. "For some reason Michael gets a satisfaction out of humiliating people," he said, wincing a little. "I think he competes even there . . . [in] personal relationships."

But Winter thought he could point to some players Jordan liked, and probably had made better, too — someone like Tyronn Lue, for whom Jordan demonstrated in public an avuncular affection he seldom displayed around the other youngsters. He'd drape an arm around Lue's shoulder after a good hustle play, reach down, with his six-inch height advantage, and rub the top of Luc's head, his hand lingering there. "I listened; I learned more about how to play with Michael this year, because sometimes before it was hard," said Lue, who had struggled last season to understand where Jordan wanted him positioned on the floor, what he wanted him to do, the uncertainty undermining his confidence.

Lue had fought back, a quality that Jordan long had admired in two other guards he'd played with, Bulls John Paxson and Steve Kerr, the latter of whom had dared to fight him once during a heated practice scrimmage. Lue backed down from no one. When he missed several games because of a separated shoulder suffered while diving for a loose ball, Jordan uncharacteristically talked at length about how much his absence meant, concluding, "That T-Lue injury really hurt us." No play by a teammate all season seemed to excite him more than when Lue dived to the floor and secured another loose ball late during a one-point overtime win at Boston in April, Jordan clapping right there on the court.

His rants of March had become his ripostes of April. He likened himself to a parent whose children didn't listen. When, for instance, an old friend, Matt Doherty, was fired as coach of North Carolina after several Tar Heel players complained of Doherty's treatment of them, Jordan disapproved of the firing, saying: "You know, kids are going to get yelled at. I got yelled at my first year."

Within three weeks, unknown to the star or his coach, Abe Pollin would talk to some of the younger players about team morale. That alone did not bode well for Jordan or Collins. Back in Los Angeles, a sympathetic Tex Winter thought that his old player had been adored for so long — by owners, by teammates, by the media — that he found criticism difficult to grasp now, even unfathomable.

As the season wound down, and the world exalted him at every stop, Jordan could not see what was coming.

The exalting took on odd forms. After games, the media assembled in a sweaty rugby-like scrum on the blue carpet of the Wizards' locker room, positioned around a gold star on the carpet. It was part of the Wizards logo but looked like a stage mark for a talk-show host. Next came the wait, twenty, thirty minutes sometimes. "Thought I was gonna wait you out," he liked to joke on the way over, the scrum swallowing him up, two or three dozen people jostling for position.

He'd done this for different parts of three decades, done it two thousand times at least.

The questions, or quasi-questions, as they were, would fly then.

"Big win tonight, Michael. Did you want to set the tone early?"

"Michael, are you guys playing with a sense of urgency?"

"Now you got the Pistons coming up. A pivotal game?"

It was not exactly *Meet the Press.*

Many reporters in the scrum — out-of-towners and television people particularly — just came for a sound bite, any sound bite, as Jordan's presence alone carried value — his actual words almost incidental to them.

He courted the media from his early college days — excitedly pushing to be on the cover of *Sports Illustrated*, generally talking to reporters and TV people when Dean Smith permitted.

It was an inclination that he brought to the NBA, where in his early years he made himself available to the media before games and lingered in locker rooms with reporters long afterward, a charming, quotable young man selling image — and shoes. On the road, he regularly invited writers to his hotel rooms to play cards with him, and on planes that the media and Bulls players rode together, he gave them time when they needed it, between hands, after happily taking their money. So close were the star and a corps of Chicago reporters that, after the birth of his first child, Jordan persuaded them not to print the news, because it was a delicate matter: he and Juanita Vanoy had yet to marry, and Jordan thought that news of the birth could damage his image.

There were limits to what could be kept from the public, however. In the early '90s, when news broke of his gambling forays on golf courses, where he had been the easy mark of slick hustlers, hard-news reporters surrounded him to demand figures and names of the disreputable. He retreated, told his old friends there would be no more pregame interviews or invitations to his hotel room, and his rules for dealing with the media changed forever.

He retired from basketball for the first time at the end of the

1992–93 season, and went off to hit about .200 for the Chicago White Sox' Class AA minor league team, but before he was done, *Sports Illustrated* would run an article saying that he and the White Sox were embarrassing baseball. It would be just one of fifty-two cover stories that *Sports Illustrated* has run on Jordan, the vast majority of which were flattering, a few even worshipful. But anybody wanting to know what Michael Jordan expects from the media needed only to watch much respected *Sports Illustrated* writer Jack McCallum approach Jordan last February.

McCallum, whom Jordan liked, hoped for a personal interview for a story about Jordan's fortieth birthday that month. He broached the idea to Jordan alongside a wall leading out of the locker room.

"Yeah, my girl told me about it," Jordan said, glancing up at the ceiling. "I don't think it's gonna happen . . ."

You're not going to talk to me, McCallum said.

"I talked to you," Jordan said, reaching down and rubbing the top of McCallum's head. What clasping elbows and shoulders was for Bill Clinton, rubbing heads was for Jordan. "I talked to you. I still love you. I just don't love your magazine." McCallum, who wasn't even the author of the baseball piece, suggested that the feud had been going on for too long.

Jordan smiled tightly. He looked at McCallum and then down the wall at a writer whose presence had come to irk him, raising his voice slightly. "I carry grudges."

During his two comeback seasons with the Wizards, that reality left much of the media, who tend to grovel for access anyway, reluctant to chronicle incidents unflattering to Jordan. It was a virtual guarantee that almost all high-profile coverage would be slavishly favorable, on Jordan's terms.

Sports reporters who had established close personal relationships with Jordan enjoyed special status, a kind of currency that flowed from a symbiotic arrangement in which coverage was flattering and absolutely devoid of controversy. "He's Jordan's guy," people would say of the favored circle, whose ranks included Ahmad Rashad, a television commentator who has famously carved out a niche doing chummy banter with Jordan. Even when he granted an interview to others, Jordan guided the discussion. Talking on the record to a visiting reporter about Boston's Antoine Walker, a laughing Jordan boasted: "I told [Walker] we were going to beat them [the Celtics] every time we played them." Jordan paused, thought about his words. "Don't write that. It might give him too much energy."

The reporter didn't write it.

Some journalists accorded Jordan this favor out of genuine respect and affection — they looked upon him the way one might look upon a comet. But a group at least as large knew that the disclosure of anything discomfiting would be regarded as heresy, that the god and his publicity machinery had the power to smite them. At its best, a moment with Jordan was akin to a struggling gold miner being allowed to take a small pan and sift in the overlord's stream for a few minutes so long as he did not cross him. Few did.

But once or twice a year, the script was violated. This past season, it happened in November, after a thirty-nine-year-old Indiana woman named Karla Knafel, already accused by Jordan in a lawsuit of trying to extort money from him, filed a counterclaim in Chicago, alleging that he had orally promised to pay her $5 million, in exchange for her silence about their two-year affair in the early '90s, and her agreement not to file a paternity suit. (She was pregnant back then with a child who turned out not to be Jordan's.) She alleged that the affair had been set in motion by a chance encounter with NBA referee Eddie F. Rush, who saw her singing in an Indianapolis club, she said, and who, shortly later, called Jordan, saying that he had someone with him whom Jordan should meet.

Jordan acknowledged in court documents that he paid Knafel $250,000 in hush money. A famous man, with an image to protect, had worried about a secret leaking.

The past season included the usual stories about athletes and courtrooms. Most notable was the ongoing saga of Sacramento Kings star forward Chris Webber, accused, along with former University of Michigan teammates from the early '90s, of accepting gifts from a university booster in violation of NCAA rules and then, in Webber's case, of lying about it before a grand jury. The Webber matter generated intense coverage: a notable athlete's image had been called into question, just as in *Jordan v. Knafel.* But scrutiny of the Jordan proceedings, in newspapers and on television outside Chicago, paled against that of Webber's case.

As his nights on the stage dwindled, the media kept some questions about him tucked away in lockboxes. It wasn't the first time an American sports idol had been accorded protection in the winter of his playing days. America had done it for DiMaggio half a century before Michael Jordan, and for Ruth before that, and for Mantle and Marciano, too. Now as then, the media did it because some truths are just too discordant when a culture is feverishly engaged in an homage fest. Truth comes later. The lockboxes open only when hagiography gives way to a hunger for knowing who the idol was, what he really meant.

Still, on a foggy March morning, a legal proceeding went forward in a small Chicago courtroom. A clerk wearing a golf-ball tie called for *Jordan v. Knafel.* The former didn't attend; the latter, now an Indiana hairstylist sporting streaked blond hair, arrived in horn-rimmed glasses, a black maxi-sweater over black hip-huggers, and a white blouse unbuttoned at the midriff.

Jordan's attorney, Frederick Sperling, argued that what Knafel had done constituted extortion. Knafel's attorney, Michael Hannafan, responded that Jordan had viewed his alleged promise of $5 million as a "bargain" meant to protect him against the "tarnishing of his public image" — and that Jordan's former attorneys certainly believed they'd entered into an agreement when their client began paying Knafel.

The Jordan side wanted to walk out of the courtroom with a dismissal of Knafel's claims, but the judge said there would be no decision that day. There was much weirdness to that morning, none greater than the sensation that Michael Jordan seemed to have nothing to do with this courtroom or event, so deftly had he distanced himself from the controversy. It was exactly the effect the Jordan team had hoped for.

On the morning that case was being heard, Jordan was headed west on his career's final big road swing, six games that would include a last dance with the Lakers and Kobe Bryant, an heir apparent as the game's best player. Jordan seemed to have difficulty with the notion, so much so that it raised the question as to whether he thought there could ever be a worthy successor.

His attitude was wait-and-see: there had been talk of heirs apparent before, like Penny Hardaway and Grant Hill, only they had faltered after suffering injuries.

But the most recent heirs, particularly Bryant and Orlando's Tracy McGrady, seemed not to be going away, just looming larger. Once, during Thanksgiving week, teammates asked Jordan: Who's the *man?* Who's better — Bryant or McGrady?

He didn't answer. It seemed he hadn't heard.

A teammate repeated the question. Who's the *man?* Jordan turned his back, not saying anything. An answer, it seemed, might open the door onto the legitimacy of a successor, and he showed no inclination to go there.

The last game between Jordan and Bryant wouldn't be forgotten. Nobody wanted to see Jordan humiliated. Nobody wanted even a moment that could call to mind something like Larry Bird abusing an old Dr. J, or Larry Holmes thrashing Muhammad Ali. The Lakers coaches would not have Kobe guarding Michael — they didn't want Kobe preoccupied with beating the king.

Everything about the game, on March 28 in Los Angeles, seemed so exquisitely timed. Jordan hit his first four shots and, late in the first quarter, stole a pass intended for Bryant and dribbled the length of the floor for a two-handed dunk. The crowd was in a frenzy, and Jordan on his way to a hellacious thirteen-point quarter.

But soon Old yielded to Young. Bryant, whom Jackson had urged to be aggressive before the start of the game, hit a three-pointer, and another, and another. He ended the first quarter with nineteen points, and the first half with forty-two. It was like watching a mudslide. The Wizards were buried by halftime.

Bryant, who cruised to fifty-five points, sidestepped suggestions of torches being passed. "I want to be like Kobe," he said neatly.

Down a hallway, somebody asked Jordan, whose game had been quiet after the first quarter, if he'd handed over his crown.

"Is he better than you?" somebody else shouted.

Subdued, Jordan kept things short: "It's easy for people to say, 'Well, the torch is in his hand.' He definitely has a share of the torch. But there are a lot of other guys who I think will have to carry that. . . . Obviously, it's tough for one guy to try to carry that."

Endings in sports are seldom pretty. But Jordan believed in the power of home-court advantage, the psychological edge that he thought it gave you, in life as well as in basketball. He had come to Abe Pollin's office to get his old job back — a position that he viewed as a stepping-stone to running the Wizards completely one day. An ex-athlete of just three weeks, he saw it as a benefit, he told one associate, that any meeting with Abe Pollin would happen at MCI Center. The owner had built the arena, but only he had filled it.

He had sat for other meetings in Pollin's office, none more illustrative of their differences than the one that took place shortly before his last season as club president, in the autumn of 2000. Pollin had assembled Jordan, Wes Unseld, their assistants, and Jordan's team of handpicked coaches, led by first-year head coach Leonard Hamilton, recently hired away from the University of Miami. One participant remembered Pollin launching into a pep talk, swiftly training his attention on the new coach. "Leonard, we are giving you three all-star players — Mitch Richmond, Rod Strickland, and Juwan Howard," Pollin said, before declaring that the team's talent meant it should make the playoffs and thrive. "I wondered," the participant recalled, "whether I should tell him that Mitch and Rod were old and shot, and that Juwan was grossly overpaid and no star. But I worried about getting in trouble if I said anything. I knew Abe didn't like dissent . . . just like Michael."

Not long after that meeting, away from Unseld, the talk among some in the group turned to the subject of Pollin: Was he deluded? Did he not understand just how weak a team he had, relative to the rest of the league? Jordan smirked, not rising to Pollin's defense, saying merely that the team better not stand pat; he hadn't come to Washington to do nothing.

Jordan's disregard for the seventy-nine-year-old Pollin exhibited itself in ways big and small. He openly viewed Pollin as a transitional figure who would bow out in time, allowing Jordan to work chiefly with Pollin's presumed successor, Ted Leonsis, the minority Wizards partner responsible for bringing Jordan to Washington. Pollin became an afterthought in Jordan conversations. Compounding strains between the two men were Jordan's occasional comments about his future ambitions, which raised questions about his long-term commitment to Washington. In early 2001, dreaming aloud about how he could see himself leaving to buy the Chicago franchise someday, he laid out how he would excitedly break the news of the prospective deal to his partners, with Pollin at the end of his thoughts. "If the [deal] is put on the table," he said, "I would sit down with Ted [Leonsis], all my guys . . . and Abe, if he's still part of the situation, and say, 'Look, the Chicago team wants to sell, it's a great fit for me. . . .'"

At that moment, however, Pollin remained very much a "part of the situation." Jordan's comment was at once gently obvious — no elderly man endures forever in ownership or in life — and completely tone-deaf to the offense it might cause a superior who said he had no plans to leave anytime soon. Jordan had a tin ear for office politics, a consequence of having been wealthy men's moneymaking machine throughout his playing days, indulged and anointed. People paid him fealty, not vice versa. At about the same time, Jordan allies began floating rumors of his disenchantment with Pollin's reluctance to cede all basketball-related decisions to him.

For a while, early this spring, Jordan's posture was that of a man believing he enjoyed leverage in the upcoming negotiations. On April 9, after a home loss to Boston, he suggested that, if a deal were not to be struck with the Wizards, he could turn elsewhere: "Obviously, my focus here is to go back upstairs, and hopefully, the way . . . we thought about and talked about." But if things didn't work out with the Wizards, Jordan added, "then, obviously, I have options."

This meant, according to conventional wisdom, a position in the NBA's new Charlotte franchise, or perhaps even back in Chicago, where an old nemesis, Jerry Krause, had just resigned as president. But something changed on April 9, irrevocably so. Something was put into motion by his words that he couldn't stop thereafter, a sense that he was less than entirely faithful to Abe Pollin's franchise, that Jordan saw his longtime dream of returning to Chicago as a viable possibility now. It did not help that the Bulls filled their position quickly, without so much as discreetly inquiring about his availability. He suddenly looked like questionable goods.

Still, if Pollin had any last questions about Jordan's leadership and issues of Wizards disunity, his handpicked coach answered them after the final home game. It came so abruptly: "I've had guys in that locker room curse at me this year, show no respect. . . ." Collins's voice shook, and that tuning-fork quiver came over him. The media assemblage, huge on this night to hear Jordan after his final game in Washington, sat stunned. Collins went on: "Any time a player disrespects a coach, everybody thinks it's all right." His public pain said nothing so much as this: he had lost the team. And lost it while executing Jordan's plan, abiding by his sentiments. Jordan was in no position, and apparently had no inclination, to play peacemaker.

Nothing Jordan could say thereafter to Pollin would much matter. Peculiarity had characterized their last awkward public minutes together in MCI, as twenty thousand looked on. The public-address announcer spoke virtually as long about Pollin and his wife, Irene, as about Jordan, noting in detail the Pollins' contribution of computers in Jordan's name, and heralding their "commitment to the environment," an unusually prolonged encomium for a couple not leaving any scene.

The man who was departing, but did not know it yet, displayed his famously imperious streak, declining to take the microphone and speak to fans screaming for him. His distance from them was never clearer. He was the visitant who had touched down, and now the one about to walk off with a wave. The smaller man next to him smiled, holding a secret between his pursed lips like a sour candy.

PETER DE JONGE

The Leap of His Life

FROM THE NEW YORK TIMES MAGAZINE

MIDWAY THROUGH THE SECOND QUARTER of an early-season game against the Memphis Grizzlies, the rookie power forward for the Phoenix Suns, Amare Stoudemire, flying diagonally across the paint, made an unlikely but life-affirming attempt to convert a low-altitude rebound into a reverse put-back dunk. Only that he's twenty and what the NBA auditors of flesh and bone call "a freak" enabled him to even imagine that he could make this play. From a little triangular section of seats right behind the Suns bench, reserved for homeboys, lovers, swindlers, and kin, Stoudemire's people looked on. Among them was Marwan Stoudemire, Amare's fourteen-year-old half-brother, whom Amare brought west with him from central Florida and enrolled in a private Phoenix day school. Marwan is not a freak. He wears a metal cast of the Cartoon Network antihero "The Brain" on a chain around his neck, has a heartbreaking smile and soft, ancient eyes, and if anything, he is small and slight for a ninth-grader. After the game, when he told his brother's towering teammates that he touched the rim that afternoon, all he got was rolled eyes.

But as his brother stretched for that rebound, Marwan, before anyone else in America West Arena, sensed the possibility of highlight-footage immortality and sprang from his seat. In his excitement, he spilled hot chocolate on his immaculate powder-blue Ecko sweatsuit; as he ruefully dabbed at the stain, his cell phone rang. The call, exhorting him to be cool, was from Michael Walker, Amare's homeboy and roommate, sitting two seats away. Unfazed, Marwan looked over at Alexi, an Arizona State sophomore Amare met at a Nelly concert, and blamed her for the spill.

"My fault?" said Alexi, a big "A" dangling from her wrist and calligraphy scrolling up her lower back.

"That's right," said their other companion, Artis Wilson. Wilson, six-foot-six, slim and stylish and a former schoolyard legend himself back in Lake Wales, Florida, is the former husband of Carrie Stoudemire, Marwan and Amare's mother. Wilson is also Marwan's temporary guardian, which might explain why he jumped to Marwan's defense. "And don't be sitting back all quiet," he went on to tell Alexi. "This ain't the opera, girl."

On television, it is easy to make the mistake of thinking that the outcome of games actually matters. In the comped pews, it's plain that every salaried second of official NBA action is pure anticlimax, a forty-eight-minute celebration of the blessed fact that the drama of getting there is finally over, and that for the millionaire players and their friends and family, it's all good now, at least for a while. When Walker yelled, "Big Al," second-year reserve forward Alton Ford pointed back, chuckling, and even Amare, who plays with a glazed-over deadpan he calls his "swagger," sneaked quick handsome grins at his girl, Alexi.

Just before the half, Carrie Stoudemire joined the party by phone from Florida, where she was serving four months at Lowell Correctional Institute. One hand cupped over his Nokia, Wilson connected his ex-wife, in prison, to her son's heroic exploits on the court. "Amare. Fifteen feet straight away. Jumper. Net. And now some Grizzly is trying to take it to the hole. *Rejected!* I tried to warn the boy before he did that, but he wouldn't listen."

Before she and Wilson were cut off by her prison curfew, the ex-couple giddily discussed her imminent transition from inmate to front-row NBA mom. I couldn't hear Carrie, but this was Wilson's end of the conversation: "You aren't going to sit here and be cool. . . . You may try to be cool, but you ain't never been cool. . . . I'll be what kind of cheerleader?. . . . Oh, that's really funny. . . . Well if I put that on, what are you going to put on? A grass skirt?"

For all the joking, there was an undercurrent of anxiety, because Carrie Stoudemire, who because of numerous convictions has been in and out of jail for much of her sons' childhoods, was getting out the next morning. At 8:00 A.M., she would step through the gates and climb into a limo that would take her to Orlando, where $40,000 worth of jewelry would be waiting along with the $100,000 Mercedes Amare bought her. Then on Saturday morning, after two days of shopping and primping, so, as Wilson put it, "Carrie can arrive in style," she had a ticket on the red-eye to Phoenix.

Female genetic lottery winners become supermodels. Male genetic lottery winners play professional basketball, and this week in Manhattan, the NBA's twenty-nine general managers will divvy up the planet's annual harvest at the league's draft. To refine their thinking, they will have reviewed ad nauseam the results of the 2002 draft, in which the first choice was a seven-foot-five twenty-one-year-old from China; the fifth, a seven-foot nineteen-year-old from Georgia (as in Tbilisi, not Atlanta); and the seventh, a six-foot-eleven behemoth from São Carlos, Brazil. But the best of all of them was the ninth pick, Stoudemire, a six-foot-ten, 245-pound teenager from Lake Wales, Florida.

It is too soon to deliver a verdict on all of last year's choices, much less fully understand the critical indicators. But one question every GM will have tried to answer is how Stoudemire, who recently became the first player directly out of high school to be named the NBA's Rookie of the Year and whose first-season numbers easily outshone previous high-schoolers turned superstars, like Kobe Bryant, Kevin Garnett, and Tracy McGrady, was still around at number nine.

One insight the GMs could take from the early returns is that getting caught up in anything but a coldblooded appraisal of genetic endowments is bound to break their hearts and get them fired. Every team knew Stoudemire was the funkiest athlete in the draft, a monstrous combination of length, hops, quickness, and power. But it was the soft data that led them astray.

And there was so much of it. For starters, Stoudemire was raw even for his age, which was only nineteen. It's one thing for a top American prospect to emerge from high school without an education, but we expect our matriculating man-children to be fluent in basketball. Stoudemire played only two years in high school, but cannily spun his inexperience as evidence of staggering potential. "When I go on to college or the NBA," he told *Slam* magazine while he was in high school, "and get somebody to teach me basketball, man, it is over." Nevertheless, his best move, which is getting the ball with his back to the basket, turning on his defender with a terrifying suddenness, and throwing it down in his wincing face, is difficult to pick up from a chalk talk.

Then there was the disquieting fact that Stoudemire's Cypress Creek High managed to win just sixteen of its twenty-nine games in his senior year. What kind of dent would Stoudemire make on the league if he could barely lift a high school team above .500?

But what had general managers really freaked was the Stoudemire family. Chaotic households are the smithies of the NBA, but Stoudemire's first coming of age was precarious by any measure. His father died when he was twelve, and his mother had been in and out of jail on a variety of convictions for theft and forgery. During Stoudemire's middle school years, his mother yanked him and Marwan out of classrooms as she moved abruptly among various towns in Florida and New York State. Between sophomore and senior years, Stoudemire switched schools seven times. What Stoudemire said about Marwan, who lost his father when he was seven, also applies to him. "Growing up without a mom or dad," Amare told me, "is going to be tough on anyone."

It was certainly tough on Amare's older brother, Hazell Jr. After spending a year in juvenile detention, he led Bradenton Southeast High School to a record of 35–0 and a Florida state championship. Yet even the bona fide prospects of pro stardom could not keep Hazell out of trouble; he is now doing three to nine years for drug dealing and sexual abuse at a prison in upstate New York.

General managers aren't shrinks, but they've absorbed enough Dr. Phil to know that some measure of childhood stability is necessary to becoming a productive, law-abiding adult. League rosters may be stuffed with the sons of absent fathers, but entering the league without either parent is pretty much uncharted terrain. Surely, empathetic GMs thought, a kid making the jump straight out of high school is going to be in over his head without his mom.

Before the draft, the Suns were leery of Stoudemire, too. "We do an extensive background check," said Bryan Colangelo, the general manager and son of the Suns owner, Jerry Colangelo. "The information that turned up was nothing I would say would cause great concern."

They also had Stoudemire sit down for a psychological test, as they do with all prospective players. "It's a brief ten- or fifteen-minute sketch of who that person is," said Colangelo, a Cornell graduate who was struggling to sell commercial real estate in New York when his father welcomed him into the fold. "It's prepared by a sports psychologist and administered by a team counselor and graded and prepared by an outside firm."

Even after they drafted him, the Suns behaved as if Stoudemire might surface on the police blotter without full-time baby-sitting and remedial input. As the season approached, they talked of weaving him "the perfect cocoon" and recruited Scott Williams, a veteran who as a teenager lost both his parents in a murder-suicide, to be his good neighbor in the locker room. The assistant GM, Mark West, was charged with monitoring his comings, goings, and cash flow.

Seemingly oblivious to all this attention, Stoudemire came in and took care of business, dunking as mercilessly on the heads of NBA all-stars as he had on overmatched schoolboys. More than that, he fired up a Suns team that had entered the season with decidedly modest expectations. And there hasn't been a whiff of off-court malfeasance. When the traffic from Scottsdale made him late to a preseason practice or two, he moved closer to the downtown arena. He organized his life around simple routines, chilling on his couch after practice, napping before games, and limiting his nightlife to trips to the mall for "something to chew on" at the Cheesecake Factory.

When I arrived in Phoenix, Amare was living with his old friend Michael Walker; he had his brother Marwan set up in a Scottsdale townhouse under the caring eye of Artis Wilson. The season was young, and things had settled into a calm rhythm. But nothing has ever stayed that way for long in the Stoudemire household.

Unlike many players' mothers, who are unwilling to uproot their lives to move to a city from which their son might be traded at the drop of a hat, Carrie Stoudemire was coming to town to reinvent herself and stay. And everything the team had heard from Stoudemire's agent, John Wolf, indicated that she would insist on being a major part of the picture, if not run the whole show.

The team got a glimpse of her volatility last summer when Frank Johnson, the Suns coach, accompanied Stoudemire to his mother's sentencing hearing in Florida. The bitter paradox of her most recent legal difficulty is that it was based on attending last year's NBA draft. When she left for New York last June without permission, she violated her probation. It seems cruel to punish the biological urge to witness the moment your son becomes a multimillionaire, as well as to give the party afterward for which Wolf got stuck for the $3,000 champagne bill. But impulsiveness had cost Carrie Stoude-mire before.

"Carrie didn't actually think they would violate her, because she had been doing so good on probation," Wilson said. "Plus she had paid back all this money for restitution and done everything she could to get off probation early. I think the problem was that the parole officer and Carrie had some words before, and I think that's 75 percent of the reason for the lady violating her. Carrie is the type, she is going to speak her mind. She may regret some of the things she says later, but at the time, she's going to say it."

Johnson said that at the hearing, Carrie Stoudemire was consid-ering trying to work out a new deal that would have allowed her to come to Phoenix and help her son set up house. It was a move, he said, that could have backfired in the form of a much longer sen-tence. In a highly emotional encounter, Amare was able to per-suade her "to just do the time and get it over with." And according to someone close to the team, Carrie Stoudemire did not help her cause at the hearing when she kept her sentencing judge waiting for half an hour.

Still, in the middle of all this drama, Carrie Stoudemire man-aged to exert her will on the organization. "We all had dinner one night," said Johnson, a former NBA journeyman who was entering his first full season as head coach. "Afterward, she and I stayed in the car and talked for two and a half hours. She filled me in on Amare and what he needs. It was extremely valuable. Carrie's a very strong-willed woman. She'll tell you what she wants. She's got very definite rules she believes in, and if they're not followed, she'll let you know."

Part of what makes Carrie Stoudemire so tough is that nothing in her past will embarrass her into receding into the woodwork. As Wilson sees it, that refusal to quietly accept the hand she's been dealt is, for better or worse, who she is. "Unless you're someone who knows that you're never going to make more than $30,000 a year your whole life, it's hard for you to judge someone like Carrie," he said. "Carrie is the boldest woman I've ever known."

All of which made the team's preparations for transforming her into a happy member of the Suns family, particularly through a program for parents dreamed up by the younger Colangelo, unlikely, if not laughable. "The idea," said Colangelo, "is to bring everyone in for a weekend and put them up in a nice hotel. It will be sometime in the year; we're still working on the dates. This is not just for Carrie, and we're going to get them to realize what our organization is about, help them understand what we expect of their sons and what they should expect of their sons and what they should expect of life in the NBA."

Colangelo is particularly proud of the name he coined for his little retreat, which he has yet to hold. "I call it NBA Moms 101," he said.

After practice one afternoon, I followed Stoudemire and Michael Walker back to a small, stone-sided ranch house with palm trees out front that Stoudemire was renting in a nondescript upper-middle-class grid ten minutes from the arena. Except for the loaner Caddy in the garage — Stoudemire's Escalade was getting the requisite NBA $50,000 Gucci makeover — the place looked abandoned. The small pool in back was half-empty, the shades drawn, and the front yard burnt to a crisp.

Once inside, my hosts disappeared into their bedrooms so Stoudemire's pit bull and I could get acquainted. After a lonely morning in the back yard, JT had abandonment issues of her own. Beside herself, she bounded off the floor to paw my chest and root between my thighs with her stony prehistoric snout.

For distraction, I scanned the minimal furniture. A couch and chair faced a big-screen TV, and between them sat a stack of video games. The only personal effects were a handful of Polaroids of Stoudemire and his older brother posing in front of a phony backdrop of palm trees and sand taken last summer at a correctional facility in New York.

Since Hazell Jr. is also six-foot-ten, and seventy pounds heavier than his brother, the two are a formidable sight, particularly staring down over huge crossed forearms. Knowledgeable observers insist that it's still not clear who is the better player. Certainly, Hazell, whose nickname in high school was Baby Shaq, was more intimidating and, according to his mother, made Amare, himself on the aggressive end of the spectrum, seem like a puppy. Maybe that is how it goes for would-be entertainers from America's gladiatorial class. Exceed a certain level of aggressiveness, you become an inmate. Stay just on the right side of it, you get a sneaker contract.

Hazell, who is just twenty-six, may still be young enough to play pro basketball when he gets out, if not here then overseas, but he has never had his younger brother's passion for the game or capacity for sidestepping trouble. Burney Hayes, a Lake Wales cop who cared for Amare and Marwan during their mother's absences, blames adults who let him down for Hazell's difficulties. "Hazell learned at the wrong time how easy it was for him to make people back up," Hayes said. "And if he sees you're intimidated, oh, he's going to play on it."

When Stoudemire emerged from his room, he said we could talk while he and Walker played video games. Before I could object, he inserted a cartridge marked "Florida vs. Florida State" into his PlayStation2 console and collapsed on the couch, he and Walker instantly deep into the game.

On the court, Stoudemire gives nothing away, barely acknowledging his defender or even his own teammates. In his best games, he plays as if in a private fury, grabbing offensive rebounds off the backs of bewildered teammates and dunking on them almost as much as his opponents.

On his couch, he rarely took his eyes off the screen. "Amare has a hard time showing emotion," Wilson told me earlier. "You can tell when he's happy sometimes, but for the most part he always has the same look. A lot of time when he's angry, you won't actually know it unless he tells you." In her long conversation with the Suns coach, Carrie Stoudemire told him she hadn't seen her son cry since the afternoon when he was twelve and learned that his father had died.

There has been a lot of hand-wringing about throwing callow teenagers into the caldron of pro sports, but watching Stoudemire, joystick in hand, you could sense that his transition from Cypress Creek High School to the Western Conference had been the one easy segue in his uneasy life.

Rigors of the NBA? That workday consisted of a two-and-a-half-hour practice, much of it at the foul line, an assistant snapping the ball back to him after each shot so he wouldn't have to step off the stripe. After a shower, a quick check of his pager and both cell phones, ten minutes in his Cadillac listening to the latest bit of re-suscitated Tupac, he was back on his couch playing video games with a pal he's had since fourth grade.

What might have been perilous was going to college, where he would have had to share a room with strangers, go to classes he wasn't prepared for, and be stone-broke and surrounded by white people who weren't. Pro basketball is one of the few venues in which a poor African American can legally make a fortune without having to spend inordinate amounts of time with people whom Stoudemire segments into "hippies and rednecks" and don't think it's not the cherry on the cake of his day. In Stoudemire's house as well as the Suns locker room, the TV is tuned to BET, and in the car in between them, the music is always hip-hop or R&B. When we discussed a proposed reality show about his first year in the league, it became clear Stoudemire has never heard of Ozzy Osbourne.

But if adjusting to life in the NBA has been a minor challenge, getting there — a dream he had been burnishing since his first reverse dunk at thirteen — required one bold calculated gamble after another. Before he got to Phoenix, Stoudemire bounced through six high schools in three years, including two brief stops at Mount Zion Academy, the North Carolina basketball factory attended by Tracy McGrady. In the various accounts of Stoudemire's development, all this moving around is often characterized as an example of how the system betrays the young men it is supposed to help. But every time Stoudemire jumped ship, he was operating less like a student than like an ambitious CEO, willing to relocate as many times as it took to find the right situation. If coaches and basketball pimps were playing him for whatever they could get, he was working them just as hard. None of it was personal, just business.

When Stoudemire was declared academically ineligible as a freshman, Hayes had Stoudemire tested for a learning disability. Instead, the test confirmed something he and his wife suspected, which is that Stoudemire has an extremely high IQ. Though that intelligence may not have shown up in his high school transcripts, it is clear in the way he threaded his way through the land mines of his high school experience.

Entering the league out of high school is about aura as well as skill, and everything Stoudemire did, and managed not to do, for five years, including the decision to participate in an HBO pro-

gram about his checkered high school career, was a play for exposure. With a father in the ground, a mother in jail, and an older
brother heading there fast, Stoudemire never stopped plotting career moves.

An example came the summer before his senior year, when
Stoudemire abandoned the Adidas-sponsored camp for the one
sponsored by Nike. "That had never been done before," Stoudemire said, the slightest trace of a smile at the corner of his mouth,
"switching camps and going like that."

HBO implied that the jump was prompted by a timely visit to
Carrie Stoudemire at a Polk County jail by George Raveling, the
former USC coach turned Nike procurer. "That's bull, man,"
Stoudemire said in his startlingly deep voice, the truth of what he's
saying so transparent there's no need to emphasize it with eye contact. "She was incarcerated at the time, bro, and nobody was really
looking out for the fam, and Rav pays a visit and puts $100 in her
commissary. She didn't even get a chance to touch the money. He
put it in so she could buy snacks here and there, you know what I
mean? I was going to the Nike All-American regardless. I am trying
to go out of high school. On the AAU circuit, I was destroying
everybody. I don't mean to sound cocky or nothing, but I was doing
me. I figured if I go to the Nike camp and get the player of the
camp, I'd be the best player in the country, no question."

The most impressive part of his high school résumé was how he
handled himself after being declared ineligible his junior year by
the Florida High School Activities Association after a controversy
over his Mount Zion transcripts, which may have been doctored by
the school. In an entire year without basketball, he managed to stay
out of trouble almost entirely. His only infraction was a ten-day suspension for pretending to hurl a basketball at a gym teacher, who
was telling him to get off the court. She claimed that while Stoudemire had her in his sights, her life passed before her eyes.

To avoid the fate of so many around him, Stoudemire has
learned to seal out the world, as if by throwing a switch. By now it
has become so ingrained that his first reaction to any entreaty from
the outside world is "No," which can make him appear chilly and
absent. Unlike the Suns star point guard, Stephon Marbury, who
has been supporting more than a dozen friends and relatives since
he turned pro, Stoudemire has kept the purse strings tight. "A lot

of my family, I'm not going to support," he said. "You know why? 'Cause just yesterday, I was doing really bad, and they didn't support me. I wasn't doing too good just last year. They didn't think I was going to go out of high school. Now that I did, I had two cousins call from New York I never even saw before. I don't know how they got my number. They didn't really want me to send them money, but I could hear in their voice, the next time they call, it will be 'Well, I need a favor.' Well, I'm going to change my number before you even ask me."

Lake Wales is a Citrus Belt town of 12,000, some forty miles southwest of Orlando. The Stoudemires, Wilsons, and Palmores (Carrie's family) have lived there and known of one another for a couple of generations. On a hot morning a few weeks after I visited Amare in Phoenix, I drove by the corner house where Carrie lived as a child and the now-empty lot just off Lincoln Avenue, the barlined heart of the town's ghetto, where Amare's father, Hazell Sr., and his nine siblings lived. Amare's grandfather moved to Lake Wales from Alabama for work in a sawmill and was later stabbed to death at a card game on Christmas morning. My guide was Earnest Stoudemire, Amare's uncle and a semiretired police officer, who told me that when he returned from Vietnam and became a cop, Lincoln Avenue was where he got "his workout on Saturday night from the fights, shootings, and cuttings."

He also pointed to the lot where the house once stood in which Amare often lived with his father, a stylish, athletic man who had a couple of years of college and had just given up on a lawn business to sign on with a trucking company when he died at forty-one. "That still makes me mad," said Earnest, who survived a heart attack at thirty-nine. "The males in our family have a problem with high cholesterol. Hazell had been having chest pains and ignored them, and he knew better. If he was alive, he'd have two sons in the NBA right now, because he was the one who could control Hazell Jr."

The main drug corridor north from Miami, Highway 27, runs straight through Lake Wales and brought a crack epidemic that touched all three families and that at one point required Amare's uncle to arrest his younger brother, Hazell Sr. Years of harassment by Earnest and his colleagues have only succeeded in moving the crack trade a few blocks over to a desolate stretch that exudes a palpable menace even in blazing sunlight.

Earnest said that when he signed on with the police department, a black person had no hope of advancement, and despite a college degree, he didn't get a promotion for seventeen years. Eventually, a new chief came in with more egalitarian standards, and Earnest spent thirteen years as a homicide detective before becoming a captain, the highest black appointment in the department's history. Now, as a part-time officer, he does some pastoring and has an outreach ministry specializing in the eradication of evil spirits. He has performed some one thousand exorcisms.

Most of the black population of Lake Wales is settled now, but Carrie's and Artis's parents, like many of their generation, were migrants working the Florida orange groves in spring and the upstate New York fruit and vegetable farms in the summer. Although Carrie and Artis dated briefly in 1984, they didn't get together seriously until half a dozen years later, when they found they had both signed on for the same summer upstate apple-picking trip organized by Wilson's uncle.

The two were married from 1990 to 1995, spending much of that time in New York State around Middletown and Newburgh, where Wilson, who had dropped out of high school and joined the Navy, worked at a chemical factory and did maintenance at night. They never had any children, but all three of Carrie's sons spent time with them. Hazell Jr. got into his trouble when he was living with Wilson, and Amare and Marwan were with Carrie and him when, over a matter of months, each boy lost his father. Wilson has a record, too, which he described as "a little bit of everything."

Amare and his younger brother spent the last couple of years of their time in Lake Wales in a corner of Burney Hayes's trailer home behind the elementary school. Their life in Phoenix is a far cry from that, and for a while at least, Artis Wilson shared in the upgrade. The afternoon after I went to Amare's house, Wilson took me to pick up Marwan after school. He sat low behind the wheel of his two-tone DeVille, gold shades fighting off the desert sun, as he made the fifty-minute drive into Phoenix. Stoudemire's high school transfers may have been self-initiated, but the earlier upheavals were not. And for Marwan, who didn't have the dream of a pro career to sustain him, they were devastating.

"Marwan almost feels like he has to keep the family together," Wilson said. "When Carrie and I first got married, he couldn't sit and watch Carrie walk outside because he didn't know whether she was going to come back, and if she went outside, he would run to the door and cry. I was, like, 'Boy, sit down; she's just going to the telephone.' Over a period of time, you know it affected him more than it did Amare, but now he's going to be all right because all this is behind Carrie now, and they're coming into this new life and whole new lifestyle, and I don't think she's ever going to leave him again."

As soon as Amare, who wears a diamond-studded "Pinky" around his neck in solidarity with his brother's "Brain," signed his contract, he made it a priority to get Marwan's education on track. When Wilson and Marwan arrived in Phoenix last July, they were met at the airport by Frank Johnson and his wife, Amy, who took them to a few private schools she had researched based on Carrie Stoudemire's criteria. Her recommendation was St. Mary's in east-central Phoenix, based on its academic and athletic strength as well as its economic and racial diversity. Wilson concurred. The downside is the lengthy rush-hour commute from the townhouse Stoudemire is renting for Wilson and Marwan in Scottsdale.

"I get him up at six o'clock, make him some breakfast, and drive him to school," Wilson said. "Most of the time, I pick him up at 2:30. Sometimes he stays after school. Like today he has a detention because I got him there late. So that was my fault this time. We come back here. He takes a nap, gets something to eat, and at seven o'clock he goes to the Sylvan Learning Center. I get him from there at nine. We come back here, watch a little TV and talk a little bit, and go to sleep by ten."

When Wilson wasn't chauffeuring Marwan, he was on the phone. "We got three lines in the house and two cells," Wilson said, "and most of the time they're pretty busy." Carrie Stoudemire called a dozen times a day from minimum-security in Florida; the more restricted Hazell Jr., once a day from medium-security in New York. Stoudemire's windfall and prospect of long-term security has given an unexpected infusion of hope to each troubled member of his immediate family, and a lot of that hope is channeled by Wilson through the phone.

For Wilson, Carrie's arrival would be the first step in a staggered reunion that won't be complete until Hazell Jr., who is up for parole early next year, also makes it west. "I want to see their family when Carrie is here and his brother is here and they're all back together again," he said. "Because over the period of their lifetime, they have been through so much, and they had so much to overcome and so much adversity and so much that has gone wrong. You know, this to me is God's way of repaying them. Saying, you know, 'Hey, it was bad, but look at it now.' So the thing for me is to see them as a family again and look at them all together."

Wilson took particular pleasure in the conversations between Amare and Hazell Jr. "I love to hear them talk," he said. "Amare is very close to his brother. His brother gives him advice about girls, talks to him about playing on the court and just about life in general — watching out for people, his money, everything. Amare respects his brother's opinion and judgment about a lot of stuff."

As the Cadillac gobbles the miles, I asked Wilson if he thinks he and Carrie are getting back together. "No, I don't think so," Wilson said. "A lot of women that know her and know me, they think it might happen, but I don't think like that, and neither does Carrie. The love, as far as being intimate, it ain't there no more. As friends, she's my best friend, and I'm her best friend."

Wilson spoke of Amare's need to be wary of women who might want him for the wrong reasons. Wilson isn't overly concerned, because of all the people cautioning him about just that possibility. Then again, getting advice about love is like weatherproofing a shack against a hurricane. "When it hits, it hits," Wilson said with a gravelly laugh, "and that's it."

Romance is something Wilson knows a little about. He was not having trouble meeting women in Phoenix. "I meet them anywhere," he said. "If I'm at a red light, I see a pretty girl, I let my window down and speak, 'Hey, what's up?' I just have fun."

One afternoon, he walked into a clothing store and came out with the phone number of a petite woman going through a rough divorce, and it did not seem like a lark anymore. "I'm crazy about her," Wilson said.

We pulled off the highway, rolled down a side street, and found Marwan, in dress-code khakis and white button-down shirt, standing outside the school in an afternoon swirl of just-released students. He bade farewell to friends, hopped into the back seat, screwed his earrings back in, and was asleep before he could be asked to divulge a detail of his day.

Carrie Stoudemire did not make it out to Phoenix as quickly as planned. She wasn't on the Saturday red-eye out of Orlando or the Sunday or Monday morning flight either. And after five months in which she had burned up long-distance minutes with hourly check-ins from Lowell, she dropped out of phone contact soon after rolling out of the prison gates.

"About eleven in the morning, I called and spoke to the limo driver, who said she was in some store," Wilson said. "And she didn't call back until eight the next night."

With her NBA-playing son on a road trip, her urgency to get to Phoenix had apparently lifted. It wasn't until Tuesday afternoon that Wilson met Carrie's plane at the airport. From there, they picked up Marwan at St. Mary's and after dinner stopped by Amare's house, which Carrie found scandalously modest, because Carrie wanted to see JT. "She's crazy about that dog," Wilson said.

When the Suns returned from the road, the team put out the welcome mat for the mother of their Rookie of the Year candidate with a little party before a home game. According to Wilson, Carrie kept to herself, as she did when the team invited mothers onto the team plane for a short trip to the West Coast to play the Clippers. "Carrie wouldn't mingle," Wilson said. "She never has. She's a loner. She'll speak to the other mothers at games, but she's not going to become friends in the way that they will do stuff together."

As for relations with Wilson, all was quiet for a couple of weeks. When he would get back from dropping Marwan off at school, the two went out for late breakfasts or stayed around the house and talked and made frequent trips to the malls. There was a little testiness about Wilson dipping into an account not allocated for his expenses, but everything was essentially copacetic, he said, until she found out about the petite woman from the store.

Carrie and Wilson hadn't been a couple for years, but Carrie gave him the age-old ultimatum to stop seeing the woman or get out. By taking sole care of Marwan since July, freeing Amare to focus on basketball, Wilson had provided a crucial service to the Suns and Stoudemire, and though he had not received the salary he says he had been promised, he considered himself an employee of the family. "And I don't know too many employers who are going to tell you who to date," Wilson said. Two days before Christmas, a female friend he had made in town offered her couch. "If it wasn't for her," he said, "I'd be sleeping under a bridge."

For Wilson, it was a precipitous fall. Overnight, he lost his home, car, and good Suns tickets and was summarily cut off by all four Stoudemires. Even Michael Walker froze him out. But the low point, he said, was when Carrie had Marwan call to tell him, "You ain't never done nothing for me."

Only Frank Johnson, the coach, and his wife, Amy, showed flickers of conscience, Wilson said, offering leads for jobs at the Phoenix airport, one of which he eventually got, and still comping him tickets to games, although they were on the far side of the arena. But Amy Johnson, who earlier in the year would talk on the phone with Wilson for two hours at a time, was in an impossible position and gradually stopped returning his calls. (The Johnsons now deny ever helping him with the job or tickets.)

And with his link to celebrity severed, Wilson lost his allure to the sales clerk. "When I was with Amare," Wilson recalled, amazed by his own naïveté, "she would make it her business to somehow get out to Scottsdale." Now that he was working the graveyard shift at National Car Rental and living in a little studio two blocks from her place, she wanted to slow things down.

Meanwhile, according to friends of the family in Phoenix and Lake Wales, Marwan had stopped attending school when Wilson moved out. When the team left town again for a six-game trip that passed through Orlando, Carrie followed them on the road and took Marwan with her. By the time she got back, she had resolved to move closer to Amare's place and saw no point in having Marwan go back to St. Mary's. "I remember coming by the house one day," Wilson said, "and seeing Marwan sitting around playing Sega. I said, 'Why are you not in school?' He just looked at me with a little smile."

Even with the tutoring, Marwan struggled at St. Mary's, and perhaps it wasn't the best school for him. But another disruption seemed to be the last thing he needed.

After pushing Wilson out of the picture, Carrie set about dealing with her son's other personal connections, like his agent, John Wolf. Wolf had been an unlikely candidate to have landed a rookie as prominent as Stoudemire. But throughout his working life, Wolf has shown a knack for seeing business opportunities in hard-pressed pockets. He invested part of the money he made from representing Dee Brown, his first NBA client, in a small chain of coin-operated laundries, and after selling that, bought a huge liquor store with a dozen cash registers in Minneapolis. Brown, who worked for the Orlando Magic after he retired and got to know the Stoudemire family, recommended Wolf to Amare.

In the time allotted to him, Wolf did an excellent job, skillfully steering Stoudemire to Phoenix, whose young team he thought was the best fit. And in a climate in which sneaker money was scarce for all but a handful of street-minded superstars, Wolf extracted from Nike a deal guaranteeing more than $1 million a year for three years. "It wasn't a good contract," Wolf told me over the phone from his office at the liquor store. "It was a *great* contract."

But it wasn't good enough for Carrie Stoudemire, and perhaps in the wake of Nike signing this year's high-schooler, LeBron James, to a $90 million contract, she's right. When she told Wolf to go back to Nike for more, Wolf remembered why he had invested his share of Dee Brown's Reebok money in those laundries and quit. According to someone close to the team, Wolf felt sufficiently abused to want to quit weeks before, but he had been talked out of it by the Suns. It is crucial for a team to have a buffer between it and the player so that it can exert influence over him without becoming the direct object of his contempt. For the Suns, the prospect of having to deal with Carrie every time they have an issue with Amare is terrifying.

Especially since, at this point, Carrie Stoudemire may be in a fouler humor than when she checked into Lowell Correctional. Despite the fairy-tale improvement in her family's fortunes, her four decades of personal catastrophe follow her everywhere she goes. In a brief phone interview, the only one she would allow, she summarized her outrage. "My life," she said, "is not a joke."

In that same conversation, which took place shortly after she arrived in Phoenix, Carrie Stoudemire had already found plenty not to like about her son's new employers. "I can't talk to you," she said, "because I'll tell you the truth about these people." Besides, she said, she has to save her story for a major cable channel, which is planning a documentary on her life.

With Carrie Stoudemire ensconced in Phoenix and Hazell Jr. set to arrive in town as early as next year, those two troubled family members could become the most delicate challenges in Stoudemire's career. Unlike Eminem, who has been so unforgiving of his imperfect mom, Stoudemire sees every line on his mother's rap sheet as proof of her commitment to provide for her family. He defiantly refers to her as "my role model," "my heart and soul," and someone who "was always there even when she wasn't" and "had my back through thick and thin." But what Stoudemire is thinking and what he tells reporters may not be the same. According to Wilson, who when last I spoke to him had begun spending time with Marwan and Carrie again, Stoudemire has already expressed interest in having his mother move to Florida or New York.

Just before the end of an early-winter practice, the Suns unlocked the doors to their pristine practice courts in the bowels of America West Arena and let in beat reporters for their routine look-see of the team. For the next ten minutes, all that could be heard in this subterranean chapel of basketball was the squeak of sneakers and the pock of basketballs.

Working with a trainer, a shirtless Marbury strengthened his release by taking tiny two- or three-foot shots with a medicine ball. At another hoop, the team's rookie swingman, Casey Jacobsen, fired up three-pointers. On a third basket, Stoudemire, wearing a black sleeveless T-shirt, black Nikes, and his trademark rubber band on his left wrist, was throwing up baby hooks, casual jumpers, and finger rolls. He was bouncing up and down so effortlessly that it seemed as if the energy that propelled him upward, higher than perhaps any other player can go, was coming from right out of the floor.

In Lake Wales, Burney Hayes told me that for Amare the court became a sanctuary and the ball itself a tangible piece of salvation. "She's a little bald-headed girl," Hayes said. "She won't complain; she just sustain. Bounce her, and she comes back. All she wants is more." And watching Stoudemire gamboling around the court, skinny legs tapering up to a thick chest and huge arms, I could see why he was so upset about being banished from that high school court. But now he had his own perfect court, and nobody was ever going to shoo him off it.

For Stoudemire, the court remains, as it probably always has been, a refuge from family turmoil. But Carrie, Hazell Jr., and Marwan gave Amare more than something to flee from. They not only gave him a desperate need to succeed, and to succeed quickly, but the precocious maturity to handle it when he did. By the time he was thirteen and his arms and legs started morphing like a cartoon superhero's, he knew that his body was not only his own best hope but also the last and only chance for his mother and two brothers.

Safely ensconced in the league, Stoudemire quickly proved that he was a hard-nosed competitor, and by the time he scored thirty-eight points against Kevin Garnett and the Timberwolves and then grabbed twenty-one rebounds against the Grizzlies, he had answered all the big questions. He was more than good enough, and his skills would translate into wins for a Suns team that went on to make the playoffs and even managed to take two games from the San Antonio Spurs in the first round. As far as basketball is concerned, the greatest suspense left is whether he will develop his left hand and a medium-range jumper. After all he has been through, it hardly matters how that part of the story turns out.

The question with something real riding on it is whether Stoudemire's success will be of lasting benefit to the beleaguered family members who did so much to inspire it. Amare can pay for all the things they have never had, but in the end, it may turn out that Carrie, Marwan, and Hazell Jr. did more indirectly for Amare than his money can do for them. In their way, they prepared him for, and sped him toward, his future.

At the very end of the practice session, Amare stepped to the stripe for his daily dose of foul shots. For a player who goes to the basket as hard as Stoudemire does, foul shooting is important, and this year he only shot 66 percent. But at practice, he knocked them down like a seasoned pro. It would have been hard for anyone but an expert to spot the flaws. Clearly, there is nothing much wrong with any part of Stoudemire's game or his head, and his success has once again tilted NBA priorities. Just ask Lebron James, the fatherless eighteen-year-old with an astounding vertical leap, whose mother bought him a Hummer with money she didn't have. Had it not been for Stoudemire, Nike would never have gambled $90 million to sign James to a sneaker deal, and the Cleveland Cavaliers would not be nearly so thrilled to be making him the number-one pick this week. Thanks to Stoudemire, talented American high-schoolers from the worst neighborhoods are just what NBA general managers are looking for again.

LISA OLSON

Making a Play for Players

FROM THE NEW YORK DAILY NEWS

CHICAGO AT THE MOMENT is swarming with millionaires — you can hear the sound of platinum credit cards brushing against mahogany — and Sheila Dent is on the prowl.

She emerges from a top-end hair salon, fingering the spun gold extensions that have literally been sewn, like delicate embroidery, into her scalp. They cost $3,000, and they are *fine*. The shoes are Manolos, four-inch daggers that cause her calves to twitch, the skirt is centimeters away from danger, and the silicone has been paid in full by a very famous baseball player who is at this very moment napping in a hotel on the higher end of Michigan Avenue.

"I could afford them myself," Dent says of her new breasts. "But he owed me. I'm ready to trade up." In ballplayers, she means.

Dent is a trust-fund baby, college-educated, a self-advertised modern-day Gloria Steinem. She travels in limousines, stays at the Four Seasons, and generously finances her girlfriends so they might accompany her on these pleasure hunts. Debby Johnson, Dent's best gal, is in major-league debt, owing nearly six figures to the banks, but a girl's got to support her habit. She has taken goddess classes, developed a mean swing in the Chelsea Pier batting cages, teaches fitness training, and is so beautiful it is frightening.

Her body is adorned with gifts from two big-time sports studs: diamonds in her ears, and an emerald bracelet on her right ankle that skims a tattoo of the number 49. Why 49? "It was his high school number," she says. "He changed it when he made it out of Double A."

He is playing tonight across town in the All-Star Game. His wife, parents, and three children will be in prime box seats, where the TV cameras can capture their adorableness. Johnson and Dent have mapped out their own seats, at the team's hotel bar, where later, when the perfect family is tucked away, there will be no danger of running into the missus.

They are predators, they are dreamers. They are two women in their early thirties who met in a baseball chat room, kindred spirits discovering they shared a single-minded pursuit.

Connoisseurs of sports and sex are hardly a new phenomenon; the choreographed bump-and-grind can be traced to Maximus's bedsheets. Wilt Chamberlain and his tales of twenty thousand women pushed the dance into the public domain, and now we barely go a minute without hearing about some athlete and his unchecked zipper.

The modern sports groupie is both high-tech and old-fashioned, generally abiding by ground rules not of their making. It's a world where wives are conditioned to look the other way, where adultery is condoned, where women are taught that dating a powerful male athlete is a noble achievement.

Player culpability, an athlete's responsibility, is often a lost art. Jeremy Shockey, the Giants' tight end, ratted out his married teammates when he told *Maxim* magazine that some had girlfriends in other cities — a claim his teammates were quick to shout down.

Dent plops herself onto a bar stool. Half a bottle of Shiraz later, the game ends and there is a rustle in the Westin lobby. Dent thinks she has it all figured out: she has turned men into sexual objects, into her little trophies.

"Deb was the first one who didn't judge me," says Dent. "I offered to help pay for some of her trips. We look out for each other 'cause it can be rough out there, you know?"

Dangers Galore

The risk for both parties goes much deeper than getting caught. There are communicable diseases, planned and unplanned pregnancies, consensual encounters that turn violent, false accusations that become dowries. Lives are ruined, zipper by zipper.

One blackmail scam in recent years involved a con man who

hired attractive women. They would meet baseball players in a bar, lure them to a hotel room, and slip them a drug that would render them unconscious.

"Then," says an FBI agent who investigated the ring, and lectures players about it during spring training, "she'd open the door for her co-conspirator, they'd undress the player and take pictures of him in what we call compromising positions with other men. The player wakes the next day — other than a headache, he has no idea what happened."

Until the manila folder arrives in the mail. One Yankee confirms details offered by the FBI agent: inside the folder are copies of the photos, and a typed letter saying they will be distributed to gossip columns unless $250,000 is sent to a certain bank account. "I think the guys pay the money and pretend it never happened," says the Yankee, who did not want to be identified.

"I Want to Make a Date"

The NBA, a high-octane synergy of monied athletes and hip music, would be the envy of Caligula, especially during All-Star week, when the host city is awash in perfume and pheromones. Even lonely winters on the road offer b-ballers afternoon delights, as Clippers forward Elton Brand discovered. He checks in under aliases, but anonymity is an easy code to crack for those with a purpose.

"I'm in my hotel room, relaxing, when this woman calls. She was, like, 'I see you're coming to my city in March. I want to make a date.' Damn. I don't even know her, and she's looking three months ahead for a hookup," says Brand.

There is another woman, he says, who has taken devotion to a higher, more frightening level. She sends mountains of faxes and e-mails, detailing intimate desires and threats. The authorities are involved, he says; maybe she'll just go away.

Steven Ortiz, assistant professor of sociology at Oregon State University, has studied the culture of groupies and its primary enabler — male entitlement.

"'Groupie' is a male term used to objectify, sexualize, subordinate, or stigmatize women in the hypermasculine world of male sports," says Ortiz, who has interviewed the wives of forty-eight professional athletes for a book he is writing.

"Being with a celebrity provides entry to a world that is otherwise off-limits," says Ortiz. "There are some women who are so desperate to be a part of these worlds that they will often allow themselves to be treated like sex objects."

Men who obsessively follow female athletes are generally referred to, simply, as stalkers, and according to law enforcement officials, are far more likely to be treated unkindly. Two WNBA players have restraining orders against male fans. Female tennis players — including Serena Williams and Martina Hingis — attract a fair share of psychotic Lotharios.

Meanwhile, the women get more daring in their pursuits.

Drowning in Letters

Sitting in front of his locker at Shea, Cliff Floyd nods toward the floor, where an ankle-high stack of correspondence remains unopened. "Pictures so explicit, I don't even want to tell you about them," he says. "I get maybe twenty a month. Some guys might respond. They rationalize it, like she might be a future wife. Sure. She might also be a stalker and drug you and do whatever."

He no longer tells his girlfriend about the, um, fan mail. "We both know the trust level has to begin at 100 percent," he says, "and that's where I plan to keep it."

Some female fans have innocent infatuations, harmless hobbies. There are, for instance, several women who have trailed Todd Zeile from team to team. They share pictures on websites devoted to all things Todd and, during batting practice, wave license plates proclaiming their love.

From her home in California, Nikki, a self-proclaimed Zeilot, says she has followed Todd since his days as a Dodger "because he is truly one of the nicest people I've ever met. Todd does not disappoint the fans."

The adoration is minuscule compared with the high heat aimed at some of Zeile's former Yankee teammates.

"The money, the exposure — there's a strange dynamic surrounding celebrities," says Zeile, who recently signed with the

Expos. "The more unaccessible you become, the more aggressive people are in trying to get near you. Especially this team. You can see they try to keep a safe distance from the fans."

Keeping Careful Watch

It is a Sunday afternoon in Boston, Zeile is still a Yankee. The Bombers are the first of any professional sports team to employ two ex-cops as full-time security guards. On the road, the club has explicit deals with five-star hotels in which rules for other guests are laid out, including no cameras in the lobby.

"People check into our hotel assuming they have the right to have access to the players," says Jerry Levering, director of team security. "There are a few of our very popular players who refuse to go out at night. We have the standard pool of groupies — men and women — that follow us from city to city. I recognize who they are and make sure they're not a threat to the players."

The Yankee caravan is surrounded by an impenetrable ring of force, but there are at least three hundred fans blocking the sidewalks that circle the Ritz.

"You'd think the Beatles were in town," says one Yankee. He does not know it, but Ringo Starr, incognito in a baseball cap, has just walked through the lobby, unrecognized.

Outside, a pudgy man wearing a Jeter shirt tramples two kids so he can pound on the team bus. A woman, her mascara running in sticky rivulets, her yellow hot pants as sheer as gossamer, says she paid $500 for a room the night before — not that it did any good.

"I even asked the room service waiter to help me out, but he refused," says the woman, who gives her name as Jill. "I had a list of guys I would have settled for."

As the bus pulls away from the curb, leaving crying, sweating, delirious fans in its fumes, Jill leans against a pole and admits she has trained diligently for this sort of moment. At the University of Maryland, where she majored in finance, she was a Black-Eyed Susan — a name for the hostesses who help the school recruit potential athletes. It's very important, explains Jill, to have life goals. "Guaranteed," she says, "in five years I'll be married to a Yankee."

CARLTON STOWERS

Friday Night Lite

FROM THE DALLAS OBSERVER

THEY ARE VISIBLE on the flatland horizon from miles away, rural beacons signaling that the fall ritual of Texas high school football is again under way. Down Farm Road 308, past the sprawling cotton fields and sun-browned pastureland that dot this region south of Dallas, the Friday-night stadium lights are luring fans to a game that is more special than any other on the schedule.

On this September evening in the tiny pickup truck–and-gimme-cap hamlet of Penelope, where they play a strange and fast-paced game called six-man football, it is homecoming.

Though rain clouds are moving in and kickoff is still almost an hour away, members of the hometown Wolverines, eleven youngsters whose weights range from the heft of a 200-pound senior to a wispy 130-pound freshman, are already in their bright red uniforms and white helmets, going through the pregame ritual. That too many practice passes are dropped, punts seldom spiral, and team speed is noticeable only by its absence doesn't seem to concern the hometown fans filing into the stands or leaning against the chain-link fence that surrounds a playing field that was a pasture for grazing cattle only a year ago.

On this evening, in fact, twenty-seven-year-old Corey McAdams, ever the optimist, believes his team, the perennial doormat of District 16 throughout his brief coaching career, just *might* have a chance to win. This despite an arm-long list of disadvantages he and the inexperienced players he coaches must contend with.

The game they play here is different. Of the estimated 10 million fans who turn out to see high school football in Texas each year, only a small percentage has seen or is even aware of the hybrid sport. Its rules differ considerably from those applied on fields where the traditional eleven-man game is played.

Six-man football is played on a field eighty yards long rather than the customary one hundred; offenses must travel fifteen yards for a first down rather than ten; a kicked touchdown conversion is worth two points and one if accomplished by run or pass; and a successful field goal earns the kicker four points rather than three. Six-man teams play ten-minute quarters instead of the twelve in the eleven-man game, and all players, center included, are eligible to receive passes. In an effort to avoid embarrassment to squads of lesser talent, there is a rule that says if one team is leading by as many as forty-five points at any time after the half, the game is ended.

It is wide-open and hard-hitting, part flag football with open-field tackles, part Arena League and heavy on end sweeps and bombs. Scores generally resemble those tallied at basketball games. And, as one of the adult railbirds watching warm-ups explains, "In six-man, if you ain't got speed, you're in big trouble."

It was only four years ago that the Penelope Independent School District, the sixteenth-poorest school district in the state, revived a football program that had been dormant for thirty-seven years. It made the decision to muster a team even before it had such basic necessities as uniforms, a coach, or even a field on which to play.

This season, however, the two seniors, two juniors, four sophomores, and five freshmen who make up the Wolverine squad are playing in a manicured and well-lighted stadium funded by grant money and a sizable bank loan, awaiting the kickoff of the third game of the new season. All that's missing is a tradition of winning.

Which is not to say that Penelope High School students haven't had their moments. Inside the nearby red brick school building, built as a WPA project in 1939, a bulging trophy case tells of past achievements. There's the picture of a smiling group of teenagers who won the 1954 state girls' basketball championship and large plaques attesting that PHS performed the best one-act play in Texas in both '51 and '76. District champions in this, regional winners in that. But you've got to search in a far corner to find the lone evidence of football glory — a game ball from the team's only win since it returned to competition. It is inscribed with the score

(Penelope 32, Cranfills Gap 20), the year (2001), and the signatures of those who played in the historic game.

That Cranfills Gap is again the opponent on this night in 2003 is not lost on any of the 211 people who call Penelope home.

———————————

In the parking lot, Superintendent Harley Johnson is busy at his regular Friday-night job directing traffic. Only a few parking spaces remain with kickoff forty-five minutes away. Smiling as he looks to the clearing skies, Johnson predicts the largest crowd of the season.

Michelle Joslin, mother of two of the players, notices the number of people making their way toward the stadium and instructs her aides in the concession stand to be prepared to sell more nachos, popcorn, and soft drinks than usual. In the deer blind–sized press box, watching the stands fill, school board member and Penelope High alumnus Karen Osborne is nervously awaiting the moment she will be called on to sing an a cappella version of the national anthem.

On the field, Coach McAdams's Wolverines stop their warm-ups to count the number of Cranfills Gap players coming out of the dressing room. Unlike most nights, when the opposition has far more in uniform, they see that the visiting team has brought only eleven. That's a good sign.

Penelope, named after the daughter of a Great Northern Railroad official who founded the community in 1902 as a watering stop for passing steam engines, was not always the ghost town it is today. Longtime postmistress Mary Dvorak remembers her mother telling stories of a thriving town that once included three grocery stores, three hotels, seven churches, a lumberyard, a pharmacy with a doctor's office upstairs, a feed and hardware store, an ice house, three active cotton gins, and a depot.

Showing a collection of faded pictures of Penelope as it once was, Dvorak notes that her tiny post office is now the only business left, flanked by weather-worn and boarded-up buildings that run the one-block length of what was once called "downtown." "There's no mystery to what happened here," the lifelong resident explains. "In 1960 the railroad shut down, and cotton was no longer king." That devastating one-two punch sent shoppers and job-seekers to nearby Hillsboro, Waco, and Dallas. Today, with the exception of a small residential area inside the city limits, most of the residents whose mail she handles live in the countryside, farming their land and sending their children off to school by bus every morning.

Even inside the city limits, the only paved streets are the intersecting farm roads that run through it.

"Still," she says, "it's a wonderful place to live. After I graduated from high school, I moved up to Dallas for a couple of years. But I got enough of the big city real quick. I came home, and I've never been sorry I did. Like I've told my kids, I'm going to be here until they take me to the cemetery."

And, she adds, she'll continue to be a regular at the Wolverine football games, win or lose. "We're proud of those young men. They may not be winning much, but they're building something for the little ones down in elementary school and junior high."

Which is how Superintendent Johnson views things. Penelope discontinued football following its 1963 season. "Frankly," he says, "the idea of us playing again never entered my mind until the spring of '99, when a student named Marvin Hill came into my office. He said he'd been sent by several of the boys in school to ask if we could have a football team. I told him to bring me a list of names of those interested in playing. He did, so I took the request to the school board."

The decision to add the sport came easy; putting the idea in motion didn't. "I don't think we even had a football, much less any equipment," Johnson remembers. Nor did the school have a stadium or anyone to coach the youngsters, who had never played the game on an organized level.

Johnson resolved each problem methodically. He persuaded members of the community to donate money needed for equipment and talked an old friend, Clifton Darden, retired and living in nearby Hubbard, into coaching the team. (Though he'd never coached the six-man game, Darden's credentials were noteworthy. At Sealy High, he'd tutored former SMU great and NFL Hall of Famer Eric Dickerson.) The stadium problem was resolved when Johnson suggested that Darden draw up a schedule with nothing but road games.

"Honestly," the superintendent says, "my thinking was to wait and see if the kids would stick with it before we went to the expense and effort of building our own football field." Last year the school purchased a two-acre pasture adjacent to the campus and, with a great deal of volunteer help, was soon planting grass, building stands, and erecting lights.

While the team was winless that first season, scoring only twenty points in ten games, it was not without its poetic moments. The first Penelope touchdown of the new era was scored by Hill, the kid who'd urged Johnson to reinstate the game. In the second season came the school's first and, to date, only win. By then, a substitute teacher named Corey McAdams was serving as a volunteer assistant to Darden.

A year later, with his teaching credentials in order, McAdams replaced Darden as head coach.

As the kickoff nears, fifth-grade teacher April McAdams, wife of the coach, is hurrying some forty elementary school youngsters to one end of the field. She calls them "The Bleacher Creatures," and it was her idea that they form a "victory line" that the teams run through onto the field. Amid youthful, high-pitched cheers, she explains that it's a way the kids too young to play can be participants. Now, she points out, during daily recess periods, the grade-school boys choose sides for quick games of football, talking of the day they'll become full-fledged Wolverines.

Since Penelope High has no band, it had never bothered to adopt a school song. So April McAdams took it upon herself to persuade officials at nearby China Springs High School to let it "borrow" theirs.

And, once the elementary kids are back in the stands with their parents and the school song has been sung (". . . The friends we've made while going here will last our whole life through / So to Penelope High and the Wolverines we pledge our hearts anew . . ."), April McAdams will be on the sidelines, clipboard in hand, keeping statistics for her husband.

Corey McAdams is no stranger to the religious fervor generated by schoolboy football in Texas. Son of a coach, he quarterbacked his dad's Sudan High team to the state championship in the mid-'90s, then went off to play college ball at Abilene's Hardin-Simmons University. After graduating with a communications degree, he took a job as promotions director at a local television station but after a couple of years realized his love for the game remained. As he'd been doing all his life, he sought the counsel of Royce McAdams. His dad suggested a career of teaching and coaching, and the son went in search of a new livelihood.

His quest would lead him to a town he'd never even heard of, to coach a brand of football he knew little about. "Before I could even start helping Coach Darden," he admits, "I had to learn the rules of the game." Like the players he now coaches, McAdams started from scratch.

The game his team plays is reserved for 102 of the state's public high schools with an enrollment of 99 students or fewer, and the battlegrounds are whistle-stop communities only a short drive from Dallas that would try the geographical knowledge of lifelong Texans — Buckholts, Coolidge, and Aquilla; Calvert, Milford, and Bynum — and the adversaries are teams of Indians, Bulldogs, and Bobcats often drilled by one-man coaching staffs. (Fellow teachers Phillip Esparza and Charles Bellows assist McAdams.) Many play on poorly lighted fields bare of grass, circled by trucks and cars filled with fans who view their weekly games through windows freshly cleaned at Gus' Grocery and Gulf. A 150-pound halfback scores a touchdown, and his effort is greeted by a chorus of honking horns.

Out in the hinterlands, where bleachers might accommodate a hundred spectators, where there are rarely enough students to field a band at halftime and admission is only three bucks, there is a strong argument to be made that rural America offers up organized sport at its purest.

"I think it's pretty obvious that our kids play for the simple enjoyment of the game, of being a member of a team," McAdams says. "It's important to them, and they work hard at it, but they're not out here in hopes of some day playing at the college level or becoming a big pro star. Having a football team is fun for the school, fun for the townspeople."

Penelope's growing enthusiasm for the game lends support to his observation. While things such as late-evening farm chores prevent organization of an official booster club like those found in most towns, McAdams is one of the few coaches in the state whose players' parents were willing to donate the money necessary to buy equipment and uniforms. He also has at his disposal someone like school board member Willie Harlin, who volunteers to scout upcoming opponents, returning with such data as the formations, heights, and weights of the next week's opponents. Harlin films the Wolverine games with his own hand-held video camera, providing McAdams and his players an opportunity to review and learn from their performances.

So while school board members in Philadelphia questioned the worth of athletics in its thirty-eight public schools a few years back and Los Angeles eliminated junior high football in the name of economics, Penelope fields a junior high and high school team with an operational budget that wouldn't even keep Highland Park High School in footballs.

"Our football program," says Superintendent Johnson, "is not a financial burden, thanks to the interest and support of the towns-people." While he'll not disclose how much McAdams earns above his base teaching salary for coaching football in the fall and track in the spring, rest assured it is light-years shy of the $90,000 report-edly earned annually by the head coach at perennial Class AAAA powerhouse Stephenville High.

In addition to coaching both the high school and junior high football teams, McAdams also directs the boys' and girls' track teams in the spring (despite the handicap of not having a running track). Toss in that he lines the field for home games, launders his players' uniforms, teaches a full course schedule (speech and health), serves as scorekeeper at home games during basketball season, and assumes an after-school bus route once football season has ended, and it's easy to see that he earns every penny the Penelope Independent School District pays him.

Patience, says the superintendent, is Coach McAdams's greatest virtue. "He recognizes the fact that our kids are far behind those they're competing against. The teams we're playing are made up of boys who have been in football at least since junior high, some as early as elementary school. They know all of the basics; they under-stand the importance of practice and teamwork. Our kids are still learning what the game's all about."

"When we first started," McAdams says, "I don't think many of our kids had any idea what they were up against. None of them had ever seen a football practice, and they didn't even know how to put on the equipment." Those who occasionally miss an after-school practice to help haul hay or drive a load of cows to auction have no understanding of the disruption their absence might cause. In Penelope, priorities are a bit different.

So McAdams resigns himself to preaching realistic goals: weekly improvement, minimizing mistakes, and striving to play beyond the first half (a goal it has accomplished in two of its three games this season). "Last week," McAdams says, "when we scored twenty-five points [in a 70–25 loss to Walnut Springs], I felt it was a major step forward.

"It's hard, but it's fun," he says. "I can't deny that it isn't difficult to take the beatings we do, but the pluses far outweigh the minuses."

If there is any criticism of the young coach or his less-than-gifted players, it is difficult to find. Parents Michelle and Tracy Joslin left Duncanville in 1999, fed up with the crime and hectic pace of the Dallas area. They purchased a four-hundred-acre cattle ranch outside Penelope and enrolled their two boys in the rural school. Morgan, now a senior, and Mason, a sophomore, enjoy being a part of the team.

"The kids here," Michelle says, "are really close. And they think the world of Coach McAdams." It also pleases her that in Penelope High's history there has never been an incident involving drugs or firearms on the school's campus. She puts the current state of the infant Wolverines into perspective: "Ask any of these boys to drive a tractor or do some welding or load cattle into a trailer, and they know exactly how to get it done. But until recently, football was something completely foreign to them. But they're learning . . . and trying."

One of the goals McAdams sets for his players is to "not get forty-five-pointed." Unfortunately, the Wolverines don't achieve their objective of completing four quarters very often. The week before, the game was called early in the fourth after a Walnut Springs touchdown extended the margin to 70–25. (Which is quite an improvement over how things were back in 1958, when Venus High scored 110 points against the Wolverines *in the first half.*)

In the four seasons the Wolverines have competed, not a single college coach has dropped by to watch a practice or attend a game. Johnson and McAdams are, however, quick to point out that Mario Herrera, the center on last year's 0–10 team and one of the star performers in school secretary Gloria Walton's one-act play troupe, did receive a drama scholarship to Lon Morris College in Jacksonville, Texas.

An elderly farmer who hasn't missed a Wolverines game since the school's return to football leans against the fence surrounding the field, looking up into the crowded stands on the home side of the field. Mums, some as big as dinner plates, are worn by mothers and girlfriends alike. Several grade-school girls are dressed in uniforms similar to those worn by the six Penelope cheerleaders.

"This," the farmer says after several minutes of silence, "is the most I've ever seen at a game. I'd say 250, maybe 300."

Either guess exceeds the town's population.

Six-man football began in 1934, the brainchild of a Chester, Nebraska, educator and coach named Stephen Epler, who recognized a void in the fall programs of small rural schools. Searching for a solution, he went to the drawing board and designed a football game that would not require the customary eleven players. A game could be played, he theorized, with three linemen instead of seven, and three backs instead of four.

As word of his new concept spread, so did interest. States throughout the Midwest adopted Epler's plan, and in 1938, Rodney Kidd, then athletic director of the University Interscholastic League, governing body of high school sports, wrote Epler for information on the game.

Kidd then contacted coaches at two small Texas schools, Prairie Lea and Martindale, and asked that they study the rules, have their kids practice for a while, and then put on a spring exhibition game for UIL officials.

He and other UIL officials liked what they saw, and the following fall the formerly nonfootball schools Dripping Springs, Harrold, and Oklaunion and the two teams that had staged the spring exhibition were celebrating their first district championships.

By halftime, Penelope freshman running back Weston Walton has scored a touchdown, but Cranfills Gap — bigger, faster, and clearly more talented — has built a 25–6 lead. The oncoming defeat, however, is put aside briefly as candidates for homecoming queen, ignoring the fact that the muddy field is certain to soil the long dresses they're wearing, are escorted to midfield by members of the team.

Smiling nervously, the girls pose for one of those yearbook moments that will be remembered long after the score.

Six-man football's popularity reached a national peak in 1953 when thirty thousand teams across the country competed in the sport. And while consolidation of rural schools ultimately turned the sport into nothing more than scrapbook memories for many states, it continues to thrive not only in Texas but in New Mexico, Montana, Colorado, Kansas, Nebraska, and throughout Canada.

Today, in fact, it is no longer the sole property of small towns. The growth of urban private schools and the desire to provide their students with athletic opportunities have given rise to seventy-four new six-man football teams in Texas alone.

And while the list of six-man graduates who've gone on to make names for themselves on a higher athletic plane is admittedly short, there have been exceptions. Jack Pardee, once the rage of little Christoval High, went on to earn national recognition as a fullback for Paul "Bear" Bryant at Texas A&M in the '50s, then enjoyed a lengthy pro career with the Washington Redskins. And more recently, a gifted Amherst running back named DeWayne Miles, who scored forty touchdowns in the six-man playoffs alone, enjoyed a record-setting career at Canyon's West Texas A&M in the late '90s before playing briefly in the NFL. It should also be pointed out that *Survivor* star Colby Donaldson got his first taste of competition as number 88 on Christoval's six-man Cougars, and Dallas photographer Laura Wilson, mother of well-known actors Owen and Luke, has a picture book, *Grit and Glory: Six-Man Football,* due out next month from Bright Sky Press. Wilson spent a season visiting small-town games, gathering black-and-white images.

If there's an ultimate authority on the sport, it is Austin's Granger Huntress, thirty-eight-year-old communications manager for the U.S. Tennis Association and keeper of a website devoted to scores, schedules, and rankings of Texas six-man football. His knowledge of the game is encyclopedic. Want to know the score of the 1979 six-man state championship game between Milford and Cotton Center? Huntress can give it to you off the top of his head. He'll tell you that tiny Marathon, in the Big Bend, once enjoyed a fifty-game winning streak but, alas, this year had to forfeit all of its games since just three players reported for the team. Remember '95, when little Mullin High, out in West Texas, played a Colorado school from Weldon Valley for the mythical six-man national championship? Huntress was there, roaming the sidelines.

Recently he rushed home from the U.S. Open Tennis Championships in New York to keep alive his routine of seeing at least one six-man game every weekend. Sometimes he manages to see several. "I try to see at least fifteen or twenty games a season," he says. His travel plans are Lone Star State–simple. "I look for the good games that will be played near some place I can get good barbecue," he says. The color and atmosphere of the rural sport fascinate him. "All the wonderful clichés are there: community pride, school spirit, good people. I love it."

And, ironically, the sport he religiously follows is thriving — but for a negative reason: small-town Texas continues to vanish, swallowed up by economic hard times and the lure of urban life. "What has happened to Penelope is a textbook example of what is happening to so many rural towns. Farming is no longer very profitable, and the job market has dried up, so people move to the city to find work. Suddenly the school enrollment is so small that it is no longer possible to field an eleven-man football team. So they drop down to six-man."

Each year, he says, he sees more and more schools with marginal enrollment downsizing to the six-man game.

Many missed tackles, fumbles, and dropped passes have contributed to the Wolverines' third lopsided defeat of the season. As the crowd winds its way toward the parking lot, Corey McAdams gathers his players at midfield. He briefly reprimands a frustrated player who has thrown his helmet onto the ground in disgust, then his voice turns soft. His comments are focused more on the brief signs of improvement than a ranting recap of mistakes. "We're making progress," he says. "We've just got to keep working."

Nearby, April McAdams shakes her head. "I know he's disappointed," she whispers. "He really thought this was a game they had a chance of winning." A week later, while playing Iredell, the Penelope team reached one of the goals Coach McAdams had set. The Wolverines established a new school single-game record by amassing forty points. Unfortunately, Iredell scored eighty-eight.

CHARLES P. PIERCE

Black Sunday

FROM SPORTS ILLUSTRATED

THE ICE SPREAD OUT of a brilliantly blue southern sky. It suffused the air. You took it in with every breath, and it got into your blood and spread to your deepest places. It made the world fragile, and you with it, until it seemed that you might shatter at the slightest sound, and all the world shatter around you. On the morning of November 22, 1963, there were things that the United States believed about itself, and those things were solid and basic and seemed as permanent as granite. By midday, as the ice spread through them, those fundamental things became delicate and crystalline. Anything loud seemed dangerous.

Cheering was loud. There had been cheering in Dallas, along the streets and on either side of that long, slow — too damned slow — turn from Houston down onto Elm Street past the book warehouse. Some of the cheering was so loud that the gunfire drowned in it. After that, for the next three days, the country breathed shallowly. It spoke to itself only in chapel whispers. Football, by contrast, is loud, and therefore it seemed a perilous thing.

On that Friday at noon, the Washington Redskins were beginning an ordinary practice in the middle of a season that was going nowhere. They'd lost seven games in a row. Their game that weekend was in Philadelphia, against the Eagles, who were even more woeful than the Redskins. Philadelphia was in a long slide in which it would lose eight of its last nine games and finish 2–10–2, slightly worse than Washington's 3–11.

Amid this hopeless flotsam, the Redskins' Bobby Mitchell was having a good season. He was on his way to sixty-nine catches and seven touchdowns. In Philadelphia, Tommy McDonald would end 1963 with forty-one catches and eight touchdowns, but neither man had any illusions about his team. "We were pretty terrible," recalls McDonald. "It wasn't the best year, anyway, before all this happened."

The players heard the news, like the country did, in a thousand ways. Raymond Berry and the Baltimore Colts heard it on their airplane, at thirty thousand feet, on their way to Los Angeles for a game with the Rams. Sam Huff, the New York Giants linebacker who'd campaigned for John F. Kennedy in 1960 before the pivotal primary in Huff's home state, West Virginia, heard it on his car radio in the middle of the Triborough Bridge. McDonald found out after practice.

In Washington, coach Bill McPeak called the Redskins together in the middle of the field outside D.C. Stadium. Mitchell was baffled. McPeak, an unemotional organization man, told everyone to take a knee and pray because the president was dead.

"The first thing I thought was, God, Mr. Marshall died," Mitchell says, referring to Redskins president George Preston Marshall. His teammates sank to the ground around him, and then he knew. "It never occurred to me," Mitchell says. "I mean, that somebody would shoot the president of the United States? It took me a couple of seconds to realize that was what he meant."

Mitchell had gone to Washington in 1962, two years after the Kennedy administration began. He'd become close friends with Robert Kennedy, the president's brother and the attorney general, and had met President Kennedy several times, once at a state dinner at the White House. Mitchell had even gone to Robert Kennedy's home in Virginia to play touch football with that boisterous and ever-expanding family. Now, as he fell to his knees on the hardening earth of autumn, Mitchell thought mostly about his friend.

"I was frozen there for a minute because I'd really fallen in love with Bobby," Mitchell says. "My thoughts turned to him, and I thought, *Damn, this is going to kill Bobby.*"

The Redskins practiced anyway, and it was terrible, and McPeak finally gave up and sent the team home. The streets of Washington were a shadow play. Cars disappeared almost entirely. Black crape began to appear in shop windows. Mitchell saw people on the sidewalk, still and weeping, as though they were afraid to move. He felt cold and numb, too. He felt close to breaking.

"It was just silence," he says. "That's what I remember. Even the playgrounds were empty and quiet. I felt, I don't know, slow, somehow, and like everything had slowed down around me."

On the way home through the stunned and silent streets, the last thing Mitchell thought about was the game in Philadelphia two days later. It had been a forgettable piece of business anyway, and now it seemed unspeakable. *Why did we even practice?* he wondered. He was home that evening, glued to his television like the rest of his frozen and fragile country, when Air Force One came back from Dallas.

Football was what they played on the New Frontier. Oh, they paid the usual obeisance to baseball, the ritual national pastime. But football ran deep in the Kennedy family mystique. All four Kennedy brothers had played the game at Harvard. John was a halfback undersized even by the standards of the Ivy League in the 1930s, but young Edward once scored a touchdown in the Yale game. Football was an integral part of Joseph Kennedy's grand plan — a demonstration of muscular Americanism that would help break down the prejudices his children would face for being rich, Irish, and Catholic.

"Politics is like football," JFK once noted. "If you see daylight, go through the hole." And photographs of John Kennedy hauling in passes from his brothers helped camouflage his myriad health problems, some of which have only recently come to light.

Moreover, the touch football games at the compound in Hyannis Port, Massachusetts, were part of the glamour of the Kennedy White House, as much as Jacqueline Kennedy's horses and the iconic PT-109 tie clips. There was a tyranny of the new at work, stretching from outer space to Southeast Asia. Football was a part of all that.

By 1963 Pete Rozelle and his National Football League already were well on their way to developing a new national pastime, changing the way Americans watched their sports, much as the Kennedy campaign had changed the way Americans elected their presidents. Both were perfect creatures of television, a medium just then coming into the fullness of its power. Rozelle tailored his games to TV the way that Kennedy tailored his press conferences to it. Both the NFL and the Kennedy administration were pure products of the brawling, confident America that had been built by the generation that had fought World War II.

The year had not been the easiest for Rozelle. In April he'd indefinitely suspended two star players, Alex Karras of the Detroit Lions and Paul Hornung of the Green Bay Packers, for gambling on their teams' games, and a bidding war for college players still raged because the renegade American Football League had stubbornly refused to fold. But on November 22 Rozelle was confronted with a decision that seemed to render all the others he'd made that year trivial.

There was no blueprint for what to do on the weekend that a president is being buried on national television. In Wisconsin more than a hundred high school basketball games were played on the night of the assassination. Pimlico Race Course in Baltimore ran all weekend, and games were played in both the NBA and the NHL. In college football Nebraska and Oklahoma played each other, but all four games in the Big Ten were rescheduled, and Iowa and Notre Dame canceled their game. The AFL wiped out its entire slate of games, but Rozelle had made Sunday afternoons the property of the NFL, and because of that he was on the hook.

He called his college friend Pierre Salinger, who was Kennedy's press secretary. Speaking from the Honolulu airport, shell-shocked by the events of the day, Salinger gave Rozelle what amounted to the dead president's permission to play. "Football," Rozelle said in making the announcement, "was Mr. Kennedy's game."

The reaction very nearly undid Rozelle. At least two owners called and begged him to reconsider. Cleveland's Art Modell wound up paying for extra security to guard the Dallas Cowboys, who were in town that weekend to play the Browns. In Philadelphia, Eagles owner Frank McNamee announced that he would miss his first game in fifteen years and Mayor James H. J. Tate, who'd shared a platform at Independence Hall with President Kennedy a year earlier on July 4, tried to get a court to stop the Eagles-Redskins game.

It also became clear that Rozelle's golden touch with the media had deserted him. He was barbecued for going ahead with the schedule. In the *New York Herald-Tribune*, Red Smith all but called

Rozelle a heartless mercenary, and Melvin Durslag of the *Los Angeles Herald Examiner* called the games that weekend "a sick joke." In the *Philadelphia Inquirer*, Sandy Grady wrote, "I am ashamed of this fatuous dreamland."

Perhaps the most significant thing of all was that players around the league began to rebel, in their hearts if not on the field. "Nobody wanted to play," says McDonald. "There wasn't anything you could do about it, but there was no way anybody wanted to go out and play a game that weekend. I'm a guy who wears his emotions on his sleeve, and I couldn't stop crying.

"It was bad enough playing, but that weekend, to be playing the Redskins, from Washington, where the president lived, that was just another reason to be upset."

For his part, Mitchell felt strange leaving Washington. "Everywhere you looked, down along the street, people would just start crying," he says. "It didn't seem like the time to leave." The Redskins drove the three hours to Philadelphia and checked into their hotel. Across town, at the Sheraton on Chestnut Street, where the Eagles always stayed before home games, the team was falling apart.

The Eagles had decided to collect money for the family of Dallas policeman J. D. Tippitt, who'd been shot to death on Friday afternoon, allegedly by Lee Harvey Oswald. A team meeting, which also reportedly dealt with the Eagles' feelings about playing the game the next day, ended with a fistfight between defensive back Ben Scotti and defensive lineman John Mellekas. The two went behind closed doors to finish it, and both wound up in the hospital that night, Scotti with a broken hand and Mellekas with severe facial cuts. In his room, McDonald watched TV and never heard a thing.

That Sunday dawned cold and surreal. In their hotels, caught up in what became the first national news miniseries of the television age, the template for CNN and Fox and for the Watergate hearings and the O. J. trial and everything that came after, the players were drowning in the coverage, and how strangely that strangest of Sundays began depended vitally on where you were playing that weekend.

Kickoff was at 1:00 P.M. Eastern Standard Time. Some players around the league were at stadiums and some were in their hotels, but wherever they were, many of them were watching television at 12:21 P.M. EST when the Dallas police were transferring Oswald to the county jail and Jack Ruby gunned him down. "That was the last thing that weekend that I couldn't believe," says McDonald.

Then people showed up to watch football. That was the remarkable thing. There were 60,671 fans at Franklin Field to see the Eagles and the Redskins play a game that didn't matter on a weekend on which almost everything else seemed to matter. There was no pregame hoo-ha; Rozelle, at least, had drawn the line at that. There were no player introductions. The Eagles and the Redskins simply walked out to midfield and joined hands. A bugler blew "Taps," which nearly finished McDonald on the spot. Then the whole stadium sang the national anthem a cappella.

After that the stadium was as silent as a football stadium can be, as if tearing themselves away from the extended obsequies on television had used all the energy the fans had left. McDonald was bawling when he went back to receive the opening kickoff, and Mitchell noticed that even his coaches' words seemed hollow. "Before the game there was a lot of what you could tell was false chatter," Mitchell says. "Coaches are always over there saying, '*Grr,* let's go get 'em.' And me, I gave them a weak yell."

He made plays. So did McDonald. They each caught four passes in the game. Once, while running down the sideline for a pass, Mitchell felt the game dissolve around him. "I was there, looking up, concentrating on the ball spiraling in the air, like you're supposed to, and then I started thinking about everything that was going on in Washington," he recalls. The ball sailed over his head.

Redskins quarterback Norm Snead had a hot hand. He pushed his team out to a 13–0 lead at halftime, hitting on 12 of his first 17 passes for 192 yards. Late in the second quarter he found Dick James for a 31-yard touchdown. The game, however, seemed to be played in a virtual vacuum. "You didn't hear anything," Mitchell says. "I don't remember any noise from the stands, and in the pile-ups, where guys are always shouting and jiving, there was none of that. It was one play after another, trying to get the game done. To this day, sometimes I can't believe that I played that game. I still think I was out there in slow motion."

It wasn't a day for coming from behind. It looked for a long while as though Washington was on its way to its first shutout since 1958.

However, playing with a stiff wind behind them in the fourth quarter, the Eagles mustered ten points, highlighted by a twenty-five-yard touchdown pass from Sonny Jurgensen to Timmy Brown. But on Philadelphia's final drive McDonald let a pass go through his hands, and Mike Clark missed a sixteen-yard field goal that would have tied the game. The Redskins won 13–10.

Out in the players' parking lot, Eagles backup quarterback King Hill discovered that all the windows in his car had been shattered. The car had Texas plates.

That night, when he got home, Mitchell was struck for the last time that weekend by how quiet the streets of Washington had become. It was the strangest game any of the players had ever played and, in some ways, the most dangerous. Football is best (and most safely) played with heedless emotion, and everyone on the field seemed to be holding back. They played like men who had become aware of some unfamiliar fragility deep in themselves — far beneath muscle and bone, ligament and tendon, where they hadn't noticed any before.

Bobby Mitchell avoided Bobby Kennedy for as long as he could. Finally, about a month after the Philadelphia game, somebody from the Justice Department called Mitchell and told him that Kennedy wanted him to help dedicate the John F. Kennedy Playground on Seventh Street in the Washington ghetto. Mitchell went, distractedly driving slowly around the block, again and again, until he realized what he was doing. He was looking at all the rooftops for someone with a gun.

At the playground Mitchell took a spot in the back of the crowd, hoping that Kennedy wouldn't see him. "I was afraid," he admits. "I didn't know what I'd say to him." Kennedy spotted him, though, and brought him up to the front of the crowd, near where they had already turned the cold earth for the groundbreaking.

Kennedy was gaunt, almost lifeless in the face. He gripped Mitchell as if with iron talons. "I don't think I can do this," he said, and he couldn't. His hands were shaking too hard to work the shovel. He handed it to Mitchell so they held it together.

"I was so nervous," Mitchell recalls, "I must've thrown that dirt fifty feet over my head behind me."

He's older now, telling his story in the lobby of the Willard, a great old history-laden pile on Pennsylvania Avenue, not far from the White House. Abraham Lincoln was taken there when he was smuggled into Washington before his first inauguration, and it was the Willard's lobby that reputedly inspired the word *lobbying* when people gathered there to ply and beg and otherwise try to sublet President Ulysses S. Grant.

History has more or less passed judgment on those three frozen days in November. Later in his life Rozelle wrote that the worst decision he ever made was to play the games that weekend. And history sits with Bobby Mitchell in the awful synchronicity of anniversaries: every commemoration of John Kennedy's death follows a commemoration of Robert's. This week will mark the fortieth anniversary of John's death, not long after the thirty-fifth of Robert's, and Mitchell knows that the ice is still there, deep within him.

"You're never sure how that kind of thing will affect you, or when," he says. "We all learned from it, I think. Back after 9/11, there wasn't any choice: teams just didn't play. That was something we learned from that weekend in 1963."

And he leaves then, across the great lobby and out into the late autumn sunshine. Washington is alive with color as this November afternoon falls toward evening. Earlier that day, across the river in Arlington, down the hill from the gravesite and the eternal flame, drums were beating deep behind the golden trees, distant and muffled, like a heartbeat encased in something that can never melt but only shatter and re-form, and then shatter again, over and over and over.

GREG COUCH

A Runaway Win Cubs Fans
Won't Appreciate

FROM THE CHICAGO SUN-TIMES

THEY CAME OUT of the courtroom after their big victory, and how did the Cubs and their attorneys celebrate? They fled. They scrambled out of the twenty-third-floor room, slithered down the hall, and pushed that button for the elevator. And pushed it. Push, push, push. Tap, tap, tap. Come on. Come on.

It was as if they just needed to get out for some reason. And fast.

Judge Sophia Hall ruled Monday that the Cubs can keep scalping tickets to Cubs fans. They set up a dummy company, Wrigley Field Premium Ticket Services, to skirt the scalping laws, and now it's legitimate. They saw your loyalty, Cubs fans, your undying loyalty, and they thanked you by running a bait-and-switch on their tickets. Yes, there is profit in your emotions.

Actually, Judge Hall ruled that there was no bait-and-switch at all. The tickets sold at Premium were advertised at one price. That price was printed on the tickets. And then no one could buy them at that price except for Premium, which paid for its original supply with a pretend $1 million. The entire transaction between team and scalping office was done as a book entry and not with money.

The Cubs' lead attorney, Jim Klenk, stopped briefly in front of a pack of microphones, cameras, tape recorders, and scribbling pens and said: "Everybody wins. Fans win on this one."

Did I mention that Naperville cab driver Randy Galles's daughter won't be going to any more Cubs games? Galles was one of the fans who felt he had to sue the Cubs. He had promised to take his daughter to a game, then went to the Cubs' box office for tickets for the whole family. He was told the game he wanted was sold out. But tickets were available at Premium.

So he ordered tickets, saw the massive bill, and realized he couldn't afford to take his family. He would meet his promise to his daughter, and that was it. He says he never will go again.

Cubs win! Everybody wins! The cameras turned my way, as I have written about this a few times, and I didn't exactly see how the fans were winners. The Cubs are reducing the number of tickets offered at face value and pushing them down the block to be scalped. For the Yankees series, a $45 ticket was for sale at Premium for $1,500.

The Cubs could have sold those tickets at whatever price they wanted at their box office. They've never answered why they needed to set up a shell company, sneak around, make payments to themselves with money that never existed.

Good news, though. A Tribune Company attorney was standing there, eavesdropping. Ask him, I said. And the cameras swung around and he said the fans won. But why set up the dummy company? Um, ah, well. He turned and fled down an empty hall toward the elevators.

Cameras still on him. Tap, tap, tap. Where's that darn elevator? Come on.

What's your name? He wouldn't say. Someone asked if it was John Doe. Tap, tap, tap.

Cubs win! Everybody wins!

His name, by the way, was Michael Lufrano.

This was the strangest victory celebration I have ever seen. Run, Cubs, run.

Did I mention that before the season, Cubs fan Oscar Ruiz worked late into the night, then drove home, showered, and drove down to Wrigley Field in the early morning hours to buy Cubs-Yankees tickets? He spent the night in his car. That's how much getting his family into the game meant to him.

He was told the game was sold out. But it was only sold out at the prices that Average Joe Cubs Fan could afford.

So why are the Cubs hiding from their victory? Because this is not something you can celebrate. The assignment was to hurt the fans through scalping and to find a way around the law. The judge ruled that the Cubs had done it. Their hands were caught in the cookie jar. Crumbs were still on their face. And they won.

Klenk and Cubs vice president Mark McGuire were chased down the hall by the elevator. Tap, tap. Klenk said they weren't going to talk. Someone asked McGuire if he thought this was really a victory for Cubs fans.

He looked at Klenk. Klenk nodded. And then McGuire said that yes, it was. Tap, tap.

The door opened and someone screamed out to Klenk, "Why are you running away?" Okay, I screamed that out.

Finally, the doors started closing, he smiled and waved. No stopping this getaway.

Did I mention that people are already sending e-mails to me and calling? One guy wrote that the way the Cubs are treating their own fans makes him want to cry. One guy was so upset that he said, "Tribune and Cubs have unlimited pull in this town." One guy e-mailed questions about Judge Hall's ethics. One woman called to say, "This is just absolute craziness."

She said if this becomes the new way to deal with fans, then "I will never go to another sporting event in my life. Why even bother? We have plenty of parks, and I may as well go be a spectator of children's sports or just participate on my own. They're absolutely disgusting and disgraceful."

Cubs win! Everybody wins!

Other teams were watching, too. This ruling will change the way ticketing is done. The Cubs can scalp as many tickets as they want and have hopes of going into business with Chicago's other teams.

An appeal is possible. But the plaintiff's attorneys, the Chicago firm of Bauch and Michaels, are paying their own bills. The Cubs have spent an estimated $500,000 in legal fees, and there's plenty more where that came from.

No, the little guy lost. In her ruling, the judge agreed that a team cannot sell tickets to its own games over face value. But she ruled that a licensed broker can. That's why the Cubs set up Premium.

It would be nice if Cubs president Andy MacPhail would stand up and say, "This isn't the type of company we want to be, or the way we want to treat our fans."

It would be nice if the state attorney general's office would press criminal charges. A rep from the office was in the courtroom. But if a civil case such as this one can't be won, surely a criminal case can't.

It would be nice if baseball commissioner Bud Selig, who has made a living blubbering about his love for baseball and the attachment the game has to fans such as himself, would stand up and say that this is a betrayal of the fans. He has been quiet all along. And every bit of silence serves as an endorsement. Meanwhile, the law protects multibillion-dollar corporations, not cabbies and late-shifters.

How does victory taste to you?

So the Cubs have no moral high ground. That's why they ran for the elevators. The doors shut on Klenk and McGuire and other suits. And inside, they pushed the button.

Going down.

BOB RYAN

Misery Has More Company

FROM THE BOSTON GLOBE

THE REWARD for all that fidelity will surely come in another life. There is no indication it will ever materialize in this one.

With five outs to go, it was *there*. It was tangible. The Red Sox were going to beat the Yankees. They were going to the World Series, and, of course, they were going to win it. The "Cowboy Up" bunch was the team of every Red Sox fan's dreams, a group capable of ignoring the history and playing the game right at the same time.

But the story never, ever changes. Whatever the formula is, the Red Sox still do not have it. Pedro Martinez couldn't hold leads of 4–0 and 5–2, and the Red Sox couldn't score against Mariano Rivera. And in the cruelest twist of fate this series could possibly have provided, Tim Wakefield, unquestionably the team's MVP in this series, threw one pitch in the bottom of the eleventh and Aaron Boone hit it in the left-field seats.

Yanks 6, Sox 5, and let the crying begin.

Thus we have another gigantic log to toss on that Eternal Flame of Red Sox Misery. This lovable, gritty team seemed to have the Right Stuff, with a season-long run of comeback wins. They came to New York needing to win two, and they came within five precious outs of doing so. The problem is the Pedro Martinez of 2003 is not the Pedro Martinez of 1999. Check that: the problem was Grady Little *thought* the Pedro Martinez of 2003 is the Pedro Martinez of 1999.

He is not.

Pedro's heart is willing, but the flesh isn't what it was at his peak. His mortality was apparent as early as the seventh inning, when

Jorge Posada hit one hard to center, Jason Giambi hit the second of his two home runs over the center-field fence, and Karim Garcia lined a hard single to right. He got out of the inning and had thrown one hundred pitches.

Grady had a choice, and his decision was to stay with Pedro. It was a bad one. Before he could get Pedro out of the game, three runs were in and the score was tied.

"Pedro Martinez has been our man all year long in situations just like this," said Little. "He's the man we want on the mound, more than anyone in our bullpen."

Everybody's going to blame Grady for everything, I'm sure, but this is never an easy decision, and there was a lot more to this game than pulling Pedro or not pulling Pedro. Baseball is a lot more complex than that.

Take, for example, the failure to capitalize on a juicy situation in the fourth. Kevin Millar led off the inning with a home run to make it 4–0. Then, with men on first and third — on a perfectly executed hit-and-run, if you can believe that — the Red Sox were in a position to blow the game open when Joe Torre summoned Mike Mussina from the pen for his first relief appearance of a career that has had exactly four hundred starts. The Moose, who has been slammed by the New York press for coming up small in the postseason while wearing a Yankee uniform, fanned Jason Varitek and induced Johnny Damon to hit into an inning-ending 6–3 double play.

"That was the turning point for me," Torre said. "It kept us there. You feel like you're getting your brains beat out, but you look at the scoreboard and you're still at arm's length."

Mussina worked three scoreless innings. The relay team just kept coming and coming. Felix Heredia, Jeff Nelson, even David Wells. Wells was brought in to face David Ortiz and saw his first pitch, a changeup that dipped down and in, blasted over the right-field fence to make it 5–2.

The Red Sox' nightly strategy against the Yankees is always the same: get a lead and keep Mariano Rivera out of the game. They were on their way to doing just that when Pedro imploded in the eighth, giving up a double to Derek Jeter, a single to Bernie Williams, a ground-rule double to Hideki Matsui, and, finally, a bloop double to center by Posada.

Enter Rivera, and while he wasn't untouchable, he was good

enough. Before the game, Torre had been asked if he would even consider using Rivera for more than two innings and he said he doubted it very much, that he would do nothing to risk Rivera's health. So what happened? Rivera pitched a scoreless ninth, a scoreless tenth, and a scoreless eleventh. File that under the heading of a manager and a closer doing what they had to do.

It was a truly great game and a truly great series, but no one in Boston wants to hear that. They would gladly have taken four dull victories, but dull was never going to be the phrase associated with any game these teams were going to play. In the hundred-year history of Boston–New York American League competition, this was undoubtedly the greatest collection of ball games. They wound up playing a major league–record twenty-six times, with New York winning fourteen, Boston winning twelve, and the deciding game, for the American League pennant, lasting into the eleventh inning.

"I think the Boston fans should be proud of their ball club," Torre said. "They were the toughest team we've faced in my eight years here."

The Red Sox *always* lose in great games. The 1975 World Series was an epic. The Bucky Dent Game was an epic. The 1986 World Series was a keeper. That's the point. The Red Sox always play in these things, but they never wind up pouring the champagne.

Seriously. *Would* it spoil some vast eternal plan if the Red Sox could win one?

IRA BERKOW

An Unconventional Tradition of Success

FROM THE NEW YORK TIMES

THE TINTINNABULATIONS of the Abbey Church tower bells mixed with voices as the only sounds heard on the football practice field. It was on a recent gray late afternoon, and the St. John's University team was running plays in this relatively isolated area in the central part of the state, located amid a forest with the trees nearly bare of leaves.

There were no whistles.

"I don't like to have someone raise his voice to me, and I believe it's the same for the players," the head coach has said. "A whistle is like raising your voice. The players can get my drift with normal tones."

For a long time in football, it was considered a resolution of toughness for coaches to withhold water from players, even on very hot days. But water was readily available here, and the coach said he has never withheld it from his players.

"I grew up in a coal-mining region in Colorado, and I remember the mules sweating like crazy when they came out of the mines," the coach said. "They were given water and it surely didn't hurt them. When the miners came out, they got water. It only helped. So I figured, how couldn't it be good for my football players, too?"

And there is no tackling in practice. Never has been. "Why risk injury in practice and not have the player ready for the game?" the coach said. "Most teams protect the quarterback in practice. We protect all the players. We assume they'll get to do enough tackling in the game."

And here the gentle coach shows another side. "And if we don't," one of his players said, "well, John tells us he'll just have to get someone in our place who does."

That's another thing. The coach insists on being called by his first name. Not the traditional "Coach." "They know I'm the coach," he said. "I don't find it necessary to keep reminding them."

When considering Vince Lombardi or Bill Parcells or even Amos Alonzo Stagg, this unconventional approach would seem to be effective maybe for a sandlot team in touch football, but for a college football team, even a Division III team, like St. John's?

But, at this school run by Benedictine monks, it works, at least for John Gagliardi. And "winning with 'no,'" as he calls it — there are about one hundred such "no's" — works so well that Gagliardi, at seventy-seven, stands to have the most coaching victories in the history of college football.

On Saturday, at home in Clemens Stadium, the red-and-white-clad Johnnies (8–0) take on Bethel, another unbeaten team in their Minnesota Intercollegiate Athletic Conference. If St. John's wins, it will be the 409th college victory for Gagliardi, in his fifty-fifth season as a head football coach. It would move Gagliardi one victory past the record he holds with Eddie Robinson, the retired Grambling coach. Gagliardi (408–114–11) is sixty-eight victories ahead of Florida State's Bobby Bowden and seventy ahead of Penn State's Joe Paterno, both of whom follow him in the victories column. Gagliardi has also won three NCAA Division III championships and has a record of 20–9 in NCAA playoff games. (Robinson's record was 408–165–15.)

"Bethel is tough," he said. "They make me nervous."

Gagliardi (pronounced guh-LAHR-dee) never underestimates an opponent, which is part of the secret of success. And sometimes he is right to be concerned. Before last Saturday's game, on the road against St. Thomas, he said he was terrified that the game might be played in the mud — rain was forecast — and that St. Thomas, a longtime rival, would be up for the game. This despite St. Thomas's being 3–5, riddled with injuries and a young squad, as opposed to the St. John's team, which has three All-American players: wide receiver Blake Elliott, quarterback Ryan Keating, and linebacker Cameron McCambridge, all seniors.

It turned out that Gagliardi had reason for alarm. The Johnnies, before an overflow crowd of some 7,300 fans, fell behind in the second half for the first time this season, and they were losing, 12–7, with eight minutes to go in the game. It hadn't rained, but it was cold, and on the sideline Gagliardi pulled his maroon parka hood over the red baseball cap that covered the sparse gray hair on his head. He stood in ankle-high winter boots with his hands behind his back, watching a play through his wire-rim spectacles, seeming as calm as someone waiting for a light to change at a street corner.

When the play would end he would take a short stroll, sometimes dipping into his pocket to check the fifteen or so note cards that he keeps his plays on — his team has no playbooks — and perhaps say something to one of his assistants. And then Gagliardi would stop to watch the next play, hands again folded behind his back.

"He looks so casual, so stoic out there," said Pat Reusse, a reporter for the *Minneapolis Star Tribune* who covers the team regularly, "but no one takes losing harder than John. He's churning up inside."

In fact, when Gagliardi was asked recently how long he thought he would stay as a coach, he replied: "As long as my health holds out, or if we start losing. And if we start losing, my health will surely not hold out."

Well, the Johnnies cut their deficit to 12–9 with a safety, and then Brandon Keller, a five-foot-seven junior place-kicker, booted a twenty-yard field goal to tie the score with three minutes sixteen seconds left. After another march downfield, Keller kicked a thirty-five-yard field goal with eight seconds remaining to give Gagliardi his 408th career victory, 15–12 — on his seventy-seventh birthday, no less.

The large St. John's contingent in the stands warbled "Happy Birthday" to him; he allowed himself a smile after the winning field goal, and gave a congratulatory pat on the back to the kicker and a little wave of appreciation to the fans. "I don't go in for celebrations," he said afterward. "I'm too old for celebrations."

Although it is not often apparent, he does derive great satisfaction from his achievements, like winning another football game. And he enjoys the attention, such as the profile on him that College Sports Television is airing throughout this month.

"I've never thought about goals, or how many games my teams

can win," he said. "Really, it's the old cliché — I play them one game at a time."

Elliott, the wide receiver, said the players "wanted to get it done for John."

"We moved it up another level in the fourth quarter," Elliott said at a news conference after the game.

Elliott also praised Gagliardi's ability to adapt to different generations and to find a variety of ways to achieve victories, "from the '50s and '60s and '70s and on to today."

Gagliardi interjected: "I'm not stupid. When I have a receiver like him I'm going to throw the ball."

Keller, the place-kicker, said he simply did what he was taught to do, that those kicks were what he practiced every day, with positive rather than negative reinforcement.

"John expects us to get the job done," he said. "Like he says, 'Just do it.'"

The players hear regularly the coach's mantra: "It's ordinary people doing ordinary things in an extraordinary way."

And if Keller didn't "just do it"?

"What he probably doesn't know," said Gagliardi, seated beside Keller at a table in the St. Thomas gymnasium, "is that we would have strung him up back at the bell towers on campus if he would have missed."

It is Gagliardi's sense of humor as well as his perspective, his assiduous preparation and his candor laced with charm that is behind much of his success. He began coaching when he was sixteen. As a junior in high school in 1943, he was quarterback and captain of the Trinidad (Colorado) Catholic team when all the coaches were called up for service in World War II.

"The school officials asked me to coach the team, or they were considering eliminating football," Gagliardi said. "So I took on the job. And I treated the players the way I wanted to be treated — since I was a player, too."

The team won the championship. Rather than work in his father's body shop — as several of his brothers did — Gagliardi went to a junior college and eventually earned a bachelor's degree from Colorado College in Colorado Springs. He was then hired by Carroll College in Helena, Montana, to coach football. His teams won (24–6–1). In 1953, at age twenty-six, he was offered the job at St. John's and accepted.

He has had offers to move on, including one with the Minnesota Vikings, as an assistant coach. What he has accomplished has been without scholarships (there are none in Division III), with recruiting primarily in-state, and no recruiting beyond phone calls and visits to the campus.

"I came here because of John," said Damien Dumonceaux, who is a sophomore defensive lineman and one of eighteen St. John's players whose fathers had played for Gagliardi. "Because he wins and he makes football fun, the way it's supposed to be."

The Rev. Timothy Backous, the monk who is athletic director at St. John's, said: "John is simply a football genius. He knows how to make a difficult situation come out right."

No greater example was when he was courting Peg Daugherty, a student nurse at St. John's nearly fifty years ago. She was twenty; he was twenty-eight. Gagliardi's mother, who came from the Calabria region of Italy, was, he said, "a great cook, especially of spaghetti." Daugherty was not Italian, but she wanted to please Gagliardi, and so she made a spaghetti dinner for him at her apartment.

"I used tomato soup for the sauce," she said. "I didn't know any better."

Gagliardi had a dilemma. "Should I tell her the truth, or not," he said. "If I didn't, she'd make it again and again for me. I couldn't stand that. And if I was straightforward, would she ever see me again?"

He decided that honesty with what gentleness he could muster was the best policy. "He said, 'I know you tried hard to get this spaghetti great,'" she said, "'and I don't want to hurt your feelings. But this spaghetti is terrible.'"

And what happened?

"She learned to make the spaghetti right," Gagliardi said. "I love her."

MITCH ALBOM

Trying to Find Yourself
in the Toughest Times

FROM THE DETROIT FREE PRESS

> It is not the critic who counts. . . . The credit belongs to the man in the
> arena, whose face is marred by dust and sweat and blood, who strives
> valiantly . . . and who, at the worst, if he fails, at least fails while daring
> greatly, so that his place shall never be with those cold and timid souls
> who neither know victory nor defeat.
> — Teddy Roosevelt

Now, THAT'S a powerful quote. You don't turn to that quote unless you need it. Adam Ballinger needed it. His father, a teacher,
sent it in a letter. That letter now hangs on Ballinger's apartment
wall in this, the last year of his college basketball career.

And more and more he thinks it's the greatest gift he has ever
gotten.

"Obviously," says the Michigan State senior, with the resignation
of someone who has had this conversation too many times, "the
season hasn't gone the way I expected."

Not unless he expected to lose his starter's role, visit a sports psychologist, be pitied, criticized, all but forgotten, and ultimately
turned into a curiosity sentence: "What's the matter with Adam?"

Ballinger, you see, had the misfortune of hitting an oil slick when
the checkered flag was in sight. College basketball is supposed to
be a linear thing. You get older, you get better, you get better, you
score more, you score more, you're the man.

Each season for Ballinger had been better than the last. He came
into this year as a senior co-captain, the second-most-experienced

player on the squad. He was a starting forward. A go-to guy. Big things were expected.

But big things never came.

Unless you count big confusion.

He was off almost from the start. His shot wasn't falling. He seemed to grow tentative. His rebounding suffered. Pretty soon, Ballinger was like that Ben Stiller character in *Meet the Parents* — no matter how earnestly he tried, nothing worked out. He was held scoreless against Loyola (Illinois). He turned the ball over three times in five minutes against Michigan. His shooting went south. And then it really went south.

"The worst part wasn't just my play," he says, after seeing his scoring and rebounding stats virtually cut in half from last season. "The worst part was we were losing games that I know, if I could have played better, we could have won."

No one could figure it out. What's the matter with Adam? Tom Izzo, his coach, tried everything — yelling, coddling, noise, quiet — until finally, he benched him.

"I don't think I've ever felt for a kid more than him," Izzo said.

Ballinger, as stumped as anyone, tried every path out of the maze. He remembers sitting with a sports psychologist, feeling foolish. He remembers friends giving him advice. "They'd say, 'Go away somewhere.' But I'm a college student, where am I gonna go?"

Sometimes, for solace, Ballinger would visit the gym late at night and just shoot, by himself, feeling the floor, the ball, the heat. It was like smoothing the dirt of a foxhole. Only, as Ballinger admits, "my enemy was thinking."

But lest you think this is some sob story, remember what college is supposed to be about: learning. Ballinger, at six-feet-nine and 250 pounds, had always been tagged "a basketball player" — from Indiana, no less — and as he advanced, the lights all seemed to be turning green.

This year he discovered that green isn't promised. He learned who really cares about him. He learned the solace of good friends and good parents. When his father mailed him the Roosevelt quote, he cherished both the letter and the unconditional support it took to send it.

And then came a night against Iowa earlier this month, senior night at the Breslin Center. And like an old dog bursting through the screen door, Ballinger's game came running back to him. He scored twenty-two points, a career high, including a one-handed slam that brought his teammates swarming happily around him.

In a Cinderella story, that game would have led to more like it. Instead, Ballinger slipped back to the bench, a few minutes here, a few shots there. Life is not Cinderella. He knows that now.

He knows something else, too: he knows he truly cares about the team, because he is able to say, "I don't care if I play ten minutes or two hundred, as long as we win" — and mean it. He knows he truly loves the sport, because instead of chucking it in disgust, he wants to keep playing somewhere, anywhere, next year.

Friday night, against Maryland in the Sweet 16, could be his last college game. Does he dream of coming off the bench and finding the old touch? Sure. But if it doesn't happen, he's ready for that, too.

"In a way, it's been a great life lesson," he says. "I feel like I could go through anything now." And, as Teddy said, his place will never be among those cold and timid souls. Adam Ballinger has taken a lot of hits this year. His character has proven bulletproof.

STEPHEN RODRICK

A Long Strange Trip

FROM RUNNER'S WORLD

JUST OUTSIDE of Hicks Junction, Arkansas, kid-filled, DVD-laden SUVs and long-range eighteen-wheelers jockey for position on U.S. I-40. Inside a 1994 Ford Dutchman RV a CB radio hums with warnings about wobbly U-Hauls, hooter jokes, and guesstimates about the distance to the closest Waffle House. The accents twang and ping in a scratchy Tower of Babel. Then the chatter turns serious.

"Break 1-9, be aware there's a guy running on the interstate eastbound side. Damn fool."

"10-4. He's being followed by an RV. Says he's across America for unity."

Pause. "What the hell is unity?"

Longer pause. "That's when we all stop mussing with each other."

Longest pause. "Where the hell is the fun in that?"

Much laughter. A driver clears his throat and launches into an exaggerated honey-dripping drawl of a certain well-known simpleton, "Uh, life is like a box of chocolates."

Two drivers at once. "Go, Forrest, go!"

Up ahead, a blissfully unaware Reza Baluchi plods on. Some 1,300 miles down, 1,700 to go. He's almost halfway through his journey from Hollywood to Ground Zero, which is a walk in the proverbial park when you consider Reza's odyssey started in Rasht, Iran, and has included stopovers in Morocco, Ecuador, and a place called Burkina Faso. All in the name of peace.

If this were the pre-PC 1970s, Baluchi would warrant a sitcom. Why did he wear a Michael Jackson T-shirt and leather pants in rural Iran when he knew the local mullahs would be coming after him? That's Reza! Why did he bicycle across fifty-six countries, fleeing a lion, contracting malaria, and accumulating girlfriends? And as an Iranian national in a post-9/11 world, why did he cross the Arizona-Mexico border illegally and camp out in the desert, earning himself several months in an Immigration and Naturalization Service detention center? Yes. That's Reza!

And now he is running across the country with the help of a forty-seven-year-old unemployed entrepreneur named Dave. Sure, dozens have made the transcontinental run before: ultramarathoners, midlife-crisis guys, and multiple everymans running for various charities. But never before has there been Reza Baluchi, an irrepressible, salsa music–loving peacenik who's hoping to score both a movie deal and a place in the record books. The man is one part humanitarian, one part superhero, and one part The Ego That Ate Tehran.

Now's the time to get on the Reza Express, because he's due in New York City on September 11. So bring along some air freshener, a hanky, and some extra Ragu for dinner. Reza Baluchi will make you laugh, cry, and, occasionally, want to bounce a water bottle off his sweaty, balding head.

Oh, you might want to get a stretch in. Reza runs between thirty and forty miles a day.

That's Reza!

He is thirty years old, about five feet, seven inches tall and 130 pounds, with sharp brown eyes, and an odd balding pattern — a tuft of black hair at the top of his head exists on an island all its own — that squares perfectly with his personality. His running routine is not one that Jim Fixx would have endorsed. Nutritionally, Reza acts like he still lives in his birthplace, Rasht, a province in northern Iran where going hungry was as natural as the sunrise. He rises most mornings around 5:30, without the benefit of an alarm clock. Sometimes, he eats a bowl of corn flakes and a banana before beginning his run. Sometimes, if Dave Hyslop (Reza's driver, publicist, and guy Friday) is still sleeping, he skips it. In restaurants, he watches Americans pack their pie holes, and it disgusts him. "American, eat way, way too much," Reza says.

Despite the massive trucks and endless white noise, he logs the majority of his miles on superhighways. Although this is technically illegal, Dave says he has obtained permission from state police. "The local roads have no shoulder and too many curves," reasons Dave. "He was going to break an ankle or get hit by a car."

After running fifteen to twenty miles, at about a twelve-minute-per-mile pace, Reza usually takes a short break. He may eat another banana before he gets moving again. Once he hits forty miles, Reza stops for the day. Then Dave makes him a mega-calorie shake with ice cream, milk, and fruit. His only real meal is consumed around 7:00 or 8:00 P.M.: two big bowls of spaghetti made with Ragu tomato sauce.

Gear-wise, Reza isn't picky, but he is a little vain. He wore donated Nikes at the beginning of the trip because he loved the way they looked. But they were too narrow for his 7EEEE feet, so he switched to New Balance. Every three hundred miles, he slips into a new pair. Reza never stretches and apparently never gets tired. "If I not running, I get angry," he says. "I run, I happy. Very happy." But things weren't always so simple.

Fresh from another forty miles and his first shower in days, Reza brings out a couple of battered binders and begins to tell his story. Dave has parked the RV — his and Reza's home for the past two months — off Exit 42 in Stanton, Tennessee, cozily between a truck stop and the gravely misnamed Countryside Inn. Conversing with Reza is tricky, as he speaks Farsi but very little English. Fortunately we have a translator. Just like Dave, Afsaneh Fathi has become swept up in Reza mania. A high-level financial analyst in Los Angeles, the Farsi-speaking Afsaneh saw Reza off in California, has kept tabs on him ever since, and has flown out to Tennessee for a few days.

The Iran that Reza was born into in 1972 was a different Iran than the one he grew up in. While the last years of the Shah's reign in Iran were marked by corruption, it was a rapidly Westernizing country open to ideas. After Ayatollah Khomeini's ascension to power in 1979, Iran became an unrecognizable place, a theocracy with an extensive cultural and moral police.

Reza, the son of a rice farmer, is one of eight children. The searing memory of his childhood is his oldest brother, Saddam, returning from the fruitless Iran-Iraqi War. "He couldn't work, he couldn't do anything," recalls Reza in Farsi. "The littlest thing would make him hysterical and violent."

At the age of nine, Reza left his family and went to the nearby city of Shiraz, a much more cosmopolitan place. He lived with an aunt and made three dollars a week as a helper in a mechanic's shop. As Reza moved into his teens, he fell in love with girls and what passed for Iranian haute couture. This did not sit well with the local clergy. One evening, Reza hit the town in leather pants and long hair. The mullahs grabbed him, he says, shaved his head, and confiscated the pants. Caught eating a sandwich during the holy days of Ramadan, when no food or water can be consumed during daylight hours, he was whipped in the city square. At sixteen, he was caught alone with a girl. They were both whipped.

By his early twenties, Reza was known as one of Shiraz's bad boys. One evening, he was caught wearing a Michael Jackson T-shirt and possessing a video of a banned Iranian film. When Reza refused to disclose where he got the contraband, he was hung by his thumbs for twenty-four hours and was later thrown in jail for eighteen months for associating with "counterrevolutionaries." Reza pulls off his shirt to show an unnatural knot in his shoulder. He explains that the police would handcuff him by pushing one arm back over his head and then linking it to his other arm. When I asked him why he would take such risks, Reza smiles and shrugs.

"I like Michael Jackson. He help Africa. He help kids. Michael Jackson good man."

It's heartbreaking to hear a man talk about being hanged by his thumbs for idolizing Wacko Jacko. But Reza's jail time didn't dampen his spirits. Throughout his youth, he had participated in cycling contests, and upon his release from prison in 1996, Reza bribed an Iranian sports official, scoring a precious exit visa under the pretext that he was a world-class cyclist pedaling across Europe, spreading good news about Iran. Apparently, Reza felt compelled to make pretext reality. He flew to Germany, where visa problems stalled him for three years. He entered cycling races, he says, and worked as a mechanic to survive.

And then Reza's story becomes a nonfiction fable. From Germany, he cycled to Turkey. From there, he flew to Pakistan and began cycling east through India, China, and eventually Singapore. From there, he flew to Australia and cycled down the coast. Then he headed back to Europe. The afternoon of September 11, 2001, found Reza spending time in a hotel in Paris. He was watching television in the lobby.

"I see big fire," Reza says in his limited English. "I think it really good movie. Turn channel, same movie. Then, I understand."

On that day, Reza decided to bike across the United States. "I show America I like peace," Reza says. "Not all Iranians [are] terrorists." Of course, this being Reza, there was a slight detour. He decided first to pedal from Morocco to Johannesburg. After recovering from malaria and a stand-off with a lion in Zimbabwe, Reza flew across the Indian Ocean and began cycling through South America, beginning in Argentina.

Reza's accounts of his journey are largely unverifiable, but his scrapbook provides enough snapshots, plus the occasional newspaper article, to support at least the basic facts. However, what Reza can't explain is why. I ask him the question through Afsaneh several times. "He doesn't like war," she explains. "He wants people of all religions to get along and live freely. He thinks we all need to compromise."

Perhaps because of his prison time, Reza has grown a bit paranoid. He fears that Afsaneh is not properly translating his answers. He repeats over and over, "I like peace. I no like war. I like freedom."

Late last year, after surviving a sinking ferry off the coast of Panama, Reza made it to Mexico. He settled for a while in Monterrey, where he met a girl, fell in love, and worked in an Iranian-run pizza shop. He applied for a visa to enter America. However, in a post-9/11 world, visa applications for transcontinental cyclists from Iran were moving very, very slowly. Impatient, Reza rode up to the border to make an in-person plea. He camped out in the desert, close to the Arizona border — apparently too close. He woke up one morning to the sound of helicopters. A flashlight tapped him awake.

"Do you know where you are?" asked a border-patrol officer.

"Mexico," replied Reza. "I wait for visa."

"No, you're fifteen miles into Arizona," replied the guard. Reza spent the next four months in the INS's compound in Florence, Arizona. To bide his time, he ran around the compound's tiny yard in street shoes. Somewhere along the way, Reza decided cycling across America was not a grand enough gesture. If freed, he would *run* across America instead.

*

If Reza doesn't rate a sitcom of his own, how about *The Odd Couple*, starring Reza and Dave?

It's a little after 7:00 on a humid and damp morning, a few miles outside Memphis. Almost two hours earlier, Reza popped out of bed and began running Highway 70. Dave slept for another hour before driving after him, heading east, as usual. After seven or eight miles, he starts checking convenience stores.

"Have you seen a short, Iranian man in jogging shorts?" asks Dave, a lanky man with salt-and-pepper hair and the patience of Job on his best day.

"Sure, with a little black dog?" responds the clerk. "He's probably two, three miles up the road."

"A black dog." Dave repeats the phrase, not quite comprehending, then climbs back into the RV. Sure enough, about three clicks up on the right, there's Reza, wearing his reflective vest with the Iranian and American flags sewn on the front. His gait is gimpish, if clock-setting regular. His left arm swings like a machete in a Hong Kong action flick, the right arm hanging close to his side as if he's guarding some bauble in his running shorts. His back is stained in blood. No, it turns out to be PowerAde leaking from his hydration pack. Nipping at his heels is a malnourished black puppy that is missing a hefty chunk of flesh near his right eye. The dog pants so violently his ribs threaten to burst through his mangy fur.

"Hey, Reza, whose dog?" Dave asks. There's trepidation in his voice.

"Rocky Balboa. He follow Reza seven miles," Reza answers. "I keep him. I call him Rocky Balboa."

Reza grins and hoofs on down the road. Dave smiles wearily. He places Rocky inside the RV, gives him some water, and stares at a plague-like skin condition on the dog's back. "Man, we have to find this boy a vet. I better check for ticks tonight," he says. "We'll see what happens the first time Rocky pees on Reza's bed." He brightens a bit. "But this should cheer him up, after what happened last night."

Last night was indeed disappointing. To promote Reza's "Run 4 Peace," Dave arranged a potluck supper with a local peace group in Memphis. The media was alerted. Reza had dreams of TV trucks dancing in his head. In many towns, supporters had joined Reza for meals or short runs. But alas, after a mad-dash, red light–running RV romp through the belly of Memphis, we arrived to an empty church basement. No TV cameras, no fellow peaceniks, and no potluck supper. Reza sank into a funk. His mood only darkened when the highfalutin restaurant where we ended up brought Reza's ravioli. Reza, who loves pasta, was hungry. But his plate held just four raviolis. He went silent for the rest of the night.

"He wants to run," says Dave. "When he stops, he wants it to be for a good reason. I think he blames me."

While Reza may run, it is Dave who carries the weight. Raised in Omaha, Nebraska, he is the child of an alcoholic father who passed away when Dave was sixteen. After graduating from high school, Dave moved to California and spent much of the past two decades working in a television-facilities business in Los Angeles. But he never gained any traction in his career, and at the beginning of 2003, he was forty-six, underemployed, and deep in credit-card debt.

Then, on the morning of February 1, he opened the door of his studio apartment and picked up the *New York Times*. Over a cup of coffee, he read about Reza's incredible odyssey for the first time. Almost immediately after reading the article, Dave wrote to Reza at the detention center in Arizona and gave him his phone number.

"He seemed so brave and alone," Dave says as he feeds bologna to Rocky. "Here was one guy with a message of peace just trying to do his little thing to make people understand each other better without fighting."

Over the next two months, the two talked often, although Reza's English made significant communication nearly impossible. Still, Dave made Reza a promise: when you're released, you have a place to stay in California. After a judge granted Reza political asylum, he set off on his Centurion bike for Dave and the Pacific Coast, with a few dollars in his pocket provided by the Iranian-American community of Arizona. Along the way, a strong gust blew Reza over, and he tore his groin. Still, he pedaled on.

When he finally arrived, he and Dave plotted Reza's run across America. Reza spent eleven days sleeping at the foot of Dave's bed. Dave helped him plan his route and coordinated his send-off. Dave's television work provided him with many contacts in ethnic broadcasting, including one with Parvis Afshar, a talk-show host who's considered the Johnny Carson of the Iranian ex-pat community in Los Angeles. Afshar started hosting Reza on *TV Tapesh* every week, trumpeting the friendship between him and Dave as a sign of American-Iranian unity. It struck a chord with the Iranian community. Lumped with North Korea, and Iraq — their sworn enemy — in President Bush's axis of evil, Iranian Americans were desperate for a symbol to show that they valued peace as much as their neighbors did. For them, Reza was a gift from heaven. Throw in an American sidekick, and they were ecstatic.

On Mother's Day, Reza was off with a pack on his back, holding a small tent, some walnuts, a cell phone, and a camcorder. Dave went home. He and his longtime business partner prepared to take a lucrative and much-needed job. But when he got home, he started crying.

"It seemed like I was abandoning the guy," says Dave. He tries to hold them back, but the tears come again. He flips his silver hair out of his face and wipes his eyes. To demonstrate his point, Dave fishes out a videocassette. (Part of the RV has been turned into a multimedia center. There's a desktop computer, a printer, a VCR, and a color television.) Dave pops in the tape, which Reza made and sent to him after Day 4 of his run.

Reza's footage is more *The Manchurian Candidate* than home movie. He had made his way through the Angeles mountain range, reaching an altitude of seven thousand feet, before descending into the seedy crossroads town of Barstow, California. In a motel room that an Iranian truck driver rented for him, Reza places the camera a few feet away from himself. A television drones in the background. Reza starts shooting close-up video of his toes, which are covered in blood blisters. Speaking in Farsi, he rambles monotonously about his aching feet. Then he pops the blisters with his fingers and watches the blood trickle into a Kleenex. "That's better," he says. He sits quietly for a few minutes, his gaunt face staring into the camera. Then, apropos of nothing, his face lights up. He speaks rapidly and with great vigor. All I understand is the word *Guinness*.

"He's saying that he wants to talk to me about whether his trip qualifies him for the *Guinness Book of World Records*," says Dave. "That would make him very happy."

Shortly after that footage was shot, friends in the L.A. Iranian community arranged for a podiatrist to treat Reza's feet. Operating in the back seat of his car, the doctor treated the blisters and cut out an ingrown toenail. The same group raised enough money to rent the RV to accompany Reza on his trip. The driver was going to be an Iranian-American chef. Dave didn't think that was such a good idea.

"I could just picture the two of them walking into some small town, not having shaved for a couple of days," says Dave. "The way John Ashcroft has everyone so paranoid you could see somebody thinking they were there to blow up a school."

Dave decided to catch up with Reza and see him to New York. First, he had to tell his business partner that he wouldn't be taking the new job they had worked so hard to land. "You're throwing over your partner of ten years for a guy who you've known for a month?" asked Dave's pal.

"Yes," answered Dave, "I am."

"My partner was always a temperamental guy," Dave tells me. "I was always the one following up with our clients and telling them he didn't really mean what he said. I got that from growing up with an alcoholic. That way of always trying to make things appear perfectly normal when there's all this chaos. I guess you could say I'm an enabler."

Alas, Dave may have jumped from the psychological frying pan into the fire. The penultimate line in the *New York Times* story he read about Reza would prove prophetic: "For some, glory is like sea water. The more one drinks, the thirstier one grows."

Reza has grown mighty thirsty.

Since leaving L.A. to join Reza, Dave has kept a journal of their travels. Much of his jottings are picayune details of people met and supplies bought. Some, however, suggest that Reza can be a handful.

June 11: He shows me the bottle of baby oil I used to massage him this morning. He wants to put it on his legs, no doubt so they will glisten a bit for the TV cameras. [A crew from Oklahoma City was on hand.] No I say, "the sun hits them, it will burn." He said, "I like" and proceeds to slather all over his legs. When he finishes he looks approvingly. "This good." He leaves a half-hour early, then returns thinking maybe it would be a good idea for him to shave his legs.

June 26: Reza almost got hit by a car this evening. He called twice and the phone didn't ring. I got to him at 8:30, and he'd peed his pants he was so scared.

Later, while driving on I-40 just outside Memphis in a rented Volvo station wagon, I get a firsthand glimpse at what caused Reza to lose the contents of his bladder. (Dave, fearful their permission to run on the highway will be revoked, doesn't allow anyone to run with Reza on the interstate.) Even in the comfort of a solid Volvo, each passing semi leaves me jonesing for a Valium. At one point, Reza needs to cross four lanes of traffic as the highway merges with another. It proves difficult enough in a car. I look back expecting to see poor Reza planted on the grill of a Cadillac Escalade. But he bides his time and scoots safely across.

Dave sighs when he recalls Reza's near-miss. "I went up ahead to send some e-mails to the media in the next town. When I reached him, he told me, 'Reza runs forty miles a day, Dave spend all day on the Internet, writing to newspapers. Dave go back to L.A., and Reza write newspapers.' But after an hour, he forgot all about it." Dave is able to forgive Reza for these lapses partly because of his own enabling personality and partly because of Reza's innate likability. For every tantrum he throws, there is an act of kindness — and not all of them involve puppies. Early in his trip, Reza found a $100 bill on the side of the road. He had Dave take him to the nearest hospital, where he bought flowers for sick children. And when Afsaneh will need to fly back to L.A., Reza will insist that we drive her to the airport in Nashville, a four-hundred-mile roundtrip. At the end of the day, Reza makes sure Dave knows he's the one man in the world Reza can count on. "Dave good to me," Reza says. "Dave only one I always trust."

And so Dave remains loyal. On the RV's dashboard is a CD he made for Reza. The tunes include Elton John's "Your Song," the Rolling Stones' "Waiting on a Friend," and the Bee Gees' "How Do You Heal a Broken Heart." "I wanted songs that reflect the loneliness of running and the courage of his journey," explains Dave. He shrugs and laughs. "I don't think he likes it. Ever since he was in Mexico, he loves salsa music."

So far, despite Dave's PR efforts, Reza's journey hasn't exactly penetrated the American media. There's been some local TV coverage and newspaper stories, but none of the national shows have

bitten. Still, Reza remains undaunted. Dave plays for me some promotional videos targeted for the morning shows. One captures
Reza at dawn, about to embark on a run. "*Good Morning America*,
from Reza." Another is pitched toward NBC: "Good morning,
Katie, I am Reza." One evening after looking at slides of Reza's travels, I jokingly ask him to tell me about the groupies he must have
left in his wake. Reza smiles and says, "Steve, I not tell you everything. Reza save for book and movie." Everyone laughs. Reza already knows who is going to play him. "Tom Cruise," he says defini-
tively. "Only Tom Cruise."

In the parking lot of a Super-8 Motel, the Midnight Riders of East
St. Louis, a group of African-American bikers, shine up their chop-
pers. Into their midst arrives Reza. It's noon, and he's already run
twenty-five miles. When he comes to a stop, there's no panting, no
sign of distress. "I rest a minute and run twenty more," says Reza. As
usual, he is constantly smiling through jumbled teeth. After a few
minutes, two bikers wander over.

"That dude is running across the country?" asks one, who calls
himself Half-Pint. "That is too much."

Reza shakes a couple of hands and smiles again. "I like peace, I
no like terrorism, I want all people to like each other."

"That's cool," says Half-Pint. "I'm for that." He signs his name on
the side of the RV, adding it to well-wishers from across the country.

Reza's message of peace doesn't go much deeper than that. It's
not as if he has a doctorate in peace studies. One day, I join him for
a few miles as he runs through downtown Memphis. We pass the
Lorraine Motel, where Martin Luther King Jr. was shot. It's now a
civil rights museum. I tell Reza that King is an American hero who
worked for peace. He looks at me quizzically and then smiles. "I not
know Martin Luther King." He runs another few strides and then
pronounces: "Reza want to be American hero."

It's one of the contradictions of Reza's journey. His English is
minimal, so he is limited to a few platitudes. In a way, that's not
a bad thing. It allows the people he meets to project what they
want onto him. There's no *Crossfire*-like quibbling about border
disputes, puppet dictatorships, or American imperialism. People
leave their encounters with him feeling good about themselves no
matter their ideological stripes.

But there are still those who have the other reaction. On a Saturday afternoon, we set out to find a vet to look over Rocky Balboa. Dave eventually locates one in Memphis, next to a tattoo parlor. Reza stays with Rocky as the vet examines him. "*Qué pasa*, Rocky?" asks Reza in a loving voice. He strokes his snout and Rocky sighs. Dave explains to the doctor Reza's story of running across America. The vet stares at Reza as if he's a Vulcan. "Mmm," he mutters. For the rest of Rocky's exam, he watches Reza out of one eye. For him, there appears to be a direct corollary between running three thousand miles and spontaneous psychotic behavior.

As the sun falls, we make a pilgrimage to Graceland. Unfortunately, tours are over for the day, even for men running across the country. However, Reza borrows a pen. He walks over to a portion of the wall surrounding Elvis's home that is covered with messages from visitors. In very careful penmanship, he writes a long and elaborate note in Farsi. When he's finished, I ask Afsaneh what it says.

"It's a beautiful Iranian saying," she says. "He wrote, 'Life is very, very hard. We struggle. Only one thing is certain. In the end, we must all die.'" It's the closest I see Reza come to connecting his own suffering with his cross-country run for peace.

We head over to a nearby souvenir shop. Reza dons big gold glasses and mugs for photos with a Vegas-era cardboard Elvis. He then has an idea: why not buy a T-shirt with Elvis's picture to run through downtown Memphis tomorrow? He grabs one and disappears into the changing room. In a minute, a sheepish Reza emerges. The garment is skin-tight and could serve as wardrobe for the next Village People revival. He looks in the mirror and shakes his head. "Reza give this to girlfriend," Reza says. "This shirt make Reza look gay." Then Reza grabs my arm. "You not write Reza is gay, okay? Reza not gay."

Wait a second. Reza, a man of peace, has a sliver of prejudice in him. How could this be? After his travels across the world? After his own struggles? I think about it for a while, and although it may be odious, it makes Reza seem more like real flesh and blood. To the humanitarian/superhero/egomaniac trifecta, add human being.

But even that doesn't capture Reza. He surely cares about peace, but that's not all this trip is about. If it were, Reza would have learned more than a few clichés — whether in Farsi, English, or Esperanto — to say on the subject, and he'd definitely be able to ID Martin Luther King Jr. No, Reza is a wanderer. As much as peace or his ambitions to become a star, that's what this trip is about. And Reza is at home in America, because from the Sooners waiting for the signal on the Oklahoma border to the bicoastal commuters of the new century, this is a country of roamers. In the land of the rootless, Reza Baluchi is king.

Reza says that when he completes his journey, he wants to go back to school and study engineering. It's depressing to picture him, short-sleeved with a pocket protector, commuting to a suburban office park in a Hyundai, and running spread sheets. Reza realizes this. There's already talk of him running back to L.A. via Canada. I get the feeling Dave would be on board, too. "I finally feel like I'm doing something with my life," he says.

On my last day, Dave asks me to drive ahead in my rental car and give Reza some cold water. It's only 10:00 A.M., but Dave estimates that Reza is about fifteen miles down the road. Later, I'll find out Reza has already had an eventful morning. A Tennessee state trooper pulled in front of him and told Reza that running on the highway was forbidden.

"It's okay," Reza replied. "I talk to big police boss, he says okay."

Amazingly, the trooper moved on. However, as I head up I-40, Reza is nowhere to be found. I pull off an exit to begin retracing my steps. Then, my cell phone rings. It's Reza. He's not pleased.

"Steve, I run twenty miles. No water. What Steve do?"

Good point. When I find him — he had ducked into a gas station — Reza is no longer mad. He gulps water and smiles. I ask him if he wants to take a break. He's only had a banana to eat. "No," he says, "I must run." With that, Reza Baluchi trots over to the onramp, merging onto the highway between a pickup truck and a Chili's eighteen-wheeler. Destination: New York City. Dave is busy, too. He's sending a video of Reza to David Letterman.

Everyone's fingers are crossed.

Fishing the Mainstream

FROM SF WEEKLY

"CALL ME ISH," he says. "I prefer Ish." He's Ishama on the dotted line and Shama with his parents, but to anyone else — to the bass fisherman in the back of his boat, to the kids bowing their heads so he can autograph their hats, to pretty much everybody he's met since that day in high school he introduced himself to a girl and she said, "Bless you" — he'd like to be known simply as Ish. More than a name, says an ex-girlfriend of his, it's a separate identity, his "fishing persona."

Ish is cool. Ish has style. Ish — twenty-nine years old, stocky, handsome, black — thinks he brings something new to the sport of bass fishing, something he calls "flavor," which may have to do with the fact that he wears wakeboard shorts and visors at his tournaments and says things like, "I *love* the camera — the camera makes me who I am." (Ish also would like you to know that some of his sponsors are Skeeter, Yamaha, and Lamiglas.) And at this moment, Ish Monroe is grabbing a fish by the lower jaw — six pounds of fat, ornery bass — and he's yelling:

"Come an' *git* you some!"

It's an overcast spring day on California's Clear Lake, in a cove known as "The Keys," and Monroe is crouched at the prow of his boat, a can of Red Bull in his veins, an ESPN camera over his shoulder. He is wearing a soaked black ball cap, a green rain jacket with matching pants, and a pair of bug-eye shades with green-tinted lenses. He begins to rise.

"Come an' *git* you some!"

This is a big moment for Monroe, and he knows it. Here he is, near the top of the tournament standings, on the verge of becoming the first black pro to qualify for the Bassmaster Classic, the sport's Super Bowl, and an ESPN camera is whirring just a few feet away. He has spent most of the tournament flipping along the margins, working so deep in the tules that at one point he could hear his fellow fishermen wonder where the hell he was. One of them swore Monroe was somewhere around here; another called him a fucking asshole. And then along comes this big, yawning fish, and Monroe sees its mouth close around his hook, and then he sees his line begin to swim, and then, ecstatic, he shouts the only thing that comes to mind. (Later, when they replay the clip on the video screens at the Classic, he'll do a double take.)

"Come an' *git* you some!" Now he is pointing at the camera, at the television viewers, the great majority of whom, unaccustomed to this sort of shit talk on their Saturday-morning fishing shows, are surely dropping their spoons in their grits.

Monroe plucks the hook out of the fish's mouth. "Like I said," he says, settling down for a second, "flippin' a little tighter."

And then (pointing again): "Come an' *git* you some!"

Then (dropping the fish in a tank): "*That's* what I'm talkin' about!"

Then (pumping his arms): "Come an' *git* you some!"

He takes a deep breath and a moment later turns to his bundled-up partner, Virgil, in the back of the boat. "Partner," Monroe says, "can I get a little high-five over there?" Virgil complies and slaps Monroe's palm with a stiff pink hand. Virgil, it's clear, could use some flavor.

In fishing circles, Monroe is described as a "breath of fresh air" and "one of the hottest properties on the Bassmaster circuit" and "more flashy than a double willow blade." *Sports Illustrated* says he "is changing the face of competitive fishing, a sport heretofore dominated by white Southerners." At the Classic this year, in New Orleans, they asked Deion Sanders — the only man ever to play in both the Super Bowl and the World Series and a self-made celebrity known variously as "Neon" and "Prime Time" — whom he'd want to fish with, if he could have his choice. Sanders, in town to promote his new ESPN show, mentioned Bill Clinton, and he mentioned Oprah, but when he said, "You know I've got to cover the brother first," he was talking about Monroe. "He's doing great things for the sport," Sanders told reporters. "He's really opened a lot of eyes." ("I'm like, 'Deion Sanders wants to go fishing with *me*? Cool!'" Monroe recalls. "I'll take him out. I'll whoop on him a little bit, but I'll take him out.")

Bass fishing has never inspired the masculine poetry of, say, trout fishing. It's not pretty or lyrical or peaceful. It's two hundred guys in their lucky underwear spread across forty thousand acres of dirty water, cussing out one side of the mouth and dangling a cigarette out the other, making three casts a minute into weeds and tules and praying the lake will cough up the fattest, ugliest shitkicker bass it's got — what some anglers call a donkey. Which is to say, bass fishing is not Hemingway, and it's not great TV either. Two years ago, ESPN bought the Bass Anglers Sportsman Society and its Bassmaster tournament trail for a reported $30 million to $40 million, and quickly set about steering the sport into NASCAR's wake, hoping to win the same kind of mainstream appeal. Of course, it's a long cast to the mainstream, especially for a sport that has yet to shed its drawl. To get there, bass needs drama, characters — "Come an' *git* you some," in other words.

Monroe, who grew up in San Francisco and now lives ninety miles southeast of the city, in Patterson, may have come along at the right time. He has fished since he was two years old, turning pro at eighteen, and insists it's all he has ever wanted to do. He once skipped his girlfriend's prom for a tournament ("I won," he says, albeit a little ruefully), and later, when the two of them were living together, he'd tape over her movies with his fishing shows. "Fishing is my *deal*," Monroe says. "Fishing's the best relationship I've ever had. It's the purest thing I have. It's my *everything*. . . . I mean, fishing is so exciting to me, I wake up every day with butterflies in my stomach. I wake up in the middle of the night, and I'm like, 'Dang, is it time yet? Can I go fishing?'"

Maybe the best place to watch Ish — the persona, at least — is the weigh-in at the end of a round. There are the board shorts and visor; his tournament shirt — the one with logos crawling up the arms and collar — will be clean and pressed. ("Guys are like, 'Dang, how do you keep your shirt so neat and clean?'" he says. "What I do is, I fold it up in a plastic bag and put it away. I won't wear my tournament shirt until weigh-in time, or unless the cameras are on me. 'Cause you go out fishing all day, driving these boats seventy-five miles per hour, you get grass on you, blood, bugs.") Monroe will banter with the MC, careful to drop the names of his sponsors whenever possible and maintain his good humor in general. At the Classic, he entered to the thump of Rob Base's "It Takes Two" and even managed to smile as he walked onto his sport's biggest stage — without a single fish to weigh. But when he has something — a fat, ornery six-pounder, say, that came and got herself some — he'll hoist it by the lower jaw and smile broadly for the cameras. Knowing the extent of Monroe's obsession, knowing that his girlfriend once popped in a tape expecting Christian Slater and instead got a screenful of bass, you have to wonder: is he holding the fish, or is the fish holding him?

As eureka moments go in the world of sports, it's certainly a humble one, with the whiff of apocrypha: on a rainy day in 1967, an insurance salesman named Ray Scott Jr. was holed up in a Jackson, Mississippi, Ramada Inn, watching a basketball game. (Or was it a pocket-billiards tournament?) "That's it," he said, snapping his fingers, instantly envisioning a new spectator sport in which people would pay thousands to compete. And thus organized bass fishing was born. It had to be bass, too. "Can you imagine a Crappiemasters Classic?" Scott once told a *Washington Post* reporter. "I knew the bass was the heart of fishing. He's the king — potbellied, ugly as a backwoods sheriff, indifferent to anything you do, unpredictable. You think you know him today, but come back tomorrow, and he's done read the paper. He's gone." By 1968, Scott had founded BASS.

Less than a decade later, in Michigan, Gregory Simpson handed his baby son a small Zebco reel. Simpson's father had taken Gregory fishing, and now Gregory was doing the same for his son. The two of them would fish around Ann Arbor, sometimes for dinner, and when Ishama (his name, his mother says, is Swahili for "firstborn") was two and a half years old, he caught his first fish, a bluegill. Simpson hooked it; Ishama reeled it in. "From that day on," says Simpson, now a San Francisco firefighter, "he was kind of sprung." Fishing, Monroe says, "was the only thing me and my dad ever had, emotionally" — a game of catch, of a different sort. And on fishing trips what would they talk about? "Fishing," he says.

Monroe moved to San Francisco with his mother, Wanda Monroe, and his father followed soon after (his parents never married). The two of them continued to fish, and Monroe would spend his summers in Michigan, rod in hand. Meanwhile, bass fishing's appeal was spreading, and a BASS television show, *The BASS-MASTERS*, debuted in 1985. (ESPN would like you to know that *The BASSMASTERS*, now in its second season on ESPN2, delivers "the most in-depth, thrilling coverage of professional bass fishing.") Monroe had a Fisher-Price tape recorder, and he'd hold it up to the TV during fishing shows, catching the dialogue so he could replay it later. "I used to just sit there for hours and listen," he says.

"This kid," says Wanda Monroe, a respiratory therapist who lives in Vacaville, sighing with feigned exasperation. "When other kids were getting bicycles, footballs, basketballs for Christmas, Ishama was getting fishing poles." She remembers buying him a pair of $100 Nikes, which he wore one day to Lake Merced and promptly lost on the shore. "That kid," she says. He was fishing every week — striper, perch, largemouth bass — and he eventually began to enter local tournaments as a nonboater (meaning he'd fish in the back of a pro's boat). At seventeen, with some help from his father, Monroe bought his first bass boat, and when the two of them would fish together, it'd be Monroe at the front, running the trolling motor, and Simpson in back.

In 1993, soon after he turned pro, Monroe met Mel Tellez through a mutual acquaintance. There was a small gathering one night, and Monroe, then just out of high school, actually *turned off* the Super Nintendo to talk to her. At one point, as Tellez remembers it, he told her he was working as a UPS loader, but he said that job was only to pay for his tournaments; what he really wanted to do was fish. "I laughed," she recalls, "and I continued laughing for the next four years."

By the time of Napa High School's prom, they had been dating for four months or so. Tellez, a senior, picked out a dress and made dinner reservations. "I naturally assumed my boyfriend would be taking me," she says. "Then he informed me, probably about a week before prom, that he had a tournament to go to. I was like, 'Okay, you're still taking me to prom.' He said, 'No, I have to go to this tournament.' I said, 'You're joking. You're taking me to my prom. You can't do this to me.' He picked the tournament."

Tellez wound up going with an old crush of hers, and Monroe didn't like that at all. The prom incident became an issue — "the prom thing" — and remained one over the course of their on-and-off relationship, which had the misfortune of turning serious at the same time as Monroe's fishing career. "It was a big issue for me — all right, this guy is always going to pick fishing over me," says Tellez, who is now engaged to a cellarmaster at Rombauer Vineyards. "That's why we never worked out." Monroe eventually had to move to Phoenix "to get away from her, because it was affecting my fishing." (He moved to Patterson two years later.)

"If I had to do it over, I would've gone [to the prom]," he admits. "It's one of those things you regret." Of course, he also says: "Most girls take offense to it — they think they can change a man, and a man'll love them more than they love anything else. And that's just not the case [with me]." And: "It was the first tournament I ever won."

Adams Marine sits on a bank of the California Delta in Suisun City, just a block or two from where Main Street cul-de-sacs. The place is a Skeeter boat dealership, and every so often, customers are treated to what is known as a Demo Day, in which staff pros hold forth on bass technique and then take potential boat buyers for a spin on the water. One Saturday in October, maybe twenty people grab plastic chairs inside Adams Marine's large, hangarlike building. Discounted boats are fanned out in front of them, like a card trick. One guy has a T-shirt with a picture of a fishing hook and the large block words "BITE ME!"; another shirt, worn by an older man with a lot of tattoos, reads "Playaz Wear."

Monroe is here today, at the request of the owner, Bob. (Bob would like you to know that Adams Marine is the only Skeeter dealer in northern California.) For about fifteen minutes, Monroe takes questions from the audience, and everyone seems faintly impressed: *Besides catching fish, how do you get a job like yours?* ("Go to school for marketing," he says.) From a boy, about six years old: *Have you ever caught a jellyfish?* ("Oh, yeah, but I cut the line.") And finally: *What happened at the Classic?* ("Ummm. . . .")

Skeeter will pay Monroe's expenses for his work today; he wasn't obligated to attend, but he did because the dealer asked, and maybe when it comes time to renegotiate his sponsorship deal, Skeeter will show its appreciation. Monroe understands, and even seems to embrace, this side of the sport. "I'm an advertiser. That's what my job is," he says (though in this case, he is, more precisely, an advertise*ment*). This year at the Classic, Monroe watched as a group of cheerleaders working for Yamaha handed out small sticker tattoos of the company logo. "I just said, 'You know, I'm going to be on camera — that would be a neat way to get some extra Yamaha [exposure],'" he says. He got a sticker for his left cheek, and as it happened the left cheek got the most airtime that day. (He also kissed one of the cheerleaders, but, he says with a sigh, "That's another story.")

"Yamaha loved it," he says. "It was one of those sponsorship things where I go above and beyond the call of duty. Nobody else did it. I got on the bus that morning with all the fishermen, and all the Yamaha guys saw [the tattoo], and they're going, 'Aww, that's a major kiss-ass right there.' I'm just like, 'What, are you mad you didn't think of it?'"

It's all very Ish, a part of the persona. Ish is a salesman, carrying all sorts of expectations. "Ish," says Monroe, laughing at himself for using the third person, "is always on his P's and Q's." Tellez, one of just a handful of people to call him Shama, is blunt about her distaste for Ish; it's what she calls him when she's trying to piss him off. "He's someone who has routine answers, someone who always wants to say the right thing," she says. "When he's Ish, he's trying to be what everybody wants him to be." But Shama? Shama's clothes don't always match. Shama will say "fuck" and not worry about losing a sponsor. Shama pulls up next to a truck in Reno, sees a few strands of blond hair, and winds up with a long-term girlfriend. (Her name is Rachel, and she calls him Ish.) "Not to say I have a split personality, but Shama's more free," Monroe says. "Shama doesn't care. He just wants to have fun, be with a whole bunch of girls, enjoy life."

For all the talk about its being the sport for the everyman, bass fishing certainly creates an odd kind of athlete, one whose athletic persona is yoked to his corporate persona; he's a salesman even on the weigh-in stage. That's out of necessity: this year, Monroe says, he has won about $60,000 at tournaments; he figures he has pulled in at least that much in endorsement deals. In return, he shows up at expos and Demo Days like this, and he makes sure to mention his sponsors whenever possible. (A rod is never just a rod — it's a

Lamiglas rod.) "You don't get paid for catching fish on that product," he says. "You get paid for pitching that product."

Monroe realized early on that this was the nature of the sport — that this, in many ways, *was* the sport. After high school, he went to Contra Costa College and took marketing and public speaking courses, knowing that's what sponsors would want. And one of his last jobs before fishing served as additional preparation: he sold cars. "Like a fish in water," he says. "I was a natural car salesman." Now he sees himself as part of a new breed of bass fishermen, "people who are businessmen, more than just bass fishermen." He cites the old-guard anglers. "You hear some of them speak," he says, "you couldn't sell nothin' that way. 'Well, Ah cawt 'em on a lizzerd, yeah, on a Carolina rig.' Now you've got guys saying, 'I was out there with my seven-and-a-half-foot Lamiglas flipping stick and twenty-five-pound Maxima line and four-inch lizard on a tungsten weight made by a PRADCO.' They do a whole infomercial right there. And that's what's gonna sell." It's something the new breed appreciates: if pro fishing is mostly marketing, isn't marketing — with its own set of lures and lines — just another kind of fishing?

Bass fishing splits in two at the left edge of Texas, East on one side and West on the other, though it sometimes seems as if the old American divide of North and South had merely been set on its ear. The rivalry is essentially cultural: western guys are just flashy kids who can talk into a microphone but don't care a whit for etiquette; the good ol' boys back east are too lazy to leave their verandas and fish out west. At this year's Classic (officially, BASS would like you to know, it's the CITGO Bassmaster Classic presented by Busch Beer), which draws anglers from all corners of the country, one fisherman would roll up to the weigh-in stage playing country music; the next would come along bobbing to rap.

The center of the sport is still Montgomery, Alabama, where BASS has its headquarters. For Monroe to fish the circuit, he has to spend much of his time out "east" — he put seventy-seven thousand miles on his last truck after just a year and a half. In other words, a young black man has to cruise through the South in an out-of-state Suburban with a twenty-foot bass boat on its hitch. "I've been pulled over in Texas twice, Georgia once, Alabama once, and Florida once," Monroe says one evening, absent-mindedly watching *COPS* on television. "Georgia — that was the worst one out of all of them." In that instance, he says, he made eye contact with a cop, and the next thing he knew, a backup had arrived and a dog was sniffing around his truck (registered, because of a sponsorship deal, in Indiana) and boat (Missouri). "*And* I had a California driver's license," Monroe says. "So you know how that went." They eventually let him go, though Monroe spent the entire time worrying the cops might plant something, which would effectively torpedo his endorsements.

On the tour, Monroe insists, he's never had any problems, outside of some grumbling that he gets perks simply because he's black. BASS, for its part, seems eager to dispel the perception that this is a white man's sport. Indeed, this August's Classic was a boon for both Monroe, who, perks or no, had gotten to his sport's Super Bowl, and for bass fishing, a sport with maybe something of a guilty conscience. This June, in *BASS Times*, Tim Tucker recalled telling Monroe five years ago "that if he ever qualified for the Classic, he would have the fishing world by the tail." Tucker wrote: "I remarked that he was exactly what this sport needed — a unique combination of youth, talent, personality, and energy.

"And Ish Monroe also happens to be an African American."

Monroe certainly got a chance to showcase himself in New Orleans, and going into the first round he expected to do even more. Everything had gone well to that point. At the hotel, the front-desk clerk had liked him so much she upgraded him to a suite. The press seemed to like him, too, and everyone had eaten up his line that "fish don't see color." In practice, he'd had a "*phenomenal* day," and his media observer had said he just might win this thing. And perhaps because of all the attention, ESPN had decided to stick a cameraman with him for his first round. "Kiss of death," Monroe says. That day, as his father puts it, he got "skunked"; he caught nothing (except hell from his grandfather for cussing on national TV). At the weigh-in, Monroe climbed the stage without a bag of fish, and the crowd gasped. The MC, a boppy guy who calls himself Fish Fishburne, said: "Wait a second. Now, now, now — are you *serious?*"

"Yeah, Fish," Monroe said into the microphone, flashbulbs popping, "it was one of those days. I mean, everything that could go wrong, went wrong. I missed probably fifteen bites today. I'm watching fish come out of the grass bed, look at my lure, and swim away from it. I'm like, 'Something's wrong — I got something on my hands, something on my boat.'" He smiled faintly, dropped two Yamaha references, and vowed to go out there the next day and catch some fish.

Monroe wound up finishing fifty-fourth in a field of sixty-one. "It was one of the most disappointing moments," he says now. "One of the best, and one of the most disappointing. . . . I definitely got me some airtime during the Classic. Can't ask for much more than that." In fact, the Classic got him a mention and a photo in *Sports Illustrated*, and probably his qualifying for the event got him a job as a color analyst during ESPN's Great Outdoor Games. In addition, Monroe guesses he's been on more Bassmaster shows this year than any other angler.

"ESPN makes its superstars," he says one recent weekday while practicing out on Clear Lake. Just then his rod doubles up, and he sticks his first fish of the day.

"I've explained to ESPN," he goes on later. "'You know what you need? You need a bad boy of bass fishing.' When I say 'bad boy' I don't mean someone who breaks rules and things like that, but a guy who, if he goes out there and misses a fish, just gets pissed off and — *ksssshhhh* — snaps a rod over his knee. It's stuff like that that would bring more people into the sport.

"They asked me if I wanted the job. I said, 'No, not really. Everybody likes me.'" (Incidentally, Monroe's cussing at the Classic — he said either "shit" or "fuck" — wasn't bleeped, which may or may not have been a conscious grab by ESPN for "edge.")

I ask Monroe if he thinks ESPN is using him. "They can use me all they want," he says. "It ain't gonna do nothing but make me more popular and put more money in my pocket." As he points out, casting from the prow of his boat, he's using ESPN, too. *Come an' git you some.*

Clear Lake and its namesake city, Clearlake, lie about one hundred miles north of San Francisco; at forty-three thousand acres, Clear Lake is the largest natural lake within California's borders and possibly the oldest in North America. (The Chamber of Commerce also would like you to know that Clear Lake is considered the "Bass Capital of the West.") The three-day CITGO Bassmaster Western

Open presented by Busch Beer rolls into town on a Wednesday evening in October, beginning with registration and a briefing at the Clearlake Senior Center, and for the next few days, the city is overrun with trucks and boats, moving mostly in schools — massing at the senior center or the Best Western, or idling, in the predawn hour before launch, along the roads leading into Redbud Park.

The event is not one of bass fishing's biggest, but on the first day, a Thursday, a handful of fans turn up for the weigh-in outside the Bassmaster trailer, dragging their lawn chairs into the shade. A group of boys run around with autographs covering their yellow ball caps, lures dangling from the sides of the hats, and as the anglers return in waves at the end of the round, the kids head down to the docks to plead for more autographs and more lures. Each day of the tournament, in fact, draws a larger crowd, and by Saturday there is actually bickering among certain spectators about who set down whose cooler where.

Out on the water, Monroe fishes a pair of unspectacular but solid rounds and on Friday sits in thirty-seventh place, high enough to qualify for Saturday's finale. (Each angler fishes for a limit of five bass in a round and is ranked based on the weight of his total catch.) "I've become Mr. Consistency," Monroe says that night. "That's the new nickname I've given myself." Mr. Consistency is eating takeout on an old living-room sofa; the house, a low-roofed affair next to a dirt road and a bunch of barking dogs, belongs to his friend Aaron Coleman, a young black pro from Oakland, who uses the place when he's in town for a tournament. This week, he's let several other fishermen sleep here, and on Wednesday night there were five guys staying at the house, four of them black, or nearly the entire contingent of black anglers at the tournament. "Got all the brothers staying in one place, huh?" one white fisherman said to Coleman after the briefing. That night, they prepared for their first rounds by eating barbecue and flipping between old fishing videos and the Weather Channel. (Monroe's girlfriend, Rachel, wanted to come; he told her no.)

In any case, Mr. Consistency is not to be confused with Mr. Big Fish. "I used to be Mr. Big Fish," Monroe continues, "used to shoot for the win, and I'd either do really, really well, or I'd do really, really bad. Now I stay consistent, and I just cash checks." It's a different style of fishing, incorporating an altogether different pattern, and it means that at the end of a tournament there will likely be a paycheck. It's how full-time fishermen remain full-time fishermen. Meanwhile, Coleman and Matt Miley, an amateur staying here, make their merry way through a bottle of cognac; neither of them qualified for the final day.

Fishing with any kind of consistency is itself a major achievement. Anglers know only a few things about bass. Bass like structure (docks, for instance); they like a nice, cool spot in the shadow of a tree; they like an easy meal. "They're like people," Monroe says. "A pizzaman shows up at your doorstep with a pizza, and you ain't gotta pay for it, you're gonna eat it." The idea is to get a bite, determine precisely how you got that bite, then develop a pattern around that bite (which, come to think of it, is also how a car salesman moves Chevys). "The only thing about that is that fish are unpredictable," he says. It's not light work either. After two days — sixteen hours — of fishing, Monroe's right leg aches from leaning on the trolling motor's pedal. The muscle between his right thumb and index finger has locked up. His hands are cut, his fingers hurt, and he just took an Excedrin for his head. "Put it this way," Coleman says. "Those people who say bass fishing isn't a sport? They have no fucking clue."

The sheer difficulty of the sport — of trying to make rent money off the whims of a few ugly fish — seems to give even Monroe doubts about his choice of career. His youngest half-brother is starting to fish, and Monroe says he'd like him to get involved in the sport, but not *too* involved. "My mom takes him fishing, and I tell her to do it as much as she possibly can, because he'll end up like me," he says. "I'd love for my brother to end up like me, as far as not having the whole drugs thing, not getting into trouble, never going to jail. But as far as fishing for a living? No. I want him to have a real job." He laughs a little. "A real *life*."

But then Monroe has a good day like this, in the final round at Clearlake, and Mr. Consistency cashes another check. His nonboater for the day is Bob Sweeney, who has lung disease and a bad back. In the afternoon, as the day grows hot and Monroe complains that the theme from *Shaft* is stuck in his head, he steers his boat into the weedy corner of a marina, where he pitches over the railing of what looks like a small footbridge. Within minutes he sticks a keeper, and in one deft motion flips it up over the post, and into the boat. Then he does it again. *Can you dig it? "That* was cool," Sweeney says later. "I was sitting back there laughing. Just laughing. I had to get my breathing machine out."

Monroe winds up with five fish weighing eleven pounds, nine ounces, giving him twenty-second place overall and a $1,450 check. At the weigh-in, Fishburne, again the MC, says, "Ish has not been a happy camper this week." But at the moment Monroe doesn't look unhappy, and for the next few minutes he and Fishburne banter about Monroe's girlfriend, and then Monroe steps down from the stage. A black man shakes his hand, and a white guy sitting in a canvas chair says, "See you next spring, Ish." Monroe walks along a roped-off path with his bag of fish, and all around him the fans have taken up nice, cool spots in the shadows of trees, and the kids bounce from dock to dock with lures in their hats, as if they had just been hooked.

GUY MARTIN

Getting Slammed

FROM FIELD & STREAM

IF YOU ARE FOOLISH enough to launch a fishing expedition in the
Florida Keys armed with a plan, you will not keep it for long. There
may be a way to blame the sun, the rain, the wind, or the tackle, but
there is a force larger than the particulars in this wilderness that
breaks down human endeavor. The Keys are an extremity, like
outer space. Nothing is supposed to work here. Nothing often
does.

On the seagrass meadows, or flats, of the mangrove islands on
the northern flank of the Keys live the tarpon, permit, and bonefish. These species are the most contrary and arguably the most
finicky saltwater gamefish in the world. That they occur in one
blessed chunk of wilderness has given rise to what the Keys guides
call the Backcountry Grand Slam, or sometimes just "the Triple,"
meaning that one angler catches each fish of the trinity on a single
trip.

Very good flats fishermen can go seasons without a grand slam.
Many have just one or two in their lives. It's hard to do with bait, it's
even harder to do on a fly, and it's tremendously hard to do in a
day. In any event it makes a splendid lifetime angling goal — but
it's a very bad idea to go to the Keys *thinking* that a grand slam is
what you will get. The reason, the flats guides know, is that these
fish can hear fishermen think. Despite this, of course, every single
fisherman who goes to the flats has a slam in mind, whether he admits it or not.

My group has what I believe is an ideal plan for a Backcountry
Grand Slam, or at least a plan that the fish won't be able to deci-

pher, namely, no plan at all. The heart of our strategy is the humble boat trailer and the even more modest trailer hitch. With it, we are going to take the war to the fish, ranging up and down the lower Keys, putting in here one day, there the next, according to the vast catalog of flats and tides in Capt. Bruce Chard's sunbaked head. The fish will never know what hit them. It's our way of not telling them what we're doing until we do it.

The Permit

"Every two miles north in the ocean is an hour later in the tide," says the affable Chard, who, at thirty-two, has been guiding in the lower Keys for the last eight years. "Sometimes they like a little water on the flat, sometimes they like a *lot* of water on the flat, and some flats fish better for bones or permit rather than both. But the big thing is current: no current, no fish."

What Chard means is that, in a sturdy, eighteen-foot flats skiff that tops out at forty-five miles an hour and draws just twelve inches of water, we can chase the tide changes north, or put ourselves at an angle to the tides and chase them east or west, increasing our access to a variety of flats at their best time of day. It does not mean that the fish will oblige us by taking our flies or bait. It does mean that we can fish many different places where they might.

With his sun visor barely containing his sun-streaked ponytail, Chard looks like a University of Florida upperclassman who has wandered off the Phi Delta Theta party raft, but he fishes so well that the Teeny Company is developing a permit fly line in his name. We also have a live well full of crab and shrimp in case the wind, or the fish, won't let us fish with flies.

Our second boat is captained by Mike Sobr, a fisherman out of Sarasota. Sobr's boat is a prototype — a Panga flats boat, built in Mexico. It's beamier than the classic Keys skiff, but at twenty-one feet long still only draws about ten inches of water, fully loaded. Sobr's angler will be *Field & Stream*'s contributing photographer and Montana trout aficionado Dusan Smetana.

This cast of characters is thinking big. At a 6:00 A.M. war council over scrambled eggs and grits, we decide to go to the Marquesas, a wilderness atoll thirty miles west of Key West, to fish for permit. The Marquesas are nothing but a tangle of bushy mangroves formed in a great necklace of green islets around a submerged limestone hilltop, but this hill lies in the middle of the ocean, miles from anywhere.

Inside the Marquesas is a pristine two-mile-by-two-mile seagrass meadow. Such fields are the habitat for the crustaceans that are the diet of bonefish and permit. Because this atoll's inner bay is sheltered, and because it offers such rich food, many larger species use the meadow for breeding grounds. Crucial to the equation is the turtle grass. More than thirty species of tropical invertebrates depend on the grass, which is the absolute rock upon which the food chain of the Keys' $34 million annual sport-fishing industry rests. The meadows of the Keys, including the big one inside the Marquesas, form the largest seagrass bed in the world.

The Marquesas are an aquatic Mojave. One dresses to fish them as one dresses for the desert: long sleeves, long pants, nose masks, kepis. As the backcountry of the backcountry, the Marquesas have for decades exerted a strong pull on the fishermen of the Keys. Hemingway took John Dos Passos there on a fishing trip in 1929. A snapshot of the two writers on that trip is framed in Hemingway's dressing room in the old Whitbread Street house in Key West. In it, both men stand on the great sea meadow in long pants, with no fish, wet to their knees.

Chard and Sobr blast their boats out of Key West Harbor, bound to fish Hemingway's flat. At Boca Grande Key, we hit the big channel water coming off the Atlantic, and Chard's eighteen-footer vaults into the air from swell to swell like an oceangoing dope runner. The only way to take it is to stand up and hang on to the console rail. Chard calls this a "calm" crossing, then smiles a little wicked smile.

At the atoll, we pass quietly through a cut between keys to Mooney Harbor, a seven-foot-deep piece of water in the southern quadrant of the great Marquesas meadow, and enter the grand amphitheater of fish. Waxy green mangroves surround us. Chard noses the boat north, to a big flat inside the elbow of the northern Marquesas. It is a white-hot day. There are no humans here except for us.

We begin by baitfishing with crab on eight-pound-test. On a fly rod or on spinning rigs, the angling routine in these skiffs is like

nineteenth-century whaling on a small scale. The guide is elevated
on his platform over the motor. Rod in hand, the angler stands at
the ready on the foredeck, exactly as the nineteenth-century Cape
Codders stood ready to harpoon whales. The difference is that
whales are a whole lot easier to see than permit.

Sobr and Smetana work the eastern side of the meadow. Chard
works west, parallel to the mangrove shore. I stand, shifting my
weight from foot to foot, ready to cast.

A lemon shark lazes by. Lemons are bone and permit predators,
so he's good to see. Then life, which is to say, everything on the
meadow, seems to sag. Chard sniffs the air and calls it: we're moving to a different section of the flat. I muse on the shimmering
knowledge of guides, how they have brains that actually think like
fish. I reel in, stow my rod, and turn to the console, and there
stands Chard, line shooting off the back of the boat, his reel emit-
ting the low moan of being punished by a large fish. It's our permit.

Chard can't pole and fight at the same time. He hands the rod to
me. I jump on the foredeck as he jumps back on his poling platform to dress the nose of the boat into the fish.

"He came from behind," Chard says, shrugging coolly. He's got a
blisteringly fast cast. His friends call him Wyatt Earp, for his quickness on the draw.

Permit fight like truck drivers whaling on you with tire irons.
Specifically, permit are huge pompano and thus are richly muscled, with a deep V tailfin cut for heavy pulling. They're fast, but
the runs are not as electric as those of a bonefish. Instead, they use
their huge lateral muscles to try to pull you in the water, or break
your leader, or yank the rod out of your hands, whichever comes
first.

This one is pulling out my line on the port side of the boat. He's
got ninety feet of it already, and he's curling around like a mule for
another go. I can feel his back working. He runs aft, then crosses to
the starboard side. Sometimes, the fish I fight remind me of certain
people because of the quality of the battle. This permit reminds me
of Secretary of Defense Donald Rumsfeld beating up a pack of reporters at a Pentagon press conference. Every time I drill down on
him, he sets his jaw, adjusts his glasses, and smacks me back.

Ten long minutes later, I've got the honorable secretary tuck-
ered out, but before he submits, he tries to run under the Panga in
a last effort to put a shadow between him and me. I work him out

from under the boat, and we land him. He's twenty pounds, a big one — blue and liquid gold and glorious in the wild Marquesas sun.

"Dude," says Chard.

"We are Marq-i-*fied*."

The Bonefish

At six the next morning we're back fishing off Little Torch Key, poling along a flat right next to the Atlantic, fishing for bones on fly rods. The permit have — clearly — telepathically radioed from the Marquesas to tell the bonefish not to show up for us here. There is nothing on this flat; even the ubiquitous cormorants have evaporated. In the distance, we can see Smetana on the upswept prow of Sobr's Panga casting his spinning rod once in a while. But to what? In an hour, they motor over.

"Let's get out of here," Chard says to them.

"Uhh, we saw maybe five groups of five bones, couple of permit," says Sobr, diplomatically. "They were coming up the other side."

It's a classic Keys moment. The boats are on the same flat, two hundred yards apart. One has multiple shots at serried pods of fish. The other gets skunked.

Still, we decide to shoot north into some better tides and some tight mangroves. A quick twelve-minute run at hyperspeed, and we're in a different aquatic arena, farther from the ocean, more vegetated. Some of the mangroves are so close that you have to lift your back cast to clear them.

"Dude! Behind me!"

I whip back to face him. Chard wants me to cast *around* his pushpole at a bone some thirty feet off the back of the boat. I throw a sidearm shot that snakes past Chard. The cast wasn't horrible, a bit to the left, maybe. I strip. The bonefish doesn't spook so much as he collects his hat and cane and saunters off.

It's midafternoon, and the heat bears down on the flats with physical weight. Chard and I bonefish, because we are men, and because we caught a permit, making the next thing on our grand slam list a bone. We pole through tight mangroves near Big Torch Key.

Smetana and Sobr have been working a rank of mangroves about a hundred yards east. We don't see them for long stretches, but then we hear a strange humanoid bark in the trees, and they heave into view. Smetana is standing stiffly over his spinning rod, fighting something.

"Bowwwwne!" Sobr hollers over the water at us.

We pole over to the party. Bonefish can sprint, thrash, and shake across a flat at thirty miles an hour, which gives them plenty of time to wrap a line around a sea fan or a rock and cut it, especially early on, before you have worn them down. Smetana works this bone for ten minutes and then calls the fish to heel. He's a hefty nine-pounder.

Smetana dances around the foredeck of the Panga in a sort of ugly Czech disco-man dance. "I caught my first bone!"

"Excellent," says Chard.

It could never be the real thing, but it's our two-thirds of a haphazard, two-boat, four-angler grand slam: a start, a seedling of a shadow of an accomplishment. Just the fact that Smetana's catch is a slam species gives it a shard of reflected glory, like fools' gold. This is just the barest taste of the siren song that makes fishermen all over the world want to go for the real deal.

The Tarpon

Since we have had no plan for our grand slam — but are, in fact (in a fake way), en route to one — we are forced to admit that we now have a goal and must fish accordingly. We must flyfish for tarpon. This is perhaps foolish, but, like everything else in this place, maybe not.

Early on our third morning, we put the four of us in the Panga and run to Howe Key. The tarpon are in a bridge season, which makes things tough. The big migratory fish are gone, but what the guides call "baby" tarpon, fifty-pounders who will stay and grow here for a season, are fishable in some north backcountry mangroves.

Five minutes after we reach the flat, we spot three baby tarpon rolling two hundred feet off the port side. Mike Sobr takes the Panga's foredeck. Chard poles the boat to the right. Sobr throws a sharp, pretty loop that lands sixty feet off the port bow. There's a small suck and rustle in the water as one of the tarpon turns to the fly. Sobr bends to strip, but it takes him a second to adjust his posture, and the tarpon noses off to his brothers.

"Dude," says Chard, consoling him.

There are big tarponlike thunderheads, thousands of feet tall, jousting at each other twenty miles east of us. Now, instead of fishing, *we* are being fished by the storm. We pole up the flat for another twenty minutes, but the tarpon have gone.

"The storm's flattened them," says Chard.

The thunderheads' march brings rain just east of us, a gray wall walking. Chard's fly rod begins to vibrate with the electric charge preceding the storm. These are the seeker charges for lightning. Keys guides say this is the sign from the gods when they want to kick you off the water.

"Waterspout," says Chard. "Back east."

Waterspouts are the most surreal, and fitting, expressions of Keys weather. The thunderheads literally suck up a column of water a couple of hundred yards tall, a baby tornado, but made of the sea. Water shouldn't, by rights, flow up to the sky, but here, it does.

One shot at a baby tarpon, less than a half-day on the water, and God's boot.

Bonefish will eat before bad weather — in fact, will eat well, Chard says, but tarpon get put down by it. Here we are part of the grand wheel of weather, tide, and wildlife: at this level of play it makes no sense to blame the small things such as the rain. There is a force larger than the particulars in this wilderness that breaks down human endeavor; the trick, if you are human, is to try to swim along with it, and be the best that you can be. Nothing is supposed to work here, except what wants to work. This is why, in the Keys, you may wake up thinking that you will be doing something that day, and a few hours later find yourself doing something entirely different.

We gun the Panga down the long storm verge, trying to outrun it. Five miles south is a sliver of sunlight on the bridge to Little Torch Key. The raindrops get fatter and thicker and beat straight into our eyes. Then the storm has us racing blind.

WILLIAM NACK

"No, Not Again!"

FROM ESPN.COM

OF ALL THE KENTUCKY DERBIES run over the past twenty-five years — from Genuine Risk's triumphant rush to the lead off the final turn in 1980 to long-shot Funny Cide's shocking charge to victory in this year's renewal — none had the truly brilliant signature moment for which the '86 running will long be remembered.

It was the year of Ferdinand, an attractive chestnut with a golden clump of forelock between his ears and a white star above his luminous brown eyes. Ferdy was a neat-looking colt, a son of the great Nijinski II, one of Thoroughbred racing's premier stallions. Of course, what gave his Derby the status of fable, an enduring place in Derby lore, was the fact that two of the most revered horsemen in America — legendary jockey Bill Shoemaker and trainer Charles Whittingham — were at his side along the way.

It was the Season of the Geezers. A few weeks earlier, the forty-six-year-old Jack Nicklaus had just become the oldest golfer ever to win the Masters, and down in Louisville the gray-haired, fifty-four-year-old Shoemaker was angling to become the oldest rider to win the Derby and the seventy-three-year-old Whittingham to finally win the roses for the very first time. The year before, when Ferdinand was two, Charlie had introduced The Shoe, his old friend and favorite jock, to the promising blueblood: "We're going to have some fun with this horse," Charlie told him. "May even win the Derby with him."

No one gave them much of a chance — the crowds sent Ferdy off at 17–1 odds — and not even as they turned for home, with the colt blocked behind a wall of horses, did he appear to have a shot.

It was right there, in one magical instant, that Shoemaker and his mount turned the classic into a rare work of Derby art. As two horses drifted apart in front of him, The Shoe reacted instinctively. Tugging on his left rein, he drove Ferdy for the breach, splitting horses along the way, then set sail on the rail in pursuit of the leaders. Pouring it on, Ferdinand ran them down in the cavalry charge to the wire and raced off to win it by two and a half lengths.

It was an unforgettable performance, and the memory of it is one of the reasons why the recent news out of Japan about the horse's demise was greeted with emotions that ranged from outrage to sadness to a keening, here-we-go-again despair. The Thoroughbred industry's most-respected trade publication, *The Blood-Horse*, recently reported that Ferdinand, exiled to a breeding farm in Japan after failing as a stallion in America, had been "disposed of" a year ago. The word "shobun," used by owner Yoshikazu Watanabe to describe Ferdinand's fate, is the Japanese horse industry's camouflage for saying Ferdy had been killed in a slaughterhouse. So, it may be assumed, America's 112th Kentucky Derby winner, at age nineteen, was either consumed as dinner filets by humans — Japanese and Europeans, unlike Americans, eat horse meat — or ground up into pet food.

"I was horrified," says Michele Oren, the manager of Exceller Farm in upstate New York, a haven for old or broken-down horses rescued from New England racetracks. "This is still allowed to go on? I couldn't believe that a horse of this magnitude was shipped overseas and his whereabouts not monitored. It's scary. Kentucky Derby winners are not meant to be a part of the food chain. No horse is. When I heard about Ferdinand's death, I thought, *No, not again!*"

Indeed, the farm where Oren works is named after a horse who had met a similar fate. Exceller was one of the finest racehorses in the sport's golden age of the 1970s. Owned by a legendary Texas oilman and Kentucky horse breeder, Nelson Bunker Hunt, Exceller won major stakes races in Europe and America, $1.64 million in purses in all, and earned his brightest laurel as the conqueror of the mighty Seattle Slew in the 1978 Jockey Club Gold Cup at Belmont Park, one of the most thrilling races run in that decade. Exceller did not achieve much success as a stallion here and, in 1991, was sold to a breeder in Sweden. When *The Daily*

Racing Form went looking for him six years later, as part of a "whatever-happened-to" series, the paper discovered that the twenty-four-year-old horse, though in good health and still able to breed, had been destroyed three months earlier on the orders of his bankrupt owner. The horse had become a liability.

The woman who befriended Exceller in his years at the farm told a wrenching story of the horse's final moments as he was led to slaughter, when he heard the screams and caught wind of the smell of blood. "I made an appointment [at the slaughterhouse] because I wanted to get it over with quick," she told *The Daily Racing Form,* "but they were very busy when we got there and we had to wait. Exceller knew what was going on; he didn't want to be there. Standing with him like that . . . it made me feel like Judas."

It was thus that Exceller became the poster-horse for a clamorous movement seeking to ban the slaughter of all horses for human consumption, and revelations on the death of Ferdinand have served to rekindle the passions of those seeking to end the slaughter of horses in America. The movement already has its own stalking horse in the form of a House of Representatives bill, HR 857, entitled "The American Horse Slaughter Prevention Act." Introduced in February by Reps. John Sweeney (R-N.Y.) and John Spratt (D-S.C.), passage of the bill would make it a crime to slaughter a horse for human consumption; to import or export horses from this country for that purpose; or to transport, sell, or purchase them to that end. It would not only shutter the two remaining horse slaughterhouses in the United States, both foreign-owned and located in north Texas, but also would prevent horses from being shipped for slaughter to Canada, where tens of thousands of U.S.-based horses are dispatched annually to be prepared for dinner tables from Paris to Tokyo. Of the seven million horses living in the United States, nearly sixty thousand are slaughtered here for human consumption every year, with thousands more sent to their deaths north of the border.

The way these horses are handled — how they are torturously transported in cramped, double-decker trailers built for shorter animals, often without water for hundreds of miles — is almost as repugnant to human values as the way in which they are killed in the abattoir. They are bludgeoned with four-inch captive bolt guns that drive spikes into their skulls. But horses tend to toss their heads a lot, especially when unnerved by the smell of blood, and repeated misses with the gun can lead to scenes beyond the macabre. "I have a tape showing a horse who did not die instantaneously," says New York breeder-owner John Hettinger, a leader in the fight to ban the butchery. "The horse is thrashing around on the ground. It's just horrible. Turning a blind eye to horse slaughter is a disgrace. What we need to do is get behind that House bill."

Hettinger is not alone in his work to stop the roving vans of "killer buyers" at the tracks. The Thoroughbred Retirement Foundation (TRF), founded in 1982, has set up a network of twenty-two farms for horses they rescue from the racetrack. Four of them are havens adjacent to reformatories or prisons, where inmates care for the animals and often bond with them, forming emotional connections with these four-legged animals that they have found so elusive with the bipeds beyond the walls. "These animals are completely nonjudgmental," explained one male prisoner at the TRF's Blackburn facility in Lexington, Kentucky. "They accept me for who I am, no questions asked, and that's a first for me."

Exceller Farm, a seventy-five-acre tract in upstate New York, was donated by Hettinger to the TRF in March of 2000, and so far it has been home to 176 rescued horses, many of them sore-legged old warriors from small racetracks in New England. "I have gotten horses in incredibly poor shape," Oren says. "Swollen ankles, swollen knees. It's amazing they could even race at all." The TRF obtained them from their owners, either as donations or by offering sums competitive with the killer buyers' bounty of $1 per pound. Of the 176 head, 138 already have been adopted by people who have turned them into eventing horses, polo ponies, jumpers, and trail horses.

No one knows for sure how many racetrack horses are swept up yearly by killer buyers, but Diana Pikulski, the TRF's executive director, figures "it is in the low thousands." That may be way too many for horse fanciers, but advocates for HR 857 have met resistance from those who believe that a horse, like a pig or a cow, is nothing more than glorified livestock, an agricultural commodity — an animal whose owner has the right to race him, or show him, or hook him to a plow, or sell him to a Texas slaughterhouse, even if he ends up a main course in Normandy. Nothing more infuriates a fancier of horseflesh than to hear such declarations.

"You see the movie *Seabiscuit?*" asks Jerry Finch, the founder of Habitat for Horses, a Texas group that rescues abused equines. "It says more than anything I can say about the connection between horses and people. Red Pollard, Seabiscuit's jockey, had a connection with that horse that people simply don't have with cows or pigs. The horse is a *companion animal.* They walked with us throughout the West. They carried us through wars. They helped us move from caves to plains. The Roman Empire would not have existed without the horse. To think that man is digging so low as to permit the slaughter and eating of our companions is atrocious. Eating horses, that's like eating dogs and cats."

Michael Blowen finds the practice particularly repellent when the horses have names like Ferdinand and Exceller. A retired movie critic for the *Boston Globe,* Blowen recently founded an organization called Old Friends, whose goal is to find homes for retired Thoroughbred stallions, buying the old studs if he must. His dream is to acquire a Kentucky farm where old stallions — especially those who had failed in America and were exiled overseas — could return to a life of ease on the rolling landscapes of the Blue Grass State. He even enlisted the help of Kim Zito, the wife of trainer Nick Zito, after she came to him worried about the eventual fate of Strike the Gold, the colt her husband had trained to win the 1991 Kentucky Derby. The horse had failed as a stallion in America and was standing at stud in Turkey, in the service of the Turkish National Stud, along with the 1993 Kentucky Derby winner, Sea Hero, another failure here. Blowen also has his eye on three other famous racehorses who won the Derby and Preakness, only to get beat in the Belmont Stakes: Alysheba (1987), Charismatic (1999), and War Emblem (2002). Alysheba is at stud in Saudi Arabia, Charismatic and War Emblem are in Japan.

Saving workaday racehorses from slaughter in North America is one matter; saving famous racehorses, who failed as stallions and are now overseas, is quite another. Through a Lexington lawyer, Blowen has been in touch with the Turkish National Stud, hoping to acquire Strike the Gold and Sea Hero once their days as stallions are over. Similarly, he plans to reach out to those foreign horsemen in charge of Alysheba, Charismatic, and War Emblem, who has turned out to be a "shy breeder," reluctant to mount his mares. Blowen created a Web site, oldfriendsequine.com, and he was getting four to six visitors a day when, suddenly, *The Blood-Horse* broke the Ferdinand story. At once he was getting seven hundred hits a day and e-mails from all over the world asking: "Where can I donate money to Old Friends?" He has raised $15,000 in less than two weeks.

The response has staggered him. "I'm totally, completely, utterly overwhelmed," Blowen says. He can see it now: a farm in Kentucky where five Derby winners have adjoining paddocks. "People from all over the world would come here," Blowen says. "Where else could you stand in one spot and see five Kentucky Derby winners at one time! Each with a two-acre paddock, each with separate living quarters. It's like having Michael Jordan, Larry Bird, Magic Johnson, and Jerry West in one place. You wouldn't even need appearance fees. We could create a tremendous tourist attraction in Kentucky."

Blowen says he would erect two monuments at the farm's main gate. One would say Exceller, the other Ferdinand. "Subtle reminders," Blowen says.

Of two surpassing horses who had earned a kinder fate.

JOAN RYAN

Galarraga Steals Base, Stops Time

FROM THE SAN FRANCISCO CHRONICLE

WHEN MEMORABLE MOMENTS of 2003 are recounted by newscasters at year's end, I hope to see Andres Galarraga's steal of second base in the Giants' 160th game of the season. If it goes unrecognized, it could only be because the newscasters were not there when it happened.

For those of us who witnessed it last week at Pac Bell Park, at least those of a certain age, the sight of the forty-two-year-old player motoring into second base ranks up there with the scientific discovery this summer that chocolate helps reduce chronic stress.

In other words, it was something resembling grace, an unexpected, even preposterous gift that, it seems to me, is reassurance that despite the ship-of-fools recall campaign and the current U.S. administration, God really does want us to be happy.

If you are just beginning to pay attention to baseball now that the playoffs have begun, you might not be familiar with Galarraga or understand why I would make a fuss over his steal. I first will tell you that Galarraga is why I love baseball. Not him only, but guys like him who give you everything you want from sports: a soap-opera story line and a luminous smile that invites you along for the ride. Galarraga is like one of those guys in the movie *Ocean's Eleven*. You root for them and have such a great time watching them because they are crazy enough and inspired enough to believe they can beat the system. And then they do.

On paper, Galarraga shouldn't still be playing baseball. He is nearly old enough to put a glint in Anna Nicole Smith's eye, and he's a bit over his fighting weight — "beefy," as one of my friends kindly puts it. He came back from cancer in 1999 and from a couple of seasons dismal enough to send lesser men running to open car dealerships in Miami.

A perennial All-Star and onetime batting champion, Galarraga made the Giants roster this spring after being offered only a non-guaranteed minor-league contract. Then he went and played in more than one hundred games this season, hitting over .300. Only two other Giants players hit over .300, and one of them is named Barry Bonds.

So, about the steal.

Galarraga had taken a lead off of first base, but the pitcher barely acknowledged the threat. Galarraga hadn't stolen a base all year. He had stolen just four in the last four seasons. Old and big, he can be timed from base to base, as the scouts like to say, with a calendar.

But just as the pitcher released his pitch, and to the gasps of the sold-out crowd at Pac Bell, Galarraga broke for second. The opposing catcher was so flabbergasted, he stood with the ball in his hand and watched Galarraga reach second safely. We leaped to our feet and cheered. Galarraga's face lit up like a kid in his first sandlot game. His teammates in the Giants dugout howled.

These are the moments you wait an entire season for: an athlete caught in the act of being absolutely happy. When it happens, the barriers of physical distance and experience between you and the athlete you are watching disappear.

For an instant, I could see in Galarraga something of my forgotten self, the girl who ran through sprinklers and ate Ding-Dongs and made perfume out of tap water and rose petals. Watching Galarraga at that moment was like getting a cross-section glimpse of time, with youth and age layered on top of one another, making an impossible joint appearance.

I don't readily admit to my weakness for guys like Galarraga. It can be misinterpreted by those who lump fans into two categories, serious and groupie, and who might figure me for the latter. I probably am neither. I'm more of a drafter, someone who hopes to ride for a moment or two in the wake of an athlete's experience, siphoning off some of their exuberance and transcendence for myself.

Galarraga's steal of second base offered just about everything I want in an athletic performance, especially now that I am older and slower myself. Like other smart athletes at the end of their careers, Galarraga is reveling in what he still has, unearthing joys in a game he has played all his life. I am watching the playoffs for the drama and the beauty of baseball, but Galarraga's steal reminded me of my real agenda. I am waiting for those moments that capture the continuum of age in a split-second, when you see the child in the aging adult, and recognize yourself.

RICK TELANDER

Playing Against the Clock

FROM SPORTS ILLUSTRATED

I AM AT THE NOTRE DAME twenty-nine-yard line and Joe Theismann's errant pass is zeroing in on me. I intercept it and run it back to the 14. Tailback Joe Hudson takes a pitch from our quarterback, Dave Shelbourne, and we, huge underdog Northwestern, are up, 10–0. Yeah? Huh? How do you like that, you screaming, green-derbied, leprechaun lunatics?

Now, all these years later, I'm the man in the middle.

And the middle is a swirling place. I am, to varying degrees, baffled, amused, overwhelmed, depressed, eager, angry, melancholy, innocent, guilty, cheerful, yearning, daffy. And I know this is a life condition.

Draw a circle and label the area outside the circumference *death* and label the inside such things as mice in the cabinet where dog food is, bad knee, 401(k) uncertainty, bald spot, bad back, proms, oil changes, credit-card shock, boy who won't listen to Dad's sex talk, woodchuck under porch, finger that bends sideways, press boxes, family's five cell phones with incomprehensible bills, tuition, thousands of hot dogs, lingering affection for Jack Daniel's, unfinished projects from books to the door that won't close on the garage that has raccoons running rampant inside, Madonna (the children's author) nausea, dog nightly rummaging through home's waste cans, stained carpets, clogged gutters, fear of darkness, girls' hair dryers everywhere, girls' hair on floor, hair everywhere, endless MTV *Real World* crap, ridiculous auto insurance premiums, basement from hell, fear of nuclear war ('60s style), memories.

But most of all label the inside of the circle *children.*
And shade everything with sports.

"Did you wear a jock?" my twelve-year-old son asks. His name is
Zack, but he doesn't like being written about, so I will call him Z.

"Hell, yes. Absolutely." I'm in the kitchen, watching *SportsCenter.*
"Boo-yah!" was the last word I heard.

"See," says my wife, Judy. Something was under discussion. As always I am, like the title of my daughters' favorite movie, clueless.

"You have to wear one," says Judy.

"But it's too hard!" Z whines. A set-to is coming. The conditions
are right.

"For what?" I ask, involvement forced.

"Football, and I don't want to."

"Why?"

"The plastic thing hurts."

"What plastic thing?"

"The hard thing. You know!"

I spin away from the tube.

"That's a cup. A jock is the soft thing."

"Oh," says Z.

I'm eleven, maybe twelve, about Z's age, and my dad has stopped
the car in our driveway. It's gravel, and I covet cement or blacktop.
I dream about a surface that is smooth and true. This is Peoria, Illinois, early '60s. My backboard is nailed to the garage wall above the
twin, pale green, hinged doors of the unheated garage connected
to our house by what was then referred to as a breezeway. My court,
such as it is, consists of the uneven, crushed-limestone trapezoid
that spreads from the garage toward Picture Ridge Road in front. I
groom the driveway often — raking, shoveling, filling in pits — but
I can't change what it is.

The sun has set, and before we go into the house for dinner my
dad is giving me the speech. "The penis of the bull . . ." he is saying,
and I want to disappear. I see my backboard through the windshield of our wood-paneled station wagon, see the garage doors,
which are so close to the hoop that a kid can demolish himself on a
lay-up, but which also can be used for Spiderman-style, two-handed
dunking.

"The egg is fertilized . . ." Dad is saying, and I am reminded, not for the first time, of the liberating vacuity and prescribed simplicity of sport. Now, so many years later, I see where Z is coming from.

There are four kids: Lauren, twenty-one; Cary, nineteen; Robin, sixteen; and Z. Last spring Lauren's and Cary's respective club water polo teams made it to the national collegiate tournament held at Carthage College in Kenosha, Wisconsin. Carthage, as fate would have it, is a mere forty-five minutes from our house in suburban Chicago.

Lauren goes to Colorado. Cary goes to Dartmouth. Their teams were on opposite sides of the bracket, so they had a chance to meet in the championship game. I had determined in advance that I would not be present for that. I would be in a hallway, or in the parking lot, or quite possibly in a Wisconsin roadhouse, talking to my friend Jack.

Well, it didn't happen. Dartmouth took third, behind Cal Poly and Michigan State. Colorado finished eighth.

But I was amazed when the entire Dartmouth team came to visit us at our house during the tournament. Two nights later the Colorado girls did the same. There were my daughters, tall and tough and pretty, with their sports buddies. I grew up when girls were cheerleaders.

How did I grow up? Like every other kid I knew. My dad was a bomber pilot in World War II. My mom took care of the household. My dad's nickname in our neighborhood — a name that stands to this day, in his eighty-third year — was Sweetie. He would come home from work, and I'd say, "Let's play catch," and he'd make a few tosses, jokingly complain about "bursitis" and "rheumatiz." Like every other kid's dad I knew, Sweetie worked. He came to my games when he could, supported me in whatever sports I wanted to play. And that was that. Guys I knew didn't play catch with their dads. They played catch with one another.

Somebody was smoking in the basement at the Friday night get-to-gether — "Not me!" comes the refrain from each of the kids — and somebody opened one of the screenless windows down there and, unbeknownst to anyone, a squirrel sneaked in. I walk downstairs today, Sunday, and nearly have a heart attack when I see something move. The crazed rodent has already chewed away at the frames of all the basement windows. Of course, the offending window is now thoughtfully closed. I crouch on one side of the messy room with the Rainbow Brite dolls and Barbie cars and plastic soldiers scattered about. The squirrel perches on the other. We stare at each other. Now what?

I am in my back yard in Key West in 1979. This is where I moved as a young single man for three and a half years because I had no responsibilities. I wanted to get away from Chicago winters, yes, but year-round seventy-game softball seasons were the spice.

I am looking through a slit in the ragged cane fence, the kind you buy at the lumberyard and unroll, at my backyard neighbor, Peter Taylor, a kindly, sixty-two-year-old writer from Tennessee, who will, in the not-too-distant future, win the Pulitzer Prize for his novel *A Summons to Memphis*.

Peter is telling me that he has been diagnosed with diabetes. "The doctor allows me one and a half ounces of vodka per day," he says stoically. "And he'd prefer nothing." He describes the way he anticipates and stretches that single, frowned-upon drink, mixed with a small portion of tonic and slice of lime, every evening on the porch with his wife. And yet, he says, the single drink, sweet as it is, is almost more pain than comfort, as it signifies in its frugality what is lost. As I look at first one then the other of his sad blue eyes as they appear through the narrow slit, I think of the recent days I had spent on assignment with Roger Maris and Mickey Mantle in Gainesville.

The three of us were in the dugout at a University of Florida game. Mantle asked Maris why he quit baseball so soon after going from the Yankees to the Cardinals.

"Aw, Mick," said Maris to his old roomie. "I hurt my wrist, and when they saw I couldn't hit the curve, I was done."

Peter Taylor and Rog — they sounded the same.

I walk into the kitchen, and Z is watching the Cubs on WGN and standing and singing. He is singing to the tune of Handel's *Messiah*, and these are his words: "And Hee Seop Choi, forever, and ever. Alleluia! Alleluia!"

*

A boy is standing inside the front door of our house. He is wearing a tuxedo or something like one that looks about as comfortable on him as a starched collar on a rapper. He is here to take one of my slender, athletic, shiny-haired daughters to the high school prom. He seems nice enough, though after saying hello, we don't speak. What could I possibly say to such a fraud?

"Dad," says Cary, "we had the homecoming bonfire last night. They wouldn't let us wear our swimsuits — the administration said it was sexist. And, I mean, that's our uniform. So we wore cutoff T-shirts and grass hula skirts instead, and we had writing on our stomachs. It was great!"
  "Didn't it snow in Hanover last night?"
  "Yeah, a little. I'll send you e-mail photos. Bye!"

I am falling, falling, falling. Mel Gray is catching a touchdown pass from Dan Pastorini over my descending body in the East-West Shrine Game many years ago. Falling, falling.

Z wants to play on the junior high heavyweight tackle football team. He weighs only 123 pounds and should be a lightweight, for which the cutoff is 130. But if he plays with the lightweights, he will have to be a lineman. As a heavy, he will be perhaps the lightest kid in the league, but he'll be able to run with the ball or catch it, and play strong safety, which is all he wants to do.
  I don't want him to play at all. And yet, I am proud that he wants to. What is wrong with me?

It is after midnight as I come down the outdoor stairs from my office above the garage. The moon is out, illuminating my yard in shades of pen-and-ink. I see a basketball next to the driveway. A Frisbee. Two bats, one a *Chicago Tribune*–sponsored giveaway from old Comiskey Park, the other an illegally weighted sixteen-inch softball bat, made by a former men's league teammate two decades ago, in his basement, with a lag bolt being the ingredient hidden beneath the epoxied sawdust. There is a skateboard, a Nerf football, a real football, a bike on its side, a hard plastic baby Jesus that was obviously stolen months ago from somebody's outdoor nativity scene. "I have no idea how it got here," Z said when I accosted him. "It was just here," agreed his friend Alex.

All this stuff was supposed to have been picked up, put away. The plastic Jesus, I don't know. It rained earlier and there are puddles in the depressions on our blacktop driveway — the driveway of my childhood dreams. They are precisely where Robin parks the girls' car, the one her sister rolled several years ago on a gravel road and that has a missing fender, an ill-fitting windshield, and a passenger-side door that doesn't close right. I drive the car into the garage, into the stall with the door that is permanently open. It is the stall into which a raccoon came two summers ago and craftily figured out how to scale the car, the door, and then steal the drying fish-head I had dangling from the ceiling on a string. It was the head of an eight-pound northern pike Z had caught on an Upper Peninsula lake on the very day his grandfather Hansen died back in Chicago. I cut the head off, propped the ferocious-looking mouth open with two pine sticks, let most of the stink evaporate in the Michigan sun, and then brought it home for final drying and shellacking. It would be a trophy of joy and sadness. Then it was gone, just the string remaining.

The puddles in the driveway wound me. Here in the still night, I feel myself sliding, slip-sliding, unable to slow anything down, to accomplish anything, to feel in control, to be more than a rider on a runaway bus. The growing dents in the pavement will fill with water, then with ice, then they will crack and split, and soon Z and I and his pals, and even Cary and Lauren and their boyfriends will no longer be able to dribble properly on this court of which I am so proud, the one Z and I laid out with a lane and blocks and free throw line, using blue and yellow and white spray paint, spending one afternoon getting the dimensions right, just like at the high school.

"I am not parking in the garage!" Robin had declared. "I was stung four times by bees when you were out of town, and my leg was so swollen! And you still haven't gotten the nest."

But I will get it. It's in a hole between the doors. I know I will. I just need time.

Cary has used my airline miles to fly to Hawaii this summer to visit one of her Dartmouth swim team pals, Kristin Simunovich. In L.A., Cary joined up with another swimmer, Nicole Zarba, from the Boston area. There was the trauma the three went through, with all the other Dartmouth swimmers and divers, male and female, when the swimming and diving programs were abruptly cut before Thanksgiving 2002. Cut for that old standby, budget reasons. Cary was a freshman and had been at school six weeks. Like the other swimmers, she freaked. She had been recruited by the school, wooed by the school, and had worked her butt off to get in. After fundraising, campuswide protests, and total student mobilization — including putting the teams up for sale on eBay (top bid: $212,000) — the humiliated administration buckled and brought the swimmers and divers back.

But we don't talk about it much. Cary is still too hurt. Especially by the administration's now acting as though this little revolt was a joyous bonding experience, a graduate course in competitive co-operation and financial adventurism. One morning in August I looked at the refrigerator door and saw a form letter of congratulations to the swimmers for their successful campaign from the school dean, the same dean who had said the team "would never be back." Cary had taped it there. Across the page she had written BULLS ——, in red ink.

The three girls in Hawaii are going to participate in something called the Roughwater Swim, off Waikiki, a storied 2.4-mile race through currents, surf, and the odd sea animal. This sounds like as much fun to me as a flogging. But this is not my race. Swimmers are different.

"Be careful," I say to Cary, from five thousand miles away. "Okay?"

"I will, Dad." The girls have been climbing mountains and surfing to stay in shape.

But Tropical Storm Jimena is sending out winds, and on the day of the race the Pacific is a treacherous hostess. Of the 947 swimmers who start the race, 590 can't finish and 361 have to be rescued, some by helicopter.

"This is the strongest current we've had in thirty-four years," Roughwater committee president Ted Sheppard will tell the *Honolulu Advertiser.*

I was frantic with worry.

"They made us quit," Cary says to me by phone, in disgust, the following day. "We went off in stages, and my group got the worst

current. We were passing people, and everyone was going backward, but we were going backward slower than they were. I'd been
swimming for over two hours when they stopped me, and I was just
getting to the easy part."

In a pool Cary can swim a mile in about eighteen minutes; 2.4
miles in probably fifty minutes. In this race she still had more than
half a mile to go. But she would have made it. No question about it.
My worry all along was that she wouldn't stop. Even with a tidal
wave on the horizon.

Somehow I am now an assistant coach for Z's football team. Before
I took that three-day-a-week volunteer job, I watched one practice
from my car, reading newspapers. Then, two days later, on a gorgeous afternoon, I watched while seated under a tree, mesmerized
by the smell, the light, the timeless machinations of this hormonal
coming-out party before me. "Hey, Mr. Telander," said one of the
rec-center staff members pleasantly, startling me in mid-reverie.
That was all it took to sign me up.

My Key West team, Blossom's Grocery, is playing a night game at
Perry Court near the naval housing over by Garrison Bight. On my
team is Richie Powell, the younger, larger brother of former major
league player Boog Powell. Richie goes about 6'4", 280. He's a
sweet guy. Between innings he sits in the dugout and smokes ciga-
rettes and drinks beer. He has a catlike quickness, even at his size
(he was once a grand discus thrower), and in this slo-pitch, limited-
arc league, when you throw him a strike, he will hit it out of the
park. The ball just goes. Guys on both teams always laugh at the
sound of the concussion. The ball, when Richie hits it in one of
these night games, will leave the ring of diamond light and disappear into the black sky before reappearing in descent — almost an
afterthought — awhile later, far, far on the other side of the fence.

But the pitchers in the league are no longer pitching to Powell.
They intentionally walk him — with the bases empty, loaded, no
outs, two outs, anything in between. Powell has been walked four
straight times tonight, on pitches he can't reach even by jumping
across the plate and flailing at like a man trying to smack a moth
with a newspaper.

"I'm not going," he tells the ump after the final ball four. He stands. He looks down. He hits the plate again and again with his bat and then digs up dirt with his shoes and covers the plate so that it is invisible.

"No," Powell says. "No more."

I watch from the dugout, fascinated. What a strange game this is, I'm thinking, that lets you do this to a man.

Powell stares at the ump, unmoving.

The ump calls the game, and we go home.

In November of last year, my meniscus tears on a three-point shot at the noon game at Barat College. A click, and there is that funny pain. You know, you just know. One of the Bears' team doctors, Gordon Nuber, scopes me before Thanksgiving. Fast, easy, and the knee feels okay thirty-six hours later. But that's all it feels today — okay. It swells all the time, and I can't hoop with the old gang. In the old days the sawbones used to say you don't need cartilage. Sure. And to think I hate, and have always hated, three-point shots.

Z was offered jersey number 34 for the heavyweight league, but he said no and took 33. "Thirty-four's Walter Payton's number," he told me when I asked why. "He was too good."

Why did Lauren and Cary become accomplished swimmers? Z, too. Even Robin, before she quit swimming for socializing. Because we were down in Key West for Thanksgiving vacation, seventeen years ago, two of the kids not even born, and there was a tiny swimming pool in the back deck of the house we'd rented on Elizabeth Street. The pool was maybe twenty feet long by ten feet wide, a nightlife lounging tub, really, with hibiscus and bougainvillaea all about, and Judy had just opened the double French doors to the deck, and Cary walked over to the pool and tried to step, in her little pink Velcro-strapped sneakers, onto the surface of the water. She sank instantly, and I jumped in fully clad and pulled her out. My heart was beating wildly. I had never felt this way.

Lauren and Cary took swimming lessons soon after at a community pool in the suburb north of ours. They were facile in the water, and the next thing I knew, they had racing suits and goggles and were entered in some summer meets, and one thing led to another. I remember Lauren winning a race, her front teeth still not all the way in, and her smiling in wonderment and confusion. Why did adults care so much? Why was her dad misty-eyed?

I remember later in that Thanksgiving trip sitting right next to three-year-old Cary, now in her tiny suit and inflated arm bands, and how she was crouched on the side of the pool, at the deeper end, splashing water with one hand toward the shallow end. What was she doing? She put her face very close to mine, as she did when serious.

"I want the blue water to go down there," she said.

Z and four of his buddies are cutting through the fence behind our house to watch the Division III Lake Forest College football team play a game on its home field. "Who are they playing?" asks Alex.

"Beloit," says Z.

"Who are they?"

"I don't know," says Z. "But they have cool jerseys."

"What would happen if I did this after a touchdown?" Z asks as he holds his Wilson TDY football and does a damn good Ali shuffle.

"You would be yanked out of the game on the spot by the man known as your father."

"What if I did this?"

He spins the ball like a top and draws imaginary six-shooters from imaginary holsters and fires at the thing.

"You would have to explain to your friends why your dad put you in the car, drove off, and you never played football again."

He smiles at me, comforted.

He gets the ball and rolls it like it is a single die and snaps his fingers.

"And what if I did this?" he says.

"You would be cast into your room and, like Byron's prisoner of Chillon, never see the light of day again. Much less a football."

He is delighted.

In our town's opening high school football game, against a highly ranked team, our fullback scores a touchdown in overtime to draw his team to within two. Make a two-point conversion and the game continues.

Z and his seventh-grade pals are watching as the fullback stands over his downed foe and taunts him, receiving an unsportsmanlike conduct penalty. The ball is moved back fifteen yards for the extra point. Of course, our team can't convert a two-point play from eighteen yards out, and the game ends 28–26.

I am worried that my son will not see the stupidity in the full-back's outburst. But it seems he does.

"That was ill," says Z.

In my Peoria-area conference, the Mid-State Nine, the toughest team was Pekin High. Pekin was good in football and most other sports, and in both my freshman and senior years it won the Illinois state basketball championship, crushing downstate and Chicago teams en route. I usually had to guard Pekin's heavy-bearded white forward, Fred Miller, when my Peoria Richwoods team played the school. Miller was a muscular six-foot-four, and he could dunk, and would. This was unheard of for white guys back then, and Pekin was all white. But Pekin was different. Times were different. The school's official nickname was the Chinks.

"You are ruining my life!" Robin yelled. And then the door slammed. The hinges have been fixed, since we've been in this house, four times. Once, I told her, or maybe it was her sister who was then in that room, that when the door came off its hinges the next time, it would stay like that. And it did, for more than a month, propped against the jam like a plywood sheet in a lumber yard. What her mother and I wanted Robin to do was go to a field hockey day camp for three days, since she was going to try out for that sport at her high school, and everybody who would make the team was going. Robin has a very active social life, and this camp, to which she had initially agreed to go, was now a cast-iron anchor on her winged soul.

"You don't care about me at all!" she hollered, having reappeared. She went back into her room. She came out again.

"I will never treat my children the way you treat me!"

Judy and I have to leave town for part of the weekend, and when we return the house looks different. "It was not a party," says Robin.

And those are not Busch Light cans in the evergreens.

Phone message: "Mr. Telander, this is Dr. Tom Wiedrich, getting back to you."

Wiedrich is a hand specialist I visited a while back. He told me then there wasn't much he could do for the damaged ring finger on my left hand other than fuse it. But then I couldn't play the guitar at all. And playing is something I enjoy, even if I don't do it well. I tore the ligament on the inside of that finger when the digit got stuck in a guy's jersey back in college, and over the years the thing has bent more each time an errant ball or body has hit it. Now it looks ludicrous and is swollen and hurts, and I can barely play a C chord.

Dr. Wiedrich told me to call him in a year or so to talk about the new artificial finger joints being developed. I'd take one of those in a flash. How cool would that be? An artificial joint. That's why I called.

Our heavyweight team's tailback, who was standing behind the fullback in the I formation, has dropped to the ground, face-first, gagging, as I was explaining a play to him. His retching noises have me petrified. I'm thinking: grand mal seizure, a burst aorta, poison. Two other dad coaches come over. We kneel down. The boy spasms, making horrible sounds. Someone needs to call the paramedics. Then the youth is silent, still facedown. Dear God. Abruptly he rises to his knees. "Whew," he says at last.

"Are you all right?" we all say again and again. "What's wrong?"

"My mouth guard was in a funny place."

Judy and I are watching the Colorado–Colorado State football game on TV. The weather is growing bad at Invesco Field, and soon the game is delayed because of lightning. I call Lauren on her cell phone, certain that she is there.

"I'm like freezing," she says. "I'm wearing summer stuff. We were tailgating. But now there's nowhere to go."

As we talk, the game is restarted. "The rivalry is pretty intense, isn't it?" I ask. Yes, Lauren replies. The CSU quarterback said some cocky stuff about the Buffs, she tells me.

How are Colorado students taking it?

"The guys around me are chanting that they want the quarterback to be a quadriplegic."

"You don't have to follow me. I can go to bed by myself!" says Z huffily. "I'm not four."

No, he's twelve. He still has a high voice, and he doesn't smell.
But he'll go days without a shower if you don't ride him.

"Don't follow me!"

It's so hot here in South Bend, but it's the Fourth of July weekend
and our seventh-grade travel basketball team has to play in a tournament at Notre Dame over the holiday. Whoopee. Myself, I'd
rather be on my deck with a beer or at the beach or a picnic someplace. In a hot little gym on the second floor of the Joyce Center we
begin our second or third game. I've lost count. My ability to care
has been severely crimped. Suddenly my friend, a former Division I
baseball player, is screaming at the ref. A onetime basketball ref-
eree himself, my pal is red-faced and furious. Not only that, he is
charging onto the floor. "You do not have the right to tell me to
shut up!" he is screaming. Mouth spray is flying. His neck veins
look like snakes.

The ref — a young, muscular black man — is coming toward
my friend. Oh, Jesus. "You cannot tell me to shut up!" shouts my
friend. My friend is himself a muscular, if paunchy, guy. Now the ref
is yelling and his neck, too, is ready to explode. "Sit down and shut
up!" he bellows.

I step onto the court and get between the two. Is this what
you're supposed to do? If I don't do it, who will? I put one hand on
each man's chest, like a contestant in one of those twisted World's
Strongest Man contests. Except I'm not very strong.

I can feel each man's heart pounding. I can feel each man flex-
ing, preparing. I can see the anger in their eyes, the outrage, fear. I
have no awareness of being at a boys' basketball game. None whatsoever.

We're three games into the football season, and Z's twiglike arms
are covered with bruises. There is a scab on his jaw. Cuts on his legs.
But last week he caught a sixty-five-yard pass and then made receptions on three plays in a row. He nailed a kid on a punt coverage.
"He's a tough kid," says one of our volunteer dad coaches, Jim Co-
vert, a two-time Pro Bowl lineman for the Bears in the '80s.

Yes, but he's a kid, a toothpick. I sometimes see him in the
chair in his room, drawing skateboards, singing to himself. He has
stuffed animals on his bed. I worry.

*

Lauren and Cary were ecstatic. Their two-hundred-yard medley relay team had just set an Illinois high school record at the prelims of the state meet in Winnetka on Friday. Lauren swam backstroke and Cary swam breaststroke, and — guess what? — Dad was pretty excited, too. Now it is Saturday, finals day, and the race is on. The screaming and splashing and echoing din are almost more than I can take. Florence Mauro, the best swimmer on our team, a state champion in the butterfly two years before, is churning through the water against Mary DeScenza, the previous year's champ, from Rosary High. DeScenza, whose team's nickname is the Beads, thrashes into the narrow lead. We are losing ground (losing water?). Now it is up to the freestylers, and they roar home in a photo finish. The times flash on the scoreboard: Rosary: 1:46.37; our team: 1:46.44. Both times break the state relay record we set less than twenty-four hours earlier.

But the Beads have won. By .07 of a second. The interval between your two hand slaps when you attempt to bang both hands down simultaneously on a table. My daughters are destroyed. How many thousands of hours have they swum for this? Then, too, what's wrong with second place? *Right.*

Three of the girls on our medley team will go on to swim in Division I — Mauro will get a full ride to Arizona State — but the damage is done. It helps only marginally when two years later DeScenza swims the United States' fastest one-hundred-meter fly at the world championships in Japan.

"I'll never get over it," Lauren said the other night while home from college. "Not really."

"The news isn't good," says Dr. Wiedrich. "The artificial joints have mostly failed. There's just too much stress on them. It's unfortunate. Check back in a year or so."

I thank him. I know for certain that I am too old for a sports injury to be cool or a status symbol or anything other than a dent in the armor that is failing, failing, failing. Before failure.

Cary calls. She is studying in her dorm room, and her roomies can be heard in the background. They are all swimmers. Nicole is icing her shoulder, as she does every day. Liz has a damaged thumb and has to tape her hand into a ball to swim. Kristin hurt her wrist while body surfing in Hawaii and is still rehabbing. Cary is just tired.

"We did twenty 100's on a minute-thirty," she says of a segment of their late practice. "And I swam 1:03's."

I know this makes her proud. She's not injured, is she?

"No, I just can't raise my arms."

On Monday, Wednesday, and Friday they swim for two hours and lift weights for an hour. On Tuesday and Thursday they lift for an hour at 6:00 A.M., then swim for an hour, then swim for two more hours in the afternoon. On Saturday they lift from 8:15 to 9:30 A.M., then swim for two hours.

What time do you get up for the 6:00 A.M. practices? I ask.

"Five-forty," she says. When do you sleep? I ask.

"Oh, you know, twice a day. Like two naps."

Not long ago I asked Cary and Lauren's Arizona State pal Florence how quickly she could fall asleep, at any time of night or day. "Oh, thirty seconds, tops," she said. "Probably less."

The players have this habit of being distracted. I am terrified for all of them, with their skinny necks and fuzzless faces, being led from childhood into this violent vortex — is there any need at all for prepubescent kids to play tackle football? — and yet I think they should at least pay attention when I talk.

Just two days ago, after our gung ho, young, and impassioned head coach had orchestrated a tackling drill, about which he rhapsodized in a way that reminded me of the ways I had heard NFL linebackers such as Mike Singletary and Dick Butkus rhapsodize about collisions, I noticed two of our guys crying silently. One was the biggest kid on the team, larger than me, and I am 6'1", 200. Why were they crying? The tackling, their grand collisions resounding with noise and hoopla, had hurt. I wanted to protect them, these boys I barely knew. But how?

Today I am running a skeleton passing drill. Our fullback isn't paying attention.

"Hey!" I yell. I walk toward him, his expression all but obscured by helmet, face mask, cheek pads, mouth guard. He isn't big. I look at his pale arms. They look odd. That's because, I notice, he has used a green ink marker and lined them from biceps to wrist with a spiderweb of thick green veins.

I start to say something. But I can't help it: I buckle in laughter.

Robin seems content with no sports in her life at the moment. There are times when I think she does nothing but brush her hair and look in the mirror. Then she tells me, as she rushes past one day, that she has gotten an after-school job working with children at a fitness center.

Another week goes by. I tell her that her long hair looks nice, so thick and lustrous.

"I'm cutting it off," she tells me. "For kids with cancer. It has to be at least a foot long. It's called Locks of Love."

Then she is gone.

The sweep has been a long time developing, and Z is closing fast from his safety position. The other team's flanker, number 32, peels back full tilt, out of Z's vision, and launches himself headfirst into Z, his helmet under Z's jaw, and both boys are flying through the air, feet off the ground, and I know that Z is unconscious before he hits the grass. I sprint onto the field, and the trainer is already there, a female with a blond ponytail, and she is kneeling beside Z as he lies flat on his back. His eyes are closed, and he is not moving. I look at his little boy's face through his big man's armor, and I feel as if I am looking at all my sins, all my stupidity, all my ignorance.

I hold Z's limp hand. Finally his left foot is moving. He is moaning. The trainer asks me to hold Z's helmet steady as she checks his legs, his arms. Earlier in this game Z had been part of a big pileup on a kickoff, and his lip had been bloodied and he had been slow to get up. The trainer had given him the concussion test. *What grade are you in?* "Sixth," he had replied. "I mean, seventh." He laughed. She didn't.

What were the three words I asked you to remember? "Textbook, car, water-bottle," he said. He was right. Even I had forgotten them. But there are no concussion tests now. None needed. There is a ragged cut on Z's jawline where the main force of the blow was focused. How could a father allow this?

Finally, Z is alert. Minutes have gone by. He is helped to his feet. We get him to the bench, and his teammates applaud, as do the few people in the stands. I want to vomit. But I can't.

*

It was five years ago when Lauren was a passenger in a full car that crashed. It was driven by a boy her age, and I was terrified and nauseous when I found out. It was a bad crash, and alcohol was involved. There was a news item about it in the local paper: "'When I pulled up to the accident scene, my first thought was how many kids were dead,' said Lake Bluff Police Sgt. David Belmonte. 'The fact that nobody was killed is unbelievable.'"

But no one was even injured. The risks we take when we become parents are perhaps indefensible, maybe inexplicable, certainly unbelievable. But we take them all the same. And we pray for luck. We pray for luck never to run out.

Cary calls from school. She is doing well in her art history classes, and she says she can simply look at slides now and tell which French painter did the work and what period it was from. "And I found a catalog where they sell swimsuits with a Matisse on them, and I'm getting one!"

It's his bedtime, and I tell Z to quit messing around, turn out the light, put down the Nerf ball he is toying with and go to sleep. He is in his oldest sister's room, in Lauren's bed, where he likes to sleep while she is at school. It's bigger than his bed, which he is outgrowing, and it is different.

"Come in and lie down beside me," he says.

"No. Go to sleep. You have school tomorrow."

"Come in and lie down."

"I can't. You have to go to sleep, and I have a lot of work to do."

"No you don't," he says.

"Yes, I do."'

"No you don't."

He is right. And so I go in and close the door and lie down beside him in the dark. I put a pillow under my head and he lies beside me and we both look up at the ceiling. Lauren has stuck hundreds of fluorescent ministars up there, and there are constellations, and I can see Orion's belt and the Big Dipper, and "I ♥ you" in the mix. We stare in silence, and Z, tucked under his blankets, puts his head on my arm.

"Tell me a story, Dad," my son says to me.

And I would. I would tell him stories forever, if I could just get my voice.

ANDY MEISLER

The Fright Stuff

FROM THE LOS ANGELES TIMES MAGAZINE

EVEN FOR A LAYMAN, the concept is fairly easy to grasp: the lower a racing airplane flies, the better its pilot can see and the closer it can come to the spindly pylons that mark the inner edge of the race-course.

Which is probably why Ramblin' Rose, a 2,000-pound, 310-horsepower two-seater was flying at an altitude of about 60 feet at 2:45 P.M. on Friday, September 13. The black Questair Venture 20 — an egg-shaped home-built craft that would look great inside a design museum but looks even better going 300 mph — was running last in an eight-plane field. It was circling a 6.3-mile course defined by ten 50-foot-tall pylons over the Nevada desert adjacent to Reno Stead Airport.

On lap two of six, as it flashed past the checkered "home pylon" in front of tens of thousands of spectators, the airplane's nose twitched down, its horizontal tail folded upward, and it plowed straight into the desert floor, a tiny plane making a tiny crash and raising a small cloud of dust. There was no noise, no fire. Just a scattering of debris, mostly aluminum. One man in the crowd speed-dialed his cell phone and said simply, to whomever he was calling, "This is a solemn moment."

The race was stopped and the other competitors landed. The crowd remained silent as the announcer enjoined spectators not to rush toward the wreck — though they gave no indication that they were about to — and risk interfering with emergency personnel. Although everyone was certain that the downed pilot, a middle-aged Mississippi businessman named Tommy Rose, was dead, no announcement was made. Improvising smoothly, the race organiz-ers piped soothing music through the public-address system, then sent a jet-powered dragster down the runway for the crowd's enjoy-ment and authorized the announcers to proclaim that the day's final race would be held as scheduled.

The next morning there was a brief request over the public-ad-dress system to "keep the family of Tommy Rose in your thoughts, your prayers, and your memories," but no further mention of the fatal accident. One observer, though, breached etiquette by asking one of the most successful airplane racers present whether the pre-vious day's accident still lingered in his mind.

"Can't go there," said Bill "Tiger" Destefani of Bakersfield. "It don't work."

Which is fair warning that this story isn't about *Survivor, Fear Factor,* or trendy "extreme" sports such as road luge or wakeboarding. It's about the National Championship Air Races — an official misno-mer since it's the only regularly scheduled closed-course pylon air-plane race in the world.

Most people who know about this annual event know it as the Reno Air Races, or simply Reno. What they also know, whether they profess to enjoy this knowledge or not, is that it poses real, not vir-tual, danger. Since its inception in 1964, fourteen competitors have been killed.

Pilots at Reno compete in several different classes, including home-built passenger planes like Rose's, tiny one-seat Formula One planes, small biplanes, 1940s-era T-6 military trainers, and even subsonic, Czech-built L-39 jet trainers. Its marquee races, the ones that attract the most spectators, are between so-called Unlim-ited class airplanes: aircraft whose only design requirement is that they be powered by piston engines. The fastest planes in this class fly more than twice as fast as any land- or water-based racing ma-chine.

Which leads to an interesting anomaly. On the one hand, air rac-ing at Reno is a semisecret, underpublicized cult passion. On the other, it's a display of numerous mainstream American obsessions, including adventure for adventure's sake, competition for com-petition's sake, expensive thrills, pure speed, high-octane fuels, souped-up internal combustion engines, home-brewed technology,

World War II worship, and the God-given right to flirt with death, preferably instant, without interference from the government or anyone else.

Oh, yes — we almost forgot. Air racing is possibly the only sport in history where nearly all of the risks — financial and physical — are shouldered by rich, occasionally grumpy, old white men.

"This is my last year for goin'," insists Tiger Destefani, a prosperous cotton and alfalfa farmer, on a typically blazing Central Valley afternoon. "I'm all through. It's gonna be twenty-three years of it. It's enough. And it gets tougher and tougher; everything costs more. The engines now are about 150,000 bucks. When I first started racing, you could get one done for 20. And sponsors are hard to come by, and I'm just tired of it. I wanna do other things in my life.

"I'm not exactly a kid anymore either," he adds. "I'm fifty-seven. You start noticing things happening. Eyesight starts goin'. I got to wear glasses now to see way out there. And the [G-forces] hurt more. And I've had enough blown engines and all that stuff, you know?"

Destefani smiles and nods crisply toward his visitor from the big city, who at the moment is trying to calculate, without success, just how much deception — self- and otherwise — is going on. Destefani, a short, bald, wiry man with piercing light blue eyes and a sizable chaw in his mouth, is a six-time Reno Unlimited class champion. Country music plays from a boombox in the hangar that he rents at Minter Field, a sleepy former U.S. Army Air Corps training base a few miles northwest of Bakersfield. Every few minutes he rises to spit a stream of tobacco juice into a trash can.

In the center of the hangar sits his red-and-white racer called Strega (Italian for "witch"), which is being tended by several members of his pit crew. Built around 1945 as a North American P-51D Mustang fighter, it was a rotting wreck in 1982 when Destefani imported it from Australia and rebuilt it with major modifications. He removed all of its guns and armor, clipped two and a half feet off each wingtip and six inches off each horizontal tail surface, and reduced the size of the pilots' cockpit canopy to an aerodynamically slick pimple.

As were most wartime P-51s, Strega is powered by a Merlin engine, a supercharged, liquid-cooled V-12 designed by Rolls-Royce in the late 1930s. But while World War II Mustangs had a maximum takeoff weight of 12,100 pounds and their Merlins were tuned to produce 1,700 horsepower, Destefani's plane weighs 8,650 pounds at takeoff and its war-surplus Merlin, running at full throttle, pumps out about 3,600 horsepower.

How the old engine's output is doubled is a highly technical and complicated subject, but a simplified way to explain it is by using a measurement called "manifold pressure." This is the barometric pressure of the air rammed into the carburetor by the supercharger. During World War II, a P-51's maximum manifold pressure was set at 60 inches of mercury, although *in extremis* a fighter pilot could push it to 67 inches for a maximum of five minutes. This was called "war emergency power," and using it meant that the engine had to be completely overhauled before it was started again.

Strega's maximum manifold pressure is 155 inches. At that setting the engine's useful life is particularly brief. "It's like riding a hand grenade with the pin pulled," says Destefani. "Every time we rebuild it [it's as if] we give it an internal fuse. Sometimes it's a long fuse, sometimes it's a short fuse. You just don't know."

That's why Destefani flies Strega only fifteen or twenty hours per year. He uses the full throttle only at Reno, where he's confident that if his engine fails he can successfully glide to a landing on any of Reno Stead's three long runways. This has happened more times than he can remember.

Destefani began taking flying lessons at age twenty-one from a local crop-duster. In 1978, while recuperating from a near-fatal bout of spinal meningitis, he made an important decision. "I said, 'You know, here I am almost dying, and I haven't done everything I wanted to do.' So when I got out of the hospital, I changed my life and started doing what I wanted."

He wanted to buy, fly, and race P-51 Mustangs, the best World War II fighter plane, and began racing in the mid-1980s. Destefani's first one, called Mangia Pane ("eats bread"), was an also-ran at Reno. The next, Dago Red, did better. He then piloted Strega to the Reno Unlimited championship in 1987, 1992, 1993, 1995, 1996, and 1997. (For the record, Destefani first announced his imminent retirement in 2000. But that year, because of mechanical problems, he did not race. In 2001, the Reno races were canceled because of the post-September 11 ban on private flying.)

Along the way he also started a side business, Warbirds Unlimited, which restores derelict World War II aircraft to flying condition, but not necessarily for racing. He has restored and delivered them all over the country.

Racing in the Unlimited class is particularly dangerous. In the past fifteen years, three Unlimited pilots have died at Reno. Another Unlimited-class plane crash-landed while being flown to Minnesota, killing its businessman owner.

The man who paid $30,000 for one week of liability insurance this year shakes his head. "This is what I do," says Destefani. "I know what I'm doing, and I do it well."

Is there any sort of death wish or thrill-seeking gene involved?

No again.

"I had a buddy," Destefani says by way of explanation, "who's dead now. He died of cancer. But he was always flying up there, too, and when somebody would come up to him and say, 'Well, aren't you afraid of dying?' his answer would be, 'We don't come here to die.' And I always thought that was a great answer because we don't. We go to [Reno to] race.

"People are always asking me if this thing is 'dangerous,'" he continues. "You know what's dangerous? I'm a farmer. That's dangerous. You don't think that's a risk? You've got all the forces of nature lined up against you. You know what else is dangerous? Driving your car down a one-lane road. With another driver coming toward you."

During race week in September, Skip Holm of Calabasas could be found sitting in his racing team's motor home parked on the Reno Stead Airport pit area. Dozens of similar vehicles formed one side of roped-in compounds containing flamboyantly painted airplanes at their center. He nodded understandingly when asked about the phenomenon of gray-haired competitors going against the flow of normal human development, becoming not more cautious but less so as they age.

"Yeah," he said. "These guys become successful and rich and then they get bored. So they have to look for something else really challenging to do."

The fifty-eight-year-old Holm flies Dago Red, Destefani's old airplane, now much improved and owned by a Utah businessman. Holm flew Dago Red to the Unlimited championship in 1998,

1999, and 2000. A retired Lockheed test pilot who flew experimental models of the U-2 spy plane and F-117 stealth fighter, Holm has gone in the opposite direction: he's filling out his own Golden Years Risk Portfolio by having started a company whose still-nascent aim is to manufacture and sell general aviation aircraft built in Poland and mainland China. The project Holm is most enthusiastic about is a lightweight plane powered by a Harley-Davidson motorcycle engine.

Holm also tests privately developed aircraft and is one of the premier pilots in the movie industry. In short, along with his old friend Destefani, he's the kind of guy you would have heard about if air racing were still in its golden age, which, unfortunately, ended fifty-three years ago.

Between World Wars I and II, air racers had the same name recognition as race car drivers. Men such as Jimmy Doolittle, Roscoe Turner (who liked to pose with his pet lion cub in the cockpit), and Hollywood stunt flier Frank Tallman were sports celebrities. Planes were sponsored by major oil and auto-parts companies. Races were held around the country, and the annual Cleveland National Air Races, home of the national championships, was a major event covered on every newspaper sports page.

Early air racers pioneered innovations such as streamlining and retractable landing gear that were incorporated during World War II, when piston-engine aircraft technology was pushed to its limits. After the war, air racing resumed. The fastest competitors used surplus fighter planes that at the time could be purchased for as little as $1,000. Fans loved watching veteran racers and young war veterans compete in the Mustangs, Lockheed Lightnings, DeHavilland Mosquitoes, Chance Vought Corsairs, and Bell Airacobras that had made the world safe for democracy. The Air Force and Navy sent their boys to race their new jets, too.

In 1949, one of the favorites for the Cleveland championship was a former U.S. Army Air Corps transport pilot named Bill Odom. He flew Beguine, a beautifully modified Mustang whose fuselage was painted with the opening notes of the Cole Porter song "Begin the Beguine." On the second lap Odom lost control and plunged into a newly built house alongside the racecourse, killing himself, a young mother inside the house, and her thirteen-month-old son, who was outside in his playpen.

That tragedy and the outbreak of the Korean War — which curtailed military participation — wiped air racing off the American sports calendar. Almost everyone assumed it was gone for good.

The first Unlimited mishap at Reno 2002 took place on Sunday, September 8, one day before the weeklong competition officially began. A retired Vietnam-era Air Force fighter pilot from Auburn, California, named Tom Dwelle went up for a test flight in Critical Mass, a Hawker Sea Fury once flown by the British Royal Navy. His landing was perfect, but while taxiing back to the pit, his landing gear collapsed. Dwelle was unhurt, but damage to his fuselage, engine, and propeller forced him to withdraw from the race.

The next day, Skip Holm went up for a qualifying run. He circled counterclockwise around the longest and widest Unlimited course (ten pylons, 8.2688 miles), skimming the ground in the crystalline desert air in 59.80 seconds. This equaled 497.797 mph, a new qualifying record.

On Tuesday, Tiger Destefani took off in Strega, warmed the engine, and called for a one-lap qualification run. His circuit was timed at 486.798 mph, so he requested and began a two-lap run, hoping to wring out more power, beat Holm, and maybe even turn in the first 500-mph lap in Reno history.

On the second lap of that run he pushed the throttle as far as it would go. At full song, a racing Merlin driving a four-blade propeller makes an unforgettable noise. It sounds like an angry monster chewing its way through a large wooden building.

Everything looked fine for Strega until the eighth pylon, when Destefani felt a slight jolt — possibly a valve breaking or a piston disintegrating. People on the ground saw a puff of black smoke from the plane's exhaust pipes. By the time Destefani got to the finish line, the Merlin had backfired violently and shot a ball of burning gas through the air-induction system. It blew apart the turbocharger and sprayed large fragments of engine and engine cowling into the air.

Destefani immediately pulled up and off the course, trading airspeed for altitude, and glided to an uneventful dead-stick landing on a far runway. The plane was towed into a hangar, where he and his mechanics quickly determined that his finely tuned $150,000 investment had been turned into a lump of scrap metal. He had no spare engine.

Destefani grabbed a beer and told a reporter from a local newspaper that he was now officially retired from air racing. "We're done now," he said.

Asked why he hadn't been content with his first qualifying lap (which was the second-fastest this year), he said, "I figured if it won't run today, what would it do on Sunday?"

In 1964, a wealthy Nevada rancher, hydroplane racer, and private pilot named William Stead invited anyone who still owned a raceworthy airplane to drop by the dirt-surfaced landing strip on his 207,000-acre Sky Ranch.

Those were the first National Championship Air Races. Eight Unlimited class planes and a gaggle of assorted biplanes, monoplane midget racers (now called Formula Ones), turned up. They did it again the following September. In 1966, the races moved to Stead Air Force Base, formerly the Reno Army Air Base, which had recently closed. (It was renamed after Stead's younger brother, a P-51 pilot for the Nevada Air National Guard, was killed in a crash there.) On April 28, 1966, Stead himself died when a mechanical failure caused him to lose control of his midget racer during a practice flight.

Hence, Bill Stead never saw his creation blossom. He never saw Reno's city fathers and gambling moguls — realizing that the event was just the right size to fill the hotel rooms and casinos of Las Vegas's little brother during a quiet autumn week — embrace the races. (They supported them financially when necessary, but, more important, they kept developers from infringing onto the Reno Stead racecourse.) He never saw crowds of nearly one hundred thousand fill the bleachers and pit areas, or his namesake airport become, once a year, a small island of tarmac and sagebrush in a sea of parked cars and RVs.

He also never suffered through several years of inept coverage by ABC's *Wide World of Sports*, which Reno insiders blame for a subsequent lack of network TV exposure. And he never saw potential corporate sponsors resist all entreaties to join the fun, since they're well aware that (a) air racing fans, unlike auto racing fans, don't go out Monday to buy the same brand of tires and engine oil their heroes had used on Sunday, and (b) a winged billboard emblazoned with their logo might negatively impact their bottom line should it fall, perhaps burning fiercely, into spectators.

Nor did he have the chance to gloat over the dozens of other promoters who tried staging air racing meets in other cities and failed. Or see spare parts for Unlimiteds become rare and expensive antiques. Or watch successive Reno Air Races organizers keep prize money at such a low level that only first-prize winners had a chance to meet expenses.

And, of course, he never saw Tiger Destefani's dramatic retirement from air racing — which lasted maybe three hours.

On Tuesday afternoon, September 10, Dan Martin, a San Jose contractor-turned-full-time Warbird restorer and race pilot, offered to lend his friend Destefani a Merlin, the one with the burnt piston that he had back home. Dave Fagoaga, a scowling, black-bearded master Merlin mechanic on the Dago Red team, volunteered to help make Strega air-worthy — with his employer Terry Bland's blessing. Strega crew chief L. D. Hughes made the first of several all-night pickup-truck runs to Martin's shop in Hollister. Their daunting task was to construct, in the four days remaining before the race, one healthy Merlin out of two dead ones.

Under Reno's complicated rules, each airplane races daily in several preliminary heats beginning on Thursday; their individual finishes and average speeds place them in either the gold, silver, or bronze finals. Because of Strega's second-place qualifying run, Destefani was allowed to stay on the ground until Saturday. If he finished first in the silver heat that morning he would be "bumped up" to the gold, or championship, final on Sunday.

By Wednesday the "old" Merlin engine had been dismounted and disassembled into hundreds of parts, not one of them even remotely electronic. That day, too, a Mustang named Miss America (which was being qualified by its owner, an Oklahoma City brain surgeon named Brent Hisey) threw a rod through its engine block, starting a small fire and necessitating a too-hasty return to the ground.

Landing hard, Miss America bounced onto and off Runway 32, ran through a ditch, wiped out its landing gear, and performed a 180-degree pirouette that nearly tossed the plane onto its back, which would have been catastrophic. After the Strega team learned that Hisey was unhurt, its members began making inquiries about borrowing some of Miss America's undamaged parts.

On Thursday the Strega team began building the "new" Merlin engine. This was also the first day of heat races for all classes and the first day that paying spectators were admitted. The meet's opening ceremonies — heavily 9/11-influenced, with four T-6s flying in "missing man" formation — were sandwiched at noon between the opening races. An unscientific survey of the crowd indicated that (a) almost everyone except the many Japanese photographers present was older than forty, and (b) about half were private pilots. Most of the rest were radio-control fliers, model airplane hobbyists, or unlicensed all-around aviation freaks.

At any one time, a dozen or more were gathered around the open doors of the Strega hangar, watching a seemingly infinite number of nuts, bolts, gaskets, valves, hoses, and wires being painstakingly examined, installed, removed, adjusted, reinstalled, safety-wired, and inspected. Some, documenting the process with their still and video cameras, watched for hours.

On Friday morning a rented crane lifted the reassembled engine up to Strega's nose. Bolting it onto the engine mount and connecting the dozens of hoses and wires of the ignition, fuel, oil, air injection, and cooling systems took until late afternoon. The process did not stop after Tommy Rose's fatal crash.

As the sun slipped behind the surrounding hills and the sky turned from cobalt to black, Strega was towed to a taxiway. A mechanic climbed into the cockpit, turned his baseball cap backward, and hit the starter switch. The Merlin caught on the first try, shooting short blue flames from its exhaust pipes. A good sign, shouted another crew member above the roar.

An Unlimited air race starts in the air. The pace plane is a forty-plus-year-old civilian-owned ex–Air Force T-33 jet trainer. It takes off to the east, climbs to about twelve thousand feet, and makes a wide, lazy 270-degree circle of the airport. The Unlimiteds take off one by one in the order they qualified, cut across the circle to form up closely behind the jet in qualifying order, and are led downward, faster and faster until they hit the starting point close to racing speed and altitude. The jet peels off a few seconds before the first pylon.

A few hours before Saturday morning's race, Strega's engine cowling was covered by several aluminum panels, including one salvaged from Miss America. "To Tiger from Miss A" was scrawled on the plane's newly polished nose.

Due to missing the qualifying heats, Strega started the silver race eighth and last, but, thrillingly, passed one opponent on each lap — four Sea Furys, two Mustangs, and one Russian Yak 11. By the eighth and final lap, Destefani was comfortably ahead, winning at an average speed of 414 mph. The inside word from the crew was that he had nearly half of the engine's power in reserve.

"When you got a whole bunch of ducks in formation, you get the back ones first because the next ones don't know it," said Destefani, grinning, back at his pit. "Next thing you know you got the whole flock. If you get the front one first, they all scatter."

Then Destefani spent about an hour signing T-shirts ("Fly Fast, Fly Low, Turn Left" and "Speed Limit 500 MPH"), hats, visors, teddy bears, women's arms and upper breasts, and Revell airplane models.

Sunday morning dawned partly cloudy, with a forecast for gusty afternoon winds. A former space shuttle astronaut won the jet race, but it aroused surprisingly little excitement, probably because the planes were identical; none had been modified, much less dangerously so, and they sounded a lot like vacuum cleaners.

The Sport class was a different matter. The fastest qualifier was sixty-six-year-old Daryl Greenamyer, who had won seven Unlimited championships, the last one in 1977. He had become bored during his long retirement and had built his own plane, called a Lancair Legacy, from a kit (it took fifteen months). After Greenamyer crossed the finish line, beating his closest competitor by a lap, he flew an "honorary victory lap" in memory of Tommy Rose.

By 4:10 P.M., the scheduled start of the Unlimited gold race, the wind was thirty-five knots with gusts up to fifty miles per hour blowing directly across the runway. Dust was flying up to several hundred feet in the air, obscuring the pylons from the spectator area all around the course. Regardless, after only a few minutes' delay, the Unlimiteds took off and circled toward the starting point. On the first lap, Skip Holm and Dago Red led easily, with Destefani and Strega last. By the beginning of the second lap, Strega was third and closing fast on second place. Then, as Destefani flashed by the second pylon, he pulled up and off the course.

"I think I heard Tiger say, 'Mayday,'" said a spectator with an air traffic control band radio.

Destefani put down his flaps and landing gear, did S-turns to avoid overshooting the runway, and landed without incident. He sat in his cockpit for eight minutes while Skip Holm breezed to his fourth straight victory with an average speed of 466.634 mph.

Holm taxied in, jumped out of the cockpit, and had a brief interview with a pit reporter. "It was really, really rough out there," said Holm. "It was rougher than a cob." That's why, he explained, at times he was racing at higher-than-usual altitudes.

"I've never been up so high!" joked the former U-2 pilot. "What do they call it when you get dizzy when you're up there so far?"

Strega was towed in fifteen minutes later, twin streaks of engine oil painting lines down the sides of the fuselage. Destefani walked alongside. "Well, that's it. I'm retired now," he said, looking a little bit older but not depressed. "I guess it was fitting that I went out with a 'Mayday.'"

Then he grabbed an outstretched Sharpie and signed the bib of a fan's sleeping grandchild.

On Monday, September 16, Destefani took a commercial flight back to Bakersfield to start the cotton harvest. Strega was fitted with yet another borrowed engine and on the following Thursday was flown gingerly home by Dan Martin. When the pit crew tore down both blown engines, they found that the same piston had burnt in each of them. The engines had failed for exactly the same reason. A fix was devised.

To test it, of course, someone will have to race it again at Reno 2003.

MICHAEL HALL

Running for His Life

FROM TEXAS MONTHLY

HE WAS ON FIRE. It was three in the morning, and most of his class-mates from the Kibimba school in Burundi were dead — beaten and burned alive by friends of theirs, kids and grown-ups they had known most of their lives. Smoldering bodies lay in mounds all over the small room. He had used some of the corpses for cover, to keep from being hit by the fiery branches tossed in by the Hutu mob outside. For hours he had heard them laughing, singing, clapping, taunting. Waving their machetes, they had herded more than a hundred Tutsi teenagers and teachers from his high school into the room before sunset. A couple dozen were still alive, moaning in pain, dreaming of death.

"There weren't that many of us left," he says. "A guy said, 'I'm going out — I don't want to die like a dog.' He jumped from a window. They cut him to pieces. Then they started a fire on the roof. After a while it started falling on me, and I held up my right arm as it came down, trying to pull bodies over me. My back and arm were on fire — it hurt so bad. I decided I had had enough. I decided to kill myself by diving from a pile of bodies onto my head. I tried twice, but it didn't work. Then I heard a voice. It said, 'You don't want to die. Don't do that.' Outside, we could hear Hutus giving up and leaving. I heard one say, 'Before we go, let's make sure everyone is dead.' So three came inside. One put a spear through a guy's heart; another guy tried to escape, and they caught him and killed him. I heard the voice say, 'Get out.' There was a body next to me, burned down to the bones. It was hot. I grabbed a bone — it was hot in my hands — and used it to break the bar on the window. The fires had been going for nine hours, so it was easy to break. My thinking was, I wanted to kill myself. I wanted to be identifiable. I wanted my parents to know me. I didn't want to be all burned up, like everyone else. I was jumping to let them kill me."

There was a fire underneath the window, set as an obstacle to escape. He jumped. And somehow, in the darkness, amid the uproar of genocide, at least for a few seconds, no one saw him. His back was on fire, his legs were smoking, and his feet were raw with pain. He ran.

If you could call it running.

"Gilbert!" Almost a decade later, on March 30, 2003, he crossed the finish line at the Capitol 10K in Austin to the sound of hundreds of people clapping, many calling his name. "Gilbert! *Woo!*" He finished ahead of some fourteen thousand runners, but it wasn't good enough, and the look on his face said that he knew it. Others knew it too. A woman off to the side yelled, "Coach, you're awesome! I love you! You're number one, Gilbert!" In fact, Gilbert Tuhabonye was number three, a minute and fifteen seconds behind the winner in a race he had won the previous year and was favored to win again. Gilbert turned and jogged back against the flow of the other finishers, shaking hands and high-fiving spectators, who all seemed to know the thin African. Then he ran the last fifty yards again with Richard Mendez, one of many runners he had trained. "Come on! Come on!" Gilbert said to Mendez. "High knee!" When Mendez finished, Gilbert went back and ran with Ryan Steglich, another of his charges. And then with Shae Rainer and Lisa Spenner. "Come on! Come on!" he yelled. "Butt kick!"

Afterward, Gilbert, who stands five-foot-ten and weighs 127 pounds, hung around talking to the other runners, many of whom wore T-shirts that read "Gilbert's Gazelles Training Group." A circle of eight stood basking in his approval, trading anecdotes about their pains and agonies, as runners do. He laughed and joked with them, accepting halfhearted high-fives and thin encouragement, which made him look down self-consciously. Eight thousand miles from home, he's a celebrity in Austin, a twenty-eight-year-old with protruding teeth and a boyish laugh, the most popular running coach in a town of rabid runners, a former national champion, both as a teenager in Africa and as a college student in West Texas.

Governor Rick Perry, himself an avid runner, seeks out Gilbert to chat. Kids ask for his autograph. Rich white ladies pay him to order them to run laps. Everybody wants him to make them go faster. They've heard his mantra: it's all about form. "If you have good form," says Gilbert, "running becomes a joy. You can go farther and faster. You can run forever."

You can run forever. This, to a runner, is heaven. Gilbert's students see him as a savior, upbeat after all that he's been through, relentless and optimistic when he has every right to be withdrawn and angry. A man on a mission: to win an Olympic medal, to tell his story, to show the world what one tribe did and what one man — set on fire and left to die — can do. A man with a last name (pronounced "Too-ha-BON-yay") almost too good to be true. "In Burundi," Gilbert says, "your last name has to have meaning. When I was born, it was a very difficult time. It was right after the war. There had been a big drought, crickets attacked the crops — and then my mother broke her ankle. When I was born, she said I was special. She said, 'This is not my son. This is a son of God.' 'Tuhabonye' means 'a son of God.'"

As the runners dispersed, Jeff Kloster, who works with Gilbert at RunTex, an Austin running store, brought him his warm-ups, and Gilbert took off his shirt to change. Though Jeff had seen them before, he could not take his eyes off the scars that cover Gilbert's back. The burns continue along his right arm, where they bubble the skin like large patches of candle wax, and then to his right leg, which gets darker along the sides of his calf, where the flames ate down to the bone. The scars are proof of the unthinkable: ten years ago, on a mountaintop in Burundi, high school kids and their teachers were stuck in a room and set on fire. For nine hours Gilbert watched his friends die, breathed their burning flesh, hid under their corpses. Then he ran for his life. People speak of crucibles and the forging of character. They have no idea.

In the living room of his two-bedroom South Austin apartment, Gilbert is beating on an imaginary drum. He's playing along with a group of drummers on a CD of Burundian music. It sounds like an army — pounding, lurching, exploding, simmering, then accelerating beats; there's no melody, only occasional yelling and chanting. "There are eleven people in a circle," he says excitedly, "each with a three-foot-wide drum." He moves his arms and his head along with the rhythm. "There's one in the center. He's calling out, jumping. Everyone is watching him, following him. There's a lot of dancing. It's *awesome.*"

Gilbert's pretty wife, Triphine, plays nearby with their daughter, Emma. At home the couple speak mostly Kirundi, their native tongue, though they try to speak English around Emma, an alternately shy and boisterous two-year-old. Gilbert also speaks French and Swahili. His English is very good, and he speaks it with a melodious lilt. He has short hair and high cheekbones — he's handsome in an earnest, youthful way. He's wearing blue denim shorts, a gray Mizuno shirt, and sandals. His legs are thin but muscular. His burns look like relief maps.

The apartment is cluttered with Emma's toys. On the walls are a tacked-up Burundi flag and photos of Gilbert running; a Bible sits on a table. Another song comes on, from the sixties, called "Yes, I Love Micombero," about a Tutsi president from back then. Gilbert sings along, and Triph, who is also a Tutsi, remembers it, too. "If you say this guy's name in front of a Hutu," says Gilbert, "he will kill you." Gilbert pretends to play some of the other instruments. "In Burundi, the music is good and the climate is beautiful. If there was peace, I'd go there to train. The lake is gorgeous — there are hundreds of types of fish. It's like Hawaii: a lot of birds, all these types of fruits. It's paradise."

Burundi is a small, poor, mountainous country in east central Africa. Gilbert was born in the southern county of Songa on November 22, 1974, the third of four children. His Tutsi parents were farmers, raising corn, potatoes, peas, and beans, and also kept milk cows. As a boy, he ran everywhere: down the valley to get water, to school five miles away. He loved to race his friends, but more than anything else, he loved to chase the family's cows. In the sixth grade, he was baptized a Catholic, and the next year he went to a Protestant boarding school in Kibimba, about 150 miles away. Of the thousand or so students, about 60 percent were Hutus and the rest Tutsis. For the most part, they got along pretty well, sharing the same dorms and playing on the same soccer team.

Though the Hutu and Tutsi tribes have squabbled for centuries, it's only in the past two generations that things have gotten brutal, both in Burundi and in its northern neighbor, Rwanda. The countries are roughly the same size and are similar in many ways (think of the Dakotas). They each have a five-to-one mix of Hutus and Tutsis, they speak Kirundi, they're roughly two-thirds Catholic, and they have shared histories. In Burundi, the Tutsis (aka the Watusi) have ruled the Hutus ever since emigrating from Ethiopia, more than five hundred years ago. The Tutsis were cattle herders and aristocrats, while the Hutus were working-class farmers. They lived together in relative peace until the Europeans came; Burundi and Rwanda were incorporated into German East Africa in the 1890s, and Belgium took over after World War I. "During colonization, they started dividing people," says Gilbert. "The Germans made the differences between Tutsi and Hutu into law: divide and govern."

Both Rwanda and Burundi became independent in 1962. While the Hutus gained some power in Rwanda, Tutsis controlled the army and the government in Burundi, making occasional attempts at parliamentary elections to give the more numerous Hutus a voice in government. Just before and after independence, ethnic violence flared up, and there were massacres by both sides. In 1972 an attempted coup in Burundi led to the slaughter of some 150,000 Hutus; many Tutsis were killed, too, including three of Gilbert's uncles. "Bad teaching," he says about the causes of the violence. "Deep hate." It's a class thing and a race thing, even though both tribes have intermingled for so long that sometimes even Burundians can't tell the difference. But usually they can. A Tutsi, says Gilbert, tends to be tall and thin, with a narrow nose; a Hutu is shorter, more muscular, and has a wider nose. Tutsis complain that Hutus lack ambition; Hutus say Tutsis are arrogant.

At the Kibimba school, Gilbert began running competitively. As a freshman, he won an 8K race running barefoot. The next year, he met a coach who showed him how to run properly — how to get his knees up and how to hold his arms. The coach told Gilbert that if he worked hard, he could make the Olympics. In his junior year, Gilbert was a national champion in the 400 and 800 meters, already a great runner in a country known for producing them. By his senior year, in 1993, all he cared about was school and running. His goal was to get a scholarship to an American college, get an education, and return home. The dream actually seemed possible, since Burundi appeared to have turned a corner on its violent past:

the latest Tutsi dictator had mandated the first-ever presidential election, and not surprisingly, a Hutu won. A new day was dawning in Burundi. Four months after the election, though, the president was assassinated by Tutsi soldiers. It was a new day, all right.

"The night before," says Gilbert, "I didn't sleep. I had two tests that day, in chemistry and biology. I was thinking, maybe I studied too hard. It was my senior year, and I had to be prepared for college. That morning I turned on the radio. Nothing. I thought the battery was dead. I went to class, and people started talking about the rumors — usually when the radio isn't working, it's a coup. A friend said there was a putsch, that the president was dead. There weren't many Hutus around, but I saw one, my teammate on the 440 relay. He showed me a machete, pulled it out of its sheath, ran it along his throat, and said, 'Tonight is the night I'm gonna cut your neck.' I said, 'Why?' He said, 'Because you guys killed our president.' I thought he was joking. I found out later that Hutus had been gathering since three in the morning, planning on killing Tutsis. By ten, a mob had gathered at the school — Hutus with machetes. They took away a Tutsi professor and said, 'We're gonna kill all these Tutsis.' I told a professor, a Tutsi, what people were saying. He said, 'Don't worry — they can't do that.'"

Sitting on his flowery couch, Gilbert recounts this story carefully, speaking slowly at some points and excitedly at others, sometimes waving his arms. "Around noon, we went to the principal to ask for help, and he told us, 'You killed the president, and you have to die.' We tried to organize a peaceful running away. We also hoped the army would come. There were hundreds of us marching — girls, boys, teachers, farmers — and we locked our arms together. We didn't get far; the mob stopped us. By then it had started raining. Everywhere we looked, there was a Hutu with a machete, a bow and arrow, or a spear. Some were my friends. They told us to go back to the school. We didn't move. All of a sudden, a woman took a spear and threw it into the crowd. And they attacked us — cutting people, their ears and noses, so they'd know who was a Tutsi.

"Many escaped. I tried to, but they were watching me. They knew I was a cross-country runner, that I could run and tell the soldiers. They got me, and the principal said I'd be the last to die. He said they'd do me like they did Jesus Christ. He said, 'You will see what

Jesus saw on the cross.' He meant I was going to get a good torture, like Jesus got. They attached us to each other, one by one, with a rope, by the arms. I said, 'Where are you taking us? I thought we were friends.' 'Not anymore.'

"Kids were bleeding, screaming, crying. My heart was beating like I don't know what, I was so scared. They took us down the hill to a highway gas station owned by a Hutu, a guy I knew — I bought stuff from him all the time. People were all around us, walking next to us, with machetes. They were singing, 'We caught the enemy! We're gonna burn them to death!' When we got there, they took our clothes. All I had on was underwear and a shirt. Before they pushed us inside, they beat every kid on the back of the neck with a big club. They hit *hard* — to stun or paralyze. Some were killed. I was one of the last ones and jumped inside, but they beat me on the chest so hard that I bled for three weeks.

"There were more than a hundred people in a room this big" — Gilbert points to the kitchen wall on the far side of his living room, a forty-by-twenty-five-foot space. "We couldn't move. It was jammed with half-naked people screaming and crying. Outside, they were dancing, clapping, singing, 'We did it!' Just after I got in, they poured gasoline in through the windows — everyone got some on them. I got it on my shirt, so I took it off. Then they threw in branches that were on fire. The flames moved so fast. People were trying to hide and put out the flames. It was horrible. Many were killed by the fire and smoke. The Hutus were waiting outside for us to try to escape, but the doors were thick and we couldn't break out.

"Because I was one of the last in, I was near the wall, banging against it, and I found a door to a kind of closet. I pushed it open, and there were more people in there. I let a few more inside. The Hutus kept throwing lit branches in through a window. I hid under the bodies of my friends. After a couple more hours, I heard a student tell the chemistry professor to get some chemicals to throw inside. The people left were gasping for air. I took a deep breath and was pushing air away from my face."

At this point, the Hutus set fire to the roof, Gilbert caught fire, and he decided to let them kill him. "But something was guiding me," he says. "When I jumped, they were outside, just a few feet away, standing by the fire they'd built under the window. But they didn't see me. As soon as I landed, I couldn't see clearly. The wind was blowing, and it was cold — I was naked. I just started moving and got around the corner. I heard someone shout, 'Gilbert is coming!' I saw a mob of people — they stood up, holding machetes. Everywhere, I saw people coming. I ran downhill. The more I ran, the wind was teasing the fire on my back. Some people were saying, 'Don't worry about him; he's gonna die anyway,' and they gave up. But not everyone. A guy came running at me with a machete. I ducked, and he just missed me and cut his own arm. I kept running, and all of a sudden I fell into a deep ditch filled with rainwater. It put out the fire on my back. I heard people talking, saying, 'Let's catch him. He knows who we are.' I heard this one guy coming — I knew his voice — and he fell into the ditch. I was leaning against the side, and he had a spear in one hand and a machete in the other. I killed him. I have never confessed this before. I was so angry. They had burned me, killed my friends. I had nothing to lose. But I don't think it was me who got that strength. God gives power to eliminate evil."

How exactly did a mild-mannered high school kid kill a man? Gilbert demonstrates — he puts one hand on his chin and the other on the back of his head, jerking and twisting hard, pantomiming the breaking of someone's neck. "I watch Chuck Norris," he says. "Chuck Norris was my favorite. The guy puked on himself, and I knew he was dead.

"The voice in my head said, 'Go away,'" Gilbert continues, "so I got up again. I was so thirsty, so dehydrated, and I started toward the hospital, about a half-mile away. It was so hard to move; every step hurt. I could barely stand up. My feet, I could see, were like meat. My right leg was so bad that I could see the bone. I was on my hands and knees, running like a monkey. There were still Hutus everywhere with machetes. The voice was telling me, 'You don't want to die.' My heart was beating so hard that I thought they could hear it. When I got to the hospital, a guy saw me going in and said, 'He runs like a monkey. He's not a human being. He's a spirit.'"

It was all about form — the years on the track, keeping his knees up and his arms back, pushing himself when he thought he was going to die. He stumbled into the sanctuary of the hospital. Soon the soldiers came, and Gilbert, with third-degree burns over 30 percent of his body, was moved to an army hospital; later he recovered in a hospital near his home, where his mother came to visit him. In the immediate aftermath of the fire, she and Gilbert's father had been told that he was dead. Then, later that night, Gilbert's father had been murdered by a Hutu gang on the road. Now, she was told, her son was alive.

"When my mother came to the hospital, I was bandaged everywhere. She said, 'I told you, you are a son of God. If it wasn't for God, you are dead.' It's a shock and also a lesson. It has meaning. I don't think I survived because I'm strong but because of the power of God. God showed up." But what about the others? Surely they were also children of God. Why weren't they spared as well? "That's the thing I didn't understand. Afterward, I asked myself, 'Why me? Why did I survive?'"

In the hospital, he lay on his stomach and left side, pondering the unknowable. When he closed his eyes to sleep, he saw flames and heard screams. He read his Bible. He figured the voice he had heard was God's, but he didn't know why it had spoken only to him. "Why did God want me to survive?"

Why do people run — that is, people who aren't being chased by a fire-throwing, machete-waving mob? Why do thousands get up early on a Sunday morning and put their knees and ankles and hearts and lungs through the hell of ten thousand meters on hard pavement?

There is no single good answer to this question. In high school, people run for glory or for girls (or boys). Maybe they're being punished. Later on, they run for exercise or just to fit into their pants. Eventually, if they're lucky, they tap into another world: the state of physical and mental grace they reach when they're cruising, when their blood is racing through their every vein. Their thoughts have never been clearer, and their limbs are snapping in rhythm; their souls are revealed, and they are striving, excellent souls. They become obsessed with this feeling. They get religious about it. It is, for some of them, as spiritual as they will ever get.

Go to a running trail in any big city in Texas, and you will see them working toward this feeling: the grimacer, the puffer, the hacker, the wheezer; the stiff-armed and the backward-leaning; the torso-barely-moving and the stumpy-legs-moving-fast; the potato on sticks, the pear-shaped, the ham-thighed; the loping underachiever and the determined overstepper; the elbows swiveling, the shoulders hunched, the whole body moving as if underwater. They are all bound together by this transforming passion and perhaps also by the fact that they look less silly if they run in numbers. They are, most of them, loners: mild-mannered, nervous, self-conscious, preoccupied with their bodies. They long to get better and faster, to raise their personal bests, even when at a certain point that becomes physically impossible (such logic does not concern the runner, who is high on the opiate of self-improvement). Their feet splay to the sides, their arms flail. They are desperate.

And in Austin, at least, they hang on Gilbert's every word. He coaches at RunTex, where he is one of twenty instructors — "the Michael Jordan" of the bunch, says the store's owner, Paul Carrozza. Some of Gilbert's students (he has about a hundred at any one time) are competitive runners, people who, say, have qualified for the Boston Marathon and want to set a personal record. They're fanatics, obsessed with every half-second, every curve of the trail, every ache and pain. They aspire to the elite. Lisa Spenner, twenty-eight, is one of these, a former triathlete who, after training with Gilbert for the Motorola Marathon, missed qualifying for the American Olympic trials by only fifty-one seconds. Most of Gilbert's students are athletic types, late bloomers who run regularly but perhaps unwisely in local races like the Capitol 10K. They don't aspire to the elite; they just want to run faster. Then there are the ones who just want to get some exercise with the enthusiastic African man. They aspire to look good.

Gilbert's methods are pretty simple, really. One of the pleasant paradoxes of running is that the more machinelike you get, the freer you feel. As he says, it's all about form: how the arms move (economically, if possible) and the feet land (heel to toe). His workouts are intense — sprinting around the track, speeding up hills, springing up and down on a bench — all to improve the basic mechanics of movement. He pushes his students hard and yells at them melodramatically as he trots alongside ("Knees up! Knees up! Knees up! I want to see you in the *air!*"). When, after eight successive sprints around the track or three inexorable ascents up a steep hill or a series of 100-yard dashes on a single breath of air, they feel like they're about to die, they look at Gilbert's scars. How bad, really, could it be? "He gets people to believe in themselves," says

Spenner. "He treats everyone like they're amazing." Sometimes they watch him as he motors like a quiet machine, his head barely bobbing, his arms swinging in perfect time, his feet making quiet patting sounds, and then they try it themselves. At the end of a workout they're breathing hard, bent over, walking slowly, wet with sweat, exhausted. They are in agony. They are happy. They are better.

"Most elite runners think it's all about them," says Carrozza. "Gilbert is so giving, so willing to coach others." If Gilbert is their savior, they are his saviors, too — or at least they help answer the question that has haunted him for a decade now: why me? "Eventually, I realized I had to help people," he says, "coaching them, telling them my story, telling what happened. When I help people, I feel good."

The Kibimba massacre was the beginning of a bloody civil war in which there were mass killings fueled by revenge on both sides. Six months later, a plane carrying the president of Rwanda and the new leader of Burundi was shot down, leading to the genocide in Rwanda of eight hundred thousand Tutsis over a period of one hundred days; there hadn't been such an efficient killing machine since the Holocaust. Burundi was lucky — the Hutus weren't as organized there, and the Tutsis controlled the army. A mere two hundred thousand, mostly Hutus, would die throughout the rest of the nineties.

Gilbert spent three months in the hospital, recovering not only from the burns but from the savage beating he had received. He was now a witness, for God and Tutsi, and he told his story to anyone who visited. His right leg was so badly burned that his knee was stuck at a ninety-degree angle. The doctor said it would take six months to heal. Frustrated, Gilbert got on a bike and forcibly unstuck it. "The blood came through; I could sleep again. If I hadn't done it, I could have been crippled." While in the hospital, he got a scholarship offer from Tulane University, in New Orleans. Gilbert wasn't healed enough yet to accept it, but he used it as motivation to run again. The biking led to walking, which led to jogging, which finally led to running a year after he had been left to die. In 1995 he ran the 400 meters at a competition in Kenya and later that year ran for Burundi in the World University Games in Japan.

He went to the University of Burundi for a year and was training for the 1996 Olympics when he was sent to an Olympic training center in Georgia, one of many such facilities established by the International Olympic Committee for athletes of developing nations. He ended up as an alternate on the team but stayed in Georgia, taking English classes at La Grange College.

The next year, he accepted a track scholarship from Abilene Christian University, the small Church of Christ school in West Texas that has a storied running history. ACU has won forty-nine NCAA Division II track-and-field championships and has sent almost three dozen athletes to the Olympics, including the great Bobby Morrow, who, as a sophomore, won the 100-meter and 200-meter dashes and the 400-meter relay at the 1956 Olympics in Melbourne, Australia. ACU has recently been home to many African runners, and it was a perfect place for Gilbert, who studied agricultural business and starred for the team. He was an All-American all three years at ACU, running the 800 and 1,500 meters, the 8K and 10K, and the mile, and he was part of seven national championship teams, winning the 800 indoors in 1999. Coach Jon Murray says Gilbert was a natural team leader. "We called him the Ambassador," he recalls. "He was always making friends, always helping people."

Gilbert liked Abilene. "It gave me time to worship and think," he says. "No distractions." He told his story to church and school groups, and eventually a Burundian student from North Texas State University in Denton visited and wrote about him for her school paper. CNN did a story on him, too. In 1999 he won an award given to courageous student athletes. He got to meet Bill Clinton and Muhammad Ali. In 2000 his girlfriend, Triph, whom he had met in the hospital, came to America and enrolled at ACU, and they were married soon after.

After graduation, Gilbert couldn't find work, so one of his professors called an old ACU roommate in Austin: Paul Carrozza, who invited Gilbert down to visit. Inspired by his story, Carrozza offered him a position — several, actually. He wouldn't just sell shoes; he would speak to kids as part of the Marathon Kids program, trying to get them to run. And he'd race. Carrozza, a former track star himself at ACU, would coach him. It was a long way from the killing fields of Burundi.

He's gone back only once — Christmas of 1999 — and he

learned a hard lesson: you can go home again, but you really shouldn't if you were a witness to genocide who's told your story on CNN. The local media found him, and relatives told him that Hutus were looking for him. Gilbert lay low and fled for good just after New Year's. "I'll never go back," he says. He doesn't trust the recent power-sharing arrangement that calls for a Tutsi and a Hutu to alternate as president every eighteen months. "If there's a Hutu in power," he says, "there's no Tutsi who could sleep at night." Gilbert was granted political asylum in the United States in 2001, and he's trying to get permanent residency.

We're accustomed to African-American athletes being superior, and we're accustomed to Africans, especially East Africans, being the best long-distance runners. Generally, they are. But they're human. They make mistakes. They get hypothermia, as Gilbert did in February at the Motorola Marathon in Austin, when he finished with a disappointing time of 2:26. They train wrong, as Gilbert did for the Capitol 10K. They get tired. On a typical day, Gilbert is up at five, coaching at six, doing a morning run by seven-thirty, selling shoes all day, coaching after work, and then doing an evening run by seven; he runs an average of twenty miles a day. He tries to give time to Triph and Emma. He almost always falls short.

And, as unbelievable as it may seem to his students, sometimes he doubts himself. "I've never seen a guy so easily psyched out," says John Conley, Gilbert's agent. "Before a race, I tell him he's done the work; he knows the strategy; he's got the speed; he's got the strength. He just has to not let the negative talk in his head get to him. It's his Achilles' heel. He thinks, *These guys are better than me,* and he puts himself in last place. If he could be like Ali and think, *I'm the greatest,* he'd be unbeatable."

In truth, runners don't race to beat other runners. They race against themselves: to conquer their wills, to transcend their weaknesses, to beat back their nightmares. Of course, a runner will never actually beat himself; he'll never be good enough to do that. But he can get better. And so Gilbert has spent the spring and summer of this year trying to do just that, racing men who are faster than he is, knowing that this makes him better. In May he went to Indianapolis to run a half-marathon against a fast field and finished tenth, with a respectable time of 1:07:50. In June he ran the prestigious Grandma's Marathon in Duluth, Minnesota, at 2:23, but he'll need to get under 2:20 to make the Burundi Olympic team. Carrozza wants to push him even further and have him train with even faster runners. One problem, according to Carrozza, is that Gilbert has been running at slower paces with his students, essentially dumbing his body down. "He's got to refocus on himself," says Carrozza, "to balance the coaching with his training. But he doesn't have to give up coaching."

That will be a relief to the Gazelles and the spud-shaped obsessives on the running trails. Of course, they see Gilbert as more than just a good coach. He's a flesh-and-blood symbol, a real-life survivor, a true son of God, a man on a mission that's both infinitely greater than and remarkably similar to their own: the daily struggle to show what you're made of.

At Ease, at Last

FROM THE LOS ANGELES TIMES

IT HAS BEEN FORTY YEARS, but he still remembers the pitch. The second pitch. The final pitch.

It was late September 1963. It was a low inside fastball. He lined it down the left-field line. He sprinted to second base. The crowd roared.

Inside a crisp new Dodger uniform, Roy Gleason's heart leaped.

He was twenty, and after his first major league plate appearance, he was batting 1.000.

"I thought I was going to be a superstar," he remembered, and how was he to know?

How does anyone know that his first chance is his last? How can anyone so young imagine a future so unimaginable that, instead of running into the dugout embrace of his teammates, he should have stayed on second base forever?

It has been forty years, and Roy Gleason is still batting 1.000.

Before he was sent to home plate again in the majors, he was plucked from spring training and shipped to Vietnam. His baseball skills were damaged in jungle fighting. His World Series ring disappeared at a base camp in the bush.

The outfielder returned to the Dodgers long enough for them to realize he would never be the same. They sold him to the Angels, who quickly shipped him to the Mexican League, his last stop before an auto accident ended his pro career with that lone plate appearance.

If only Roy Gleason could have stayed on second base forever.

He retired in Orange County, in obscurity, working as a furniture mover, a bartender, a car salesman.

He is the only Los Angeles Dodger to have earned a Purple Heart, yet when the team needed a hero for an old-timers' game or autograph session, nobody called.

Records indicate he was the only player with major league experience who fought in Vietnam, yet when the team needed somebody to throw out a pitch on Memorial Day, nobody remembered.

Disconnected from the organization, tethered to his remorse, Roy Gleason finally stopped going to Dodger Stadium in 1984.

"I just couldn't bear it," he said. "I thought I was through with baseball forever."

Then, an innocent phone call, an inquiring historian, and a giant embracing tradition.

A couple of years ago, Wally Wasinack, an Orange County businessman, bought a car from Gleason. The salesman's story was so compelling, Wasinack decided to write a book about him.

This summer, Wasinack phoned the Dodgers in search of records and photos.

"I had no idea what they would say, I didn't know whether they had even heard of him," Wasinack said.

Answering the phone, Dodger historian Mark Langill had indeed heard of Gleason but knew little else. About five minutes into the conversation, his jaw dropped.

"I knew the name, I knew the one-for-one, but to hear the rest of it, I was fascinated," he said. "That this story was out there for forty years and nobody had written about it was unbelievable."

Langill invited Gleason to Dodger Stadium. Gleason hesitantly accepted. Once there, he reluctantly shared.

"He was so humble, so genuine," Langill said. "It was like pulling teeth to get him to talk about his accomplishments."

Then, slowly, amazingly, walking from the clubhouse to the upper press dining room, Gleason realized something about this team he had tried to forget.

They had never forgotten him.

Tom Lasorda spotted him in a hallway and reminded him of his big signing bonus. Bruce Froemming, an umpire, recognized him immediately and remembered a minor league rhubarb. Aging scouts stood up from their dinners to pat his back and tell him stories.

Their visit eventually ended up in the tunnel behind the Dugout

Club, next to a wall bearing most of the names from the Dodgers' all-time roster.

Gleason scanned the montage and said, "I'm sure I'm not up here."

Langill stood behind him thinking, *Please be up there. Please be up there.*

After a few minutes, they found it, above Roy Campanella, below Delino DeShields.

Roy Gleason

"I didn't really feel like I played enough to warrant being called a major leaguer," he said.

He touched the wall gently, with a finger that has been numb since he took shrapnel in Vietnam. His eyes glazed. The truth hit.

Once a Dodger, always a Dodger, even if only momentarily a Dodger.

He had never left second base after all.

Sgt. Gleason looked at Langill and shook his head.

"I'm glad I'm on this wall, instead of the other wall," he said.

As a kid at Garden Grove High, he was so talented, he would pitch batting practice to the big leaguers at the Coliseum.

As a prospect, he was so valued, Ted Williams recruited him personally for the Boston Red Sox.

But Roy Gleason wanted to be only a Dodger, so he signed quickly, and was promoted quickly from the lower minor leagues, getting a September call-up to the big league team after only his second full minor league season.

Once here in 1963, he realized he was faster than everyone but Willie Davis. He was used seven times as a pinch-runner, once as a batter, and everything was possible.

"I knew they had a great team, and I knew it might be a while before I got back," Gleason said. "But I knew I could eventually play here."

He was not on the World Series roster, spending that time in the Arizona Instructional League with the other top prospects. He then spent the next three years moving up the ladder, waiting for an opening on a major league team featuring an outfield that included, at various times, Willie Davis, Tommy Davis, Frank Howard, and Lou Johnson.

In 1967, after Sandy Koufax retired and Maury Wills was traded, the Dodgers were finally starting a rebuilding phase that would include still-young Gleason.

He arrived at Dodgertown that spring, thinking this would be his chance.

Then he received a letter from the government saying he had been drafted.

"I went from the highest of highs, to the absolute low," he said.

Most baseball players avoided Vietnam because their teams arranged for them to serve in the National Guard. But because Gleason was the sole support of his mother and two sisters, he was already ineligible. Or so he thought.

At his induction ceremony, he was the only recruit in the room who would not recite the pledge or take that traditional one step forward.

"I told the officers that they had made a mistake, that I needed to be home to support my family," he said. "They told me to put in for a hardship discharge."

It took more than a year for that paperwork to be processed. By then, he had already been to hell and back.

While his Dodger buddies were throwing fastballs, Gleason was throwing hand grenades in the jungle during an eight-month stint there.

"That was one way my baseball abilities helped," he said. "They used to say that I didn't need to shoot out of a cannon, that I already had one."

While Don Drysdale was fashioning his scoreless-innings streak, Gleason could only read about it in letters from former Dodger executive Buzzie Bavasi and members of the Dodger fan club.

"It was so hard, sitting in the jungle and thinking about what could have been," he said.

And instead of competing for rookie-of-the-year honors, Gleason was being named soldier of the month. In a photo of the ceremony, he can be seen wearing his World Series ring with his fatigues.

But as his reward, he was made a point man on dangerous missions, even at six-foot-four.

"I walked small," he said. "And they were running out of guys."

On one such mission, on July 24, 1968, a shell exploded out of a tree above him, tearing a hole in his left calf and left wrist. He kept fighting even though he couldn't walk, and blood was spurting from both wounds.

He was whisked from the battlefield in a chopper, his foot locker with his World Series ring left behind.

Less than a year later, honorably discharged, he was back in spring training, still hopeful at twenty-six, still trying to make the Dodgers, even as team doctors were removing bits of bulging shrapnel from his leg.

His injured left leg affected his speed. His numb finger affected his batting grip. And then the freak accident — a buddy drove a car over a cliff, with Gleason in the car — tore his right shoulder and finished his career.

"He could have been a big hero in this town, but it was the wrong time for him," Bavasi said. "The Army took a lot out of him."

Gleason's family had lost the house while he was at war, so he wasn't rich.

He'd had only one major league at-bat, so he wasn't famous.

After bouncing around at various odd jobs, Gleason, with the help of former Dodger Jimmy Campanis, became a car salesman at a Honda dealership, where he worked until recently.

He married twice, raised two boys, lived a quiet life that somehow felt like an unfulfilled life.

"I think he originally thought his life was a waste," Wasinack said.

Saturday night at Dodger Stadium, he will again be reminded of his error.

Before the game against the San Francisco Giants, Roy Gleason will throw out the first pitch.

He's a senior citizen now, gray hair, glasses, a slight limp.

But for one moment, he will be twenty again. For one moment, he will hear the cheers he was denied, bask in the glow that was stolen away.

For the first time, his family will see him in his natural surroundings.

For the first time, Dodger fans can give him a proper greeting.

Ladies and gentlemen, introducing the Dodgers' all-time leading hitter, batting 1.000 forever, the great Roy Gleason.

Biographical Notes

Notable Sports Writing of 2003

Biographical Notes

MITCH ALBOM is the author of *Tuesdays with Morrie* and the novel *The Five People You Meet in Heaven*. A longtime columnist for the *Detroit Free Press*, he is also the host of a nationally syndicated radio program.

IRA BERKOW is a columnist for the *New York Times* and author of *To the Hoop: Seasons of a Basketball Life* and the collection *The Minority Quarterback and Other Lives in Sports*.

GREG COUCH is a columnist and feature writer for the *Chicago Sun-Times*. His profile of a can't-miss tennis player who missed appeared in *The Best American Sports Writing 1996*. "A Runaway Win Cubs Fans Won't Appreciate" is part of a fifteen-column series uncovering a ticket-scalping scam run by the Chicago Cubs, his lifelong favorite team. He has a wife, Lisa, and children Michael and Jenny.

Long-distance swimmer LYNNE COX was the first person to swim the Straits of Magellan, the Bering Strait, and around the Cape of Good Hope. She is the author of *Swimming to Antarctica: Tales of a Long-Distance Swimmer.*

TOMMY CRAGGS joined *SF Weekly* as a staff writer in October 2002 after interning at the *Wall Street Journal*, *Harper's Magazine*, and the *Times-Picayune* in New Orleans. He graduated in 2001 from Northwestern University.

PETER DE JONGE is a frequent contributor to the *New York Times Magazine*. He has collaborated with James Patterson on two novels, *Miracle on the 17th Green* and *The Beach House*. He lives in New York.

ROBERT DRAPER is a writer-at-large for *GQ* and author of the novel *Hadrian's Walls*. Before joining *GQ* in 1997, he wrote for *Texas Monthly*. He lives in Texas.

STEVE FRIEDMAN is a correspondent for *Outside* and a writer-at-large for the Rodale sports group of magazines. His work has also appeared in *Esquire, GQ*, the *Washington Post*, and many other publications. This marks his fourth appearance in *The Best American Sports Writing*.

MICHAEL HALL has written for the *Austin Chronicle*, the *Austin American-Statesman, Trouser Press, Blender*, and *Men's Journal*. Since 1997 he has been a senior editor at *Texas Monthly;* his December 2003 story "Death Isn't Fair" was nominated for a National Magazine Award. Hall is married and lives in Austin.

PETER HESSLER is a Beijing correspondent for *The New Yorker* and the author of *River Town: Two Years on the Yangtze*. A native of Columbia, Missouri, he studied English literature at Princeton and Oxford before going to China as a Peace Corps volunteer in 1996. Hessler's work has appeared in the *Atlantic Monthly*, the *New York Times*, the *Asian Wall Street Journal*, the *Boston Globe*, the *South China Morning Post*, and *National Geographic*.

MICHAEL LEAHY has been a staff writer for the *Washington Post* since 1999. In 2001 his story on the life of a paroled murderer won the Washington D.C. Society of Professional Journalists' best feature story award. He lives with his wife Jane and son Cameron in Virginia. His new book, *When Nothing Else Matters: Michael Jordan's Last Comeback*, will be published in 2004. This is his fourth appearance in *The Best American Sports Writing*.

GUY MARTIN lives in Brooklyn. He is a frequent contributor to *Field & Stream, Rolling Stone, Condé Nast Traveler*, and *The New Yorker*.

ANDY MEISLER is a staff writer at *Workforce Management* magazine. His articles have appeared in many national publications, including the *New York Times*, the *Los Angeles Times Magazine, TV Guide*, and *GQ*. He is the co-author with Norma McCorvey of *I Am Roe: My Life, Roe v. Wade*, and *Freedom of Choice*. He lives with his wife Emily in Los Angeles.

WILLIAM NACK was formerly a senior writer at *Sports Illustrated*. He is the author of *Secretariat: The Making of a Champion* and a collection of his work, *My Turf*.

LISA OLSON joined the *New York Daily News* sports staff in 1997. Previously, she was a sports columnist for the *Sydney Morning Herald* and the *Daily Telegraph* and a foreign correspondent based in Australia. She also was a sports reporter for the *Boston Herald*. She has covered everything from cricket in Pakistan to baseball in Mexico to rugby in New Zealand. She lives in Manhattan.

Susan Orlean has been a staff writer for *The New Yorker* since 1992. Orlean graduated from the University of Michigan and wrote for alternative newsweeklies before breaking into magazines. She lives in New York City and is the author of *The Orchid Thief.*

Charles P. Pierce is the author of *Hard to Forget* and *Sports Guy* and makes regular appearances on National Public Radio's *Only a Game* and *Wait, Wait, Don't Tell Me.* A frequent contributor to *Sports Illustrated,* the *New York Times Magazine,* and other national publications, Pierce is a staff writer for the *Boston Globe Sunday Magazine.*

Bill Plaschke is a columnist for the *Los Angeles Times.* This is his third consecutive appearance in *The Best American Sports Writing.*

Joe Posnanski has been a sports columnist for the *Kansas City Star* for eight years. Before that, he worked as a columnist in Cincinnati and Augusta. Joe was named best sports columnist by the Associated Press Sports Editors in 2003, and he won APSE first-place awards for both feature and project writing in 2004. He and his wife Margo have a daughter, Elizabeth, and a dog named Hilton.

Stephen Rodrick is a senior writer for *Philadelphia* magazine and a contributing editor at *Men's Journal, Runner's World,* and *ESPN: The Magazine.* His work has also appeared in the *New York Times Magazine, GQ,* and *George.* This is his third appearance in *The Best American Sports Writing.* He splits his time between Brooklyn and Philadelphia.

Bob Ryan is a sports columnist for the *Boston Globe* and author of *When Boston Won the World Series* and, with Larry Bird, of *Drive: The Story of My Life.*

Joan Ryan wrote sports for thirteen years at the *Orlando Sentinel,* the *San Francisco Examiner,* and the *San Francisco Chronicle,* where she is now the metro columnist. She is the author of *Little Girls in Pretty Boxes: The Making and Breaking of Elite Gymnasts and Figure Skaters* and co-authored *Shooting from the Outside: How a Coach and Her Olympic Team Transformed Women's Basketball* with Stanford coach Tara VanDerveer, who coached the 2000 Olympic women's basketball team. Ryan lives in Marin County with her husband, sportscaster Barry Tompkins, and their fourteen-year-old son.

This is Gary Smith's ninth appearance in *The Best American Sports Writing.* A senior writer at *Sports Illustrated,* he is a past winner of a National Magazine Award for feature writing and the author of *Beyond the Game: The Collected Sports Writing of Gary Smith.*

PAUL SOLOTAROFF is the author of *Group: Six People in Search of a Life* and *The House of Purple Hearts: Stories of Vietnam Vets Who Find Their Way Back.* His story "The Power and the Gory" appeared in *The Best American Sports Writing of the Century.* He lives in Brooklyn.

CARLTON STOWERS has spent much of his lengthy journalism career alternately writing about sports and true crime. He has twice won the Mystery Writers of America's Edgar Award for the best fact crime book of the year (*Careless Whispers* and *To the Last Breath*), and *Within These Walls,* co-authored with former prison chaplain Carroll Pickett, received the 2002 Violet Crown Award as the year's best book of Texas nonfiction. Also among the over two dozen books he has authored is the best-selling *Marcus,* written with NFL Hall of Fame running back Marcus Allen. Stowers resides in Cedar Hill, Texas.

RICK TELANDER, a columnist for the *Chicago Sun-Times,* has two daughters in college, one in high school, and a son in junior high. His book on New York street basketball, *Heaven Is a Playground,* has now been in print for twenty-nine years.

Notable Sports Writing of 2003

SELECTED BY GLENN STOUT

ALLEN ABEL
Love of the Game and Flying.
National Post, December 13, 2003

ELLIOTT ALMOND
Unbridled Ride. *San Jose Mercury News,* November 9, 2003

CHRIS BALLARD
"That Is Going to Make You Money Someday." *New York Times,* August 31, 2003

JOHN BARTON
Putt-Putt: The Other U.S. Open. *Golf Digest,* June 2003

GREG BISHOP
Unbreakable Bonds. *Seattle Times,* June 29, 2003

RACHEL BLOUNT
Spirit of Teamwork. *Minneapolis Star-Tribune,* November 27, 2003

THOMAS BOSWELL
Destiny Gets Big Assist from Little. *Washington Post,* October 17, 2003

GEOFF BOUVIER
B-Ball. *San Diego Weekly Reader,* November 6, 2003

GEOFF BROWN
Art Modell Just Wants to Be Loved. *Baltimore,* September 2003

RIC BUCHER
American Idol. *ESPN: The Magazine,* February 17, 2003

SCOTT BURTON
Far from Heaven. *ESPN: The Magazine,* March 3, 2003

MORGAN CAMPBELL
Long Shots. *Toronto Star,* May 31–June 7, 2003

JON CARROLL
Some New Names for the Old Ball Yard. *San Francisco Chronicle,* October 3, 2003

JIM CARTY
Upset of Century Renewed a Rivalry. *Ann Arbor News,* November 20, 2003

LIZ CLARKE
The Last Beauty Standing. *Washington Post,* November 16, 2003

ROY PETER CLARKE
Cauliflower and the Champ. *St. Petersburg Times,* June 1, 2003

KEVIN CONLEY
NASCAR's New Track. *The New Yorker,* August 18, 2003

TOMMY CRAGGS
Contending with Life. *SF Weekly,* March 5–11, 2003

MIKE DOWNEY
For Carrasquel, Sox Are Always

There. *Chicago Tribune,* July 14,
2003

GORDON EDES
How the A-Rod Negotiations Ended.
Boston Globe, December 31, 2003

JASON FAGONE
The Secret Life of Kobe Bryant.
Philadelphia, November 2003
ALAN FERGUSON
Lost in Translation. *Naperville Sun,*
November 30, 2003
BILL FIELDS
The High Life and Hard Times of
John Schlee. *Golf World,* June 6,
2003
DAVID FONG
A Mother's Love. *Troy Daily News,*
February 9, 2003
SCOT FOWLER
Seventeen Seconds. *Charlotte Observer,*
September 28–30, 2003
LEW FREEDMAN
A Grueling, Grinding Race. *Chicago
Tribune,* August 3, 2003
TOM FRIEND
Rematch. *ESPN: The Magazine,* March
31, 2003
CAL FUSSMAN
Ali Now. *Esquire,* October 2003

MICHAEL GEFFNER
Robbed of Glory. *Billiards Digest,* June
2003
JONATHAN GREEN
You'll Be Cruising at an Altitude of
Thirty Thousand Feet. *Men's
Journal,* October 2003

ERIC HAGERMAN
Force Majeure. *Outside,* June 2003
JUSTIN HECKERT
Arrested Development. *ESPN: The
Magazine,* 2003
A Way with Words. *Atlanta,*
November 2003

JOHNETTE HOWARD
Enter the Tigress. *Golf for Women,*
January–February 2003
ROBERT HUBER
Julius Erving Doesn't Want to Be a
Hero Anymore. *Philadelphia,*
October 2003

MARK JENKINS
The Hard Way. *Outside,* August 2003
SALLY JENKINS
Still Ticking. *Washington Post
Magazine,* December 7, 2003
CHRIS JONES
The Passion of Tiger Woods. *Esquire,*
October 2003

JESSE KATZ
Master of Illusion. *Los Angeles,*
October 2003
TIM KEOWN
Atta Way. *ESPN: The Magazine,*
November 24, 2003
PETER KERASOTIS
Ted Williams's Ordeal Drags On.
Florida Today, July 5, 2003
DAVE KINDRED
The Pen That Broke Down Bars. *The
Sporting News,* May 26, 2003

JULIET MACUR
An Unlikely Legend of the NFL.
Dallas Morning News, April 20,
2003
JIMMY MCGAHERN
I'll Take Care of Your Kids. *Phoenix
New Times,* May 8, 2003
THOMAS MCINTYRE
Hunting Scared. *Field & Stream,* April
2003
ZACK MCMILLIN
Timeless Tigers. *Commercial Appeal,*
March 30–April 6, 2003
GERALD P. MERRELL
John Mackey's Fading Limelight.
Baltimore Sun, December 4, 2003
IRVIN MUCHNICK
Welcome to Plantation Football. *Los*

Angeles Times Magazine, August 31, 2003

SPENCER NADLER
Sweet Mayhem. *The American Scholar*, Spring 2003

RYAN O'LEARY
It Had to Be a UFO. *The Times*, August 2, 2003
JOSE DE JESUS ORTIZ
Pain Continues to Linger for Darryl Kile's Widow. *Houston Chronicle*, January 31, 2003

MICHAEL PATERNITI
The Cold Man and the Sea. *GQ*, February 2003
ERIC PRISBELL
Bulldog Academic Fraud Alleged. *Fresno Bee*, February 10, 2003

DAVID QUAMMEN
The Bear Slayer. *Atlantic Monthly*, July–August 2003

DAN RALEY
George Jugum Relives the Fatal Night. *Seattle Post Intelligencer*, June 13, 2003
PHILIP RAMATI
Breaking Barriers. *Macon Telegraph*, June 10, 2003
PETER RICHMOND
The Fall of Kobe. *GQ*, September 2003
LINDA ROBERTSON
Backlash vs. Burk as Sad Master's Policy. *Miami Herald*, April 14, 2003
CHARLES ROBINSON
Looking for Another Chance. *Orlando Sentinel*, December 21, 2003

JOE SCALZO
Heeding (Your) Calls for Change. *The Vindicator*, August 30, 2003

MIKE SIELSKI
Extreme Ordeal. *The Morning Call*, March 9–11, 2003
BILL SIMMONS
Paradise Lost, Again. *ESPN.com*, October 17, 2003
BRYAN SMITH
2 Fast 2 Furious. *Chicago*, November 2003
STEVEN COLE SMITH
The End of Innocence. *Speedway Illustrated*, June 2003
ANDY STAPLES
Coach Anway Worth Words. *Tampa Tribune*, November 2, 2003
STUART STEVENS
Drug Test. *Outside*, November 2003
MIKE SULA
Collision Course. *Chicago Reader*, August 15, 2003

TIMOTHY TAYLOR
Sting Like a She. *Toro*, April–May 2003
CRAIG TEPPER
An Evening with Oscar "Ringo" Bonavena. *Chattahoochee Review*, 2003
WRIGHT THOMPSON
Man Hid in Plain Sight as a Chief's Fan. *Kansas City Star*, November 23, 2003
ANDREW TILLIN
Run for It. *Outside*, July 2003
KIM TOWNSEND
Starting to Ride at Sixty-five. *The American Scholar*, Spring 2003

MICHAEL WEINREB
Off the Wall. *Newsday*, August 3, 2003
GRANT WAHL AND L. JON WERTHEIM
A Rite Gone Terribly Wrong. *Sports Illustrated*, December 22, 2003
EVAN WEST
Ewwww That Smell. *Indianapolis Monthly*, January 2003

JACK WILKINSON
    Warren Spahn: "I Never Really Knew
    How Good I Was." *Atlanta Journal-
    Constitution*, March 30, 2003
CHRISTINE WILLMSEN AND
MAUREEN O'HAGAN
    Coaches Who Prey. *Seattle Times*,
    December 14–17, 2003

SHAWN WINDSOR
    Saddest Summer. *Detroit Free Press*,
    September 25, 2003
GENE WOJCIECHOWSKI
    Staying Home. *ESPN: The Magazine*,
    September 28, 2003

THE BEST AMERICAN SHORT STORIES® 2004

Lorrie Moore, guest editor, Katrina Kenison, series editor. "Story for story, readers can't beat *The Best American Short Stories* series" (*Chicago Tribune*). This year's most beloved short fiction anthology is edited by the critically acclaimed author Lorrie Moore and includes stories by Annie Proulx, Sherman Alexie, Paula Fox, Thomas McGuane, and Alice Munro, among others.

0-618-19735-4 PA $14.00 / 0-618-19734-6 CL $27.50
0-618-30046-5 CASS $26.00 / 0-618-29965-3 CD $30.00

THE BEST AMERICAN ESSAYS® 2004

Louis Menand, guest editor, Robert Atwan, series editor. Since 1986, *The Best American Essays* series has gathered the best nonfiction writing of the year and established itself as the best anthology of its kind. Edited by Louis Menand, author of *The Metaphysical Club* and staff writer for *The New Yorker*, this year's volume features writing by Kathryn Chetkovich, Jonathan Franzen, Kyoko Mori, Cynthia Zarin, and others.

0-618-35709-2 PA $14.00 / 0-618-35706-8 CL $27.50

THE BEST AMERICAN MYSTERY STORIES™ 2004

Nelson DeMille, guest editor, Otto Penzler, series editor. This perennially popular anthology is a favorite of mystery buffs and general readers alike. This year's volume is edited by the best-selling suspense author Nelson DeMille and offers pieces by Stephen King, Joyce Carol Oates, Jonathon King, Jeff Abbott, Scott Wolven, and others.

0-618-32967-6 PA $14.00 / 0-618-32968-4 CL $27.50 / 0-618-49742-0 CD $30.00

THE BEST AMERICAN SPORTS WRITING™ 2004

Richard Ben Cramer, guest editor, Glenn Stout, series editor. This series has garnered wide acclaim for its stellar sports writing and topnotch editors. Now Richard Ben Cramer, the Pulitzer Prize–winning journalist and author of the best-selling *Joe DiMaggio*, continues that tradition with pieces by Ira Berkow, Susan Orlean, William Nack, Charles P. Pierce, Rick Telander, and others.

0-618-25139-1 PA $14.00 / 0-618-25134-0 CL $27.50

THE BEST AMERICAN TRAVEL WRITING 2004

Pico Iyer, guest editor, Jason Wilson, series editor. *The Best American Travel Writing 2004* is edited by Pico Iyer, the author of *Video Night in Kathmandu* and *Sun After*

Dark. Giving new life to armchair travel this year are Roger Angell, Joan Didion, John McPhee, Adam Gopnik, and many others.

0-618-34126-9 PA $14.00 / 0-618-34125-0 CL $27.50

THE BEST AMERICAN SCIENCE AND NATURE WRITING 2004

Steven Pinker, guest editor, Tim Folger, series editor. This year's edition promises to be another "eclectic, provocative collection" (*Entertainment Weekly*). Edited by Steven Pinker, author of *The Blank Slate* and *The Language Instinct*, it features work by Gregg Easterbrook, Atul Gawande, Peggy Orenstein, Jonathan Rauch, Chet Raymo, Nicholas Wade, and others.

0-618-24698-3 PA $14.00 / 0-618-24697-5 CL $27.50

THE BEST AMERICAN RECIPES 2004–2005

Edited by Fran McCullough and Molly Stevens. "Give this book to any cook who is looking for the newest, latest recipes and the stories behind them" (*Chicago Tribune*). Offering the very best of what America is cooking, as well as the latest trends, timesaving tips, and techniques, this year's edition includes a foreword by the renowned chef Bobby Flay.

0-618-45506-x CL $26.00

THE BEST AMERICAN NONREQUIRED READING 2004

Edited by Dave Eggers, Introduction by Viggo Mortensen. Edited by the best-selling author Dave Eggers, this genre-busting volume draws the finest, most interesting, and least expected fiction, nonfiction, humor, alternative comics, and more from publications large, small, and on-line. This year's collection features writing by David Sedaris, Daniel Alarcón, David Mamet, Thom Jones, and others.

0-618-34123-4 PA $14.00 / 0-618-34122-6 CL $27.50 / 0-618-49743-9 CD $26.00

THE BEST AMERICAN SPIRITUAL WRITING 2004

Edited by Philip Zaleski, Introduction by Jack Miles. The latest addition to the acclaimed Best American series, *The Best American Spiritual Writing 2004* brings the year's finest writing about faith and spirituality to all readers. With an introduction by the best-selling author Jack Miles, this year's volume represents a wide range of perspectives and features pieces by Robert Coles, Bill McKibben, Oliver Sacks, Pico Iyer, and many others.

0-618-44303-7 PA $14.00 / 0-618-44302-9 CL $27.50

HOUGHTON MIFFLIN COMPANY www.houghtonmifflinbooks.com